Neil LaBute

PLAYS TWO

Neil LaBute received his Master of Fine Arts degree in dramatic writing from New York University and was the recipient of a literary fellowship to study at the Royal Court Theatre, London. He also attended the Sundance Institute's Playwrights Lab and is the Playwright-in-Residence with MCC Theater in New York City.

LaBute's plays include: *bash: latter-day plays*, *The Shape of Things*, *The Mercy Seat*, *The Distance From Here*, *Autobahn*, *Fat Pig* (Olivier Award nominated for Best Comedy), *Some Girl(s)*, *This Is How It Goes*, *Wrecks*, *Filthy Talk for Troubled Times*, *In a Dark Dark House*, *Reasons to Be Pretty* (Tony Award nominated for Best Play), *The Break of Noon*, *In a Forest, Dark and Deep*, *Lovely Head*, *Reasons to be Happy*, *The Money Shot*, *The Way We Get By* and *All the Ways to Say I Love You*. He is also the author of *Seconds of Pleasure*, a collection of short fiction which was published by Grove Atlantic in the US and Faber and Faber in the UK.

His films include *In the Company of Men* (New York Critics' Circle Award for Best First Feature and the Filmmaker Trophy at the Sundance Film Festival), *Your Friends and Neighbours*, *Nurse Betty*, *Possession*, *The Shape of Things*, a film adaptation of his play of the same title, *The Wicker Man*, *Lakeview Terrace*, *Death at a Funeral*, *Some Velvet Morning* and *Dirty Weekend*. He has also created the TV series *Full Circle*, *Ten X Ten* and *Billy & Billie* for DirecTV.

by the same author

plays

PLAYS ONE
(*Filthy Talk for Troubled Times, The Mercy Seat,
This Is How It Goes, Some Girl(s), Helter Skelter,
A Second of Pleasure*)

BASH: LATTERDAY PLAYS
THE SHAPE OF THINGS
THE DISTANCE FROM HERE
THE MERCY SEAT
SOME GIRL(S)
FAT PIG
THIS IS HOW IT GOES
LAND OF THE DEAD *and* HELTER SKELTER
IN A DARK DARK HOUSE
IN A FOREST, DARK AND DEEP
REASONS TO BE PRETTY
REASONS TO BE HAPPY

screenplays

IN THE COMPANY OF MEN
YOUR FRIENDS AND NEIGHBOURS

fiction

SECONDS OF PLEASURE

NEIL LABUTE

Plays Two

The Shape of Things
Fat Pig
In a Dark Dark House
In a Forest, Dark and Deep

with an introduction
by the author

FABER & FABER

First published in 2017
by Faber and Faber Limited
The Bindery, 51 Hatton Garden,
London EC1N 8HN

Typeset by Country Setting, Kingsdown, Kent CT14 8ES
Printed in England by CPI Group (UK) Ltd, Croydon CR0 4YY

This collection © Neil LaBute, 2017

The Shape of Things
First published in 2002 by Faber and Faber Limited
© Neil LaBute, 2002

Fat Pig
First published in the USA by Faber and Faber inc., 2007
© Neil LaBute, 2004, 2016

In a Dark Dark House
First published in the USA by Faber and Faber Inc.
© Neil LaBute, 2005, 2007

In a Forest, Dark and Deep
First published in 2011 by Faber and Faber Limited
© Neil LaBute, 2011

Neil LaBute is hereby identified as author
of these works in accordance with Section 77
of the Copyright, Designs and Patents Act 1988

All rights whatsoever in this work, amateur or professional,
are strictly reserved. Applications for permission for any use
whatsoever including performance rights must be made
in advance, prior to any such proposed use, to Joyce Ketay,
The Gersh Agency, 41 Madison Avenue, 33rd Floor,
New York, NY 10010, USA. No performance may
be given unless a licence has first been obtained

*This book is sold subject to the condition that it shall not,
by way of trade or otherwise, be lent, resold, hired out
or otherwise circulated without the publisher's prior consent
in any form of binding or cover other than that in which
it is published and without a similar condition including
this condition being imposed on the subsequent purchaser*

A CIP record for this book is available from the British Library

ISBN 978-0-571-33571-8

Printed and bound in the UK on FSC® certified paper in line with our continuing
commitment to ethical business practices, sustainability and the environment.

For further information see faber.co.uk/environmental-policy

Our authorised representative in the EU for product safety is
Easy Access System Europe, Mustamäe tee 50, 10621 Tallinn, Estonia
gpsr.requests@easproject.com

Contents

Introduction, vii

The Shape of Things, 1

Fat Pig, 93

In a Dark Dark House, 195

In a Forest, Dark and Deep, 285

Introduction

I'm not going anywhere.

Now that can be a good or a bad thing, depending on how you feel about me or how you read that sentence (I guess the same can be said of just about any sentence ever written) and I suppose that's just the way I like it. I have spent a good part of my career as a writer – for stage, screen, print and now television – trying to tell stories that can be taken in various ways, depending on who you are and how you see the details. I'm no Agatha Christie, mind you – much to the chagrin of my business manager – but no one likes turning the tables on a reader or viewer any more than I do. O. Henry might have, in his heyday, but he's dead and gone and I'm still here.

As I said, I'm not going anywhere.

I hope that doesn't mean I'm spinning my wheels but I don't think so – that's for you to decide, I suppose, in the long run. You the reader or you the viewer. Whoever you are. Some of us have met and some of us haven't yet, but I thank you for coming here for the first time or returning to take a look again at a text or two of mine. I think the four plays represented here are some of the best and most honest work I've written for the stage in the past twenty years, so that's saying something.

It's strange to say 'honest' when all of this stuff is a big fat lie – a lie that hopefully helps us see something close to the truth, to crimp a phrase from Picasso (who was a vastly original artist but also a bit of a thief as it turns out – even at one time being considered a possible suspect in the theft of the Mona Lisa herself from the Louvre). Yes, what you'll be reading here is all made up, little stories to thrill and delight, but they touch on concerns of mine and so no doubt some shreds of honesty have fallen into the mix. When I write about art or love or abuse or sex or cowardice, I'm tapping into things that matter to me and that I've maybe even faced to some lesser (or greater) degree than my fictional protagonists. That's just the way it goes when you're a writer. You don't always steal from yourself or those around you, but just remember: it's not safe to leave things lying about when an author is around. It's all fair game, depending on how they were raised and how desperate they are for a good story.

I'm not a thief, though, at least not in the traditional sense. I haven't whisked away the details of any of my friends or loved ones or acquaintances for money and fame. Not yet, anyway. I wrote the four plays enclosed in this volume all on my own from ideas that sprang into my odd little brain and no one was hurt due to their creation – not due to plagiarism, anyway.

It's hard for me to believe that *The Shape of Things* is already sixteen years old. It came to life on the London stage in a wonderful and surprising way: I'd been lucky enough to have a play premiere at the Almeida Theatre (*Bash*) in 2000 and I was in town working on a new film (*Possession*) when I received a call from the co-artistic directors of the theatre (the wonderful Jonathan Kent and the equally great Ian McDiarmid) saying that they were looking for a script as something already scheduled had fallen by the wayside. This call came on my English cell phone and, as luck would have it, I'd just spent my Christmas holiday writing a new play. When I heard their message I immediately sent *The Shape of Things* and the play was up and on its feet within a few months. I was lucky enough to get the dream cast of Rachel Weisz, Paul Rudd, Fred Weller and Gretchen Mol. We spent the better part of one happy year together, working first on the British production, then moving the show to New York (under the

INTRODUCTION

heavy cloud of 9/11) and finally ending up in Los Angeles making a film with the same actors. I had a wonderful time with the four of them and I think we created something really special. The play tried to say something about love and art and we had a blast, working first in a beautiful old bus depot that had been converted into a set of temporary theatres by the Almeida (as their home base was being refurbished) and then at the now-extinct Promenade Theatre on the Upper West Side in New York. The Smashing Pumpkins led the musical charge and we didn't provide the audience with a curtain call and it was a creative experience I won't soon forget.

The next play represented in this volume is *Fat Pig*, which has had a wonderful life around the world in a variety of productions. It began at MCC, my home base in New York, and moved to London's Trafalgar Studios not long after. I was lucky enough to direct that production and I was even luckier to meet a young actress named Ella Smith. What a find. She was a brilliant 'Helen' and one of the easiest people I've ever had the pleasure of collaborating with. With her were three other terrific actors who made up a hilarious foursome with Ms Smith: Robert Webb, Kris Marshall and Joanna Page. The show transferred to the Comedy Theatre (now the Pinter) and added the beautiful and talented Kelly Brook to the cast; the sad truth is that more ink was spilled talking about Ms Brook in a bikini than about her acting skills but I thought she was clever and funny and sweet in the role of Jeannie. The rest of the West End ensemble was the madcap Kevin Bishop, the dashing Nicholas Burns and, eventually, the lovely Katie Kerr. Christopher Oram built us a revolving set (something that brilliantly mirrored the ever-changing cycle of courage and cowardice displayed by the main character) and I employed the sonic stylings of The White Stripes to memorably loud effect. The play was also supposed to make its way to Broadway but due to the back-handed dealings of one potential financier, that moment is still to come. Either way, I've written new material for *Fat Pig* (another office scene that gives Jeannie and Carter more room to grow as characters and also allows Helen to step briefly into Tom's workspace and, perhaps more importantly, a final monologue for Helen that alters the original ending and gives this wonderful character a clear and honest voice when she needs it the most). Incidentally, this volume of plays is the first one to include that new material for your reading pleasure – I hope you enjoy it.

In a Dark Dark House is another thing entirely – a play that hits as close to home as any has thus far. I'm definitely not an autographical writer (as mentioned above) but the family dynamic, the sibling connection and even the history of abuse at the core of this piece all mean something very real and special to me. It's not something I like to talk about, so I decided to write about it in a fictional way instead – dump all that pain and guilt and suffering on somebody who doesn't really exist. That seems fair, doesn't it? Works for me. Like many others before me, I was able to tap into some personal darkness that had previously eluded me by conjuring up a pair of fictive brothers and by using some working knowledge I had about psychiatric facilities and various kinds of abuse (I worked at a few hospitals in my college days and I lived through some abuse in my younger years). The play began its stage life at MCC again (thanks to the great artistic directors Bernie Telsey, Robert Lupone and Will Canter, who have championed my work for fifteen years now) under the direction of Carolyn Cantor and the fine cast of Fred Weller, Ron Livingstone and Louisa Krause, but really found itself under the painstaking care of my dream director, Michael Attenborough. Michael was a good enough friend to tell me honestly that the play still needed work and together we found the heart of the text and beat the thing into submission. His production, starring David Morrissey, Stephen

INTRODUCTION

Mackintosh and Kira Sternbach, really cut to the quick. Michael's work and this trio of actors made even me cry, no easy feat (I promise you). *In a Dark Dark House* is a play I don't read often any more – it's too hard to go back to those places – but reading it for inclusion in this volume made me glad that it exists.

And finally we come to *In a Forest, Dark and Deep*. Having written a play about brothers, I decided to tackle the combo of brother and sister, something up until then (2011) I hadn't really written about. The play has a mystery at its core – there I go again, trying to be Dame Christie – but it's really the sibling relationship that most interested me. Never having had a sister, it was fascinating to try and imagine how the connection works between two people of different genders who are tied together by blood. I didn't want to dabble in incest but I did want to walk a different sexual tightrope and tension – the actual love that can grow between two people who are united by birth. The character of Bobby loves his sister and desperately wants to be needed by her and that drives him throughout the play; when that character is embodied by someone as brilliant as Matthew Fox, you just have to consider your life blessed. Mr Fox was as breathtaking to watch on stage as any actor I have ever seen, and trust me, I've seen a few of them by now. He was well matched in our West End production by Olivia Williams as Betty, even though having an American and an English actor playing siblings was trickier than you might imagine. We were given a dream set by the genius known as Soutra Gilmour (who created a towering, two-storey A-frame cabin on the stage of the Vaudeville Theatre, complete with blowing wind and pelting rain) and all of this was accompanied by a rock soundtrack featuring the best of Pearl Jam, Bush and Led Zeppelin. I directed *In a Forest, Dark and Deep* myself and I think we made the play come fully to life, releasing all the lies and pain and forgiveness from the pages, but it remains chiefly in my mind as a testament to the towering talent of Matthew Fox, whose only crime as an actor is that he doesn't tread the boards nearly often enough.

And there you have it: my thoughts on the four plays committed to paper here. I have another thousand or so stories I could tell you about them, but it's really just the plays that will matter, in the end, because I lied before: I am going somewhere. I won't be around forever but with any luck these four plays will continue to be discovered and revived by actors and readers alike for the next however many years. Rejoiced or reviled, they show me at my near best and I like to think that they've held up reasonably well, so far at least. The first two, *The Shape of Things* and *Fat Pig*, were part of a loose trilogy of plays (along with *Reasons to Be Pretty*) that I wrote on the subject of 'beauty', but I've now written two sequels to that last play so perhaps one day they will deserve their own Faber collection bearing another attractive Roy Lichtenstein print on the cover.

Who knows?

Life is short, but for now it's true: I'm not going anywhere and I will keep writing (so throw your hands in the air in thanks or gnash your teeth in despair, it doesn't matter to me). I'm a storyteller and that's what I'm here to do. To tell stories, no matter where they lead me or what I have to do to tell them (or who I might offend in the telling).

I'll try not to steal too much of your own lives while I do it, but for God's sake don't trust me . . .

I'm a writer.

Neil LaBute
10 March 2017

THE SHAPE OF THINGS

The Shape of Things premiered in London at the Almeida Theatre on 24 May 2001 with the following cast:

Evelyn Rachel Weisz
Adam Paul Rudd
Jenny Gretchen Mol
Phillip Frederick Weller

Director Neil LaBute
Set Design Giles Cadle
Costume Design Lynette Meyer
Lighting Mark Henderson
Sound Fergus O'Hare
Casting Fiona Weir
Assistant Director David Salter

This production transferred to the Promenade Theatre, New York, opening on 10 October 2001, with the above cast and creative team.

Characters

Evelyn
Adam
Jenny
Phillip

Author's Note

The / in certain lines denotes
an attempt at interruption or overlap
by a given character

A MUSEUM

Silence. Darkness.
  A young woman stands near a stretch of velvet rope. She has a can in one hand and stares up at an enormous human sculpture. After a moment, a young man (in uniform) steps across the barrier and approaches her.

Adam . . . You stepped over the line. Miss? / Umm, you stepped over . . .

Evelyn I know. / It's 'ms'.

Adam Okay, sorry, ms, but, ahh . . .

Evelyn I meant to. / Step over . . .

Adam What? / Yeah, I figured you did. I mean, the way you did it and all, kinda deliberate like. / You're not supposed to do that.

Evelyn I know. / That's why I tried it . . .

Adam Why?

Evelyn . . . To see what would happen.

Adam Oh. Well . . . Me, I s'pose.

Evelyn 'Me'?

Adam No, I mean, I'm what happens, I guess. I have to walk over, like I've done, and ask you to take a step back. Could you, please? / Step back?

Evelyn And if someone doesn't? / What then?

Adam . . . You're not gonna step back?

Evelyn No . . . I mean, yes, I probably will, but just for interest's sake, what would you do if?

Adam I'm . . . Geez, I'm not sure. I've never had anyone not step back. I've only said it, like, four times, and every time they've done it. Stepped back.

Evelyn What if I'm your first? Non-stepper, I mean. Then what?

Adam Hell, I dunno . . . I'm off in, like, ten minutes, I'd probably just stand here, make sure you didn't touch anything.

Evelyn Really?

Adam Pretty much, yeah. I'd let next shift talk to you, kick you out or whatever.

Evelyn You wouldn't grab me or anything?

Adam Nah. That's too . . . you know. That's a total hassle, you end up rolling around on the ground, you'd probably sue the place, or me, and then . . . I'd get fired for doing my job. Screw that . . . (*Beat.*) Could you do that for me, though?

Evelyn Which, roll around on the ground or sue you?

Adam No, step back behind the line there . . . I'd appreciate it.

Evelyn Not really.

Adam No, seriously, I would. I'd definitely appreciate it . . .

Evelyn I mean, 'not really' I'm not going to . . .

Adam I thought you just said you probably will . . .

Evelyn Yeah, 'probably'. I decided not to.

Adam Hey, you're not gonna mess up my weekend with this, are you?

Evelyn I wasn't planning on it, but . . . I'm not completely against it, either.

Adam See, if you get all crazy, then I gotta write up a report and stuff, I'm here till six, six-thirty easy, and I have a second job to get to.

Evelyn Tonight? *Friday* night?

Adam Yep. Right after this, at the video store . . .

Evelyn Why would anyone work two jobs on Friday night?

Adam . . . For money.

Evelyn Of course . . . Sorry. (*Looks at him again.*) Oh . . . Oh, right! That's where I . . . I've seen you in there. You helped me once, I think.

Adam Yeah? / With what?

Evelyn Uh-huh. / *The Picture of Dorian Gray* . . . You found it in classics, not drama. / Somebody'd misplaced it . . .

Adam Right, I remember that. / Yes . . . Behind *Cabaret*. The 'Joel Grey' fiasco . . .

Evelyn Yeah, you said you found it with *Dirty Dancing* once, too, or something . . .

Adam I did, you're right . . . That's funny.

Evelyn Anyway, you helped me, that was nice . . .

Adam Thanks. But, you're not gonna return the favour, right?

Evelyn You mean the . . . ?

She points back toward the velvet rope.

Adam Yeah.

Evelyn No, sorry, I can't.

Adam Why is that? (*Pointing*) It's a pretty good-sized sculpture. You can see it just fine from there . . .

Evelyn Truthfully? I'm building up my nerve, and if I go back over, I'll probably be a big wuss about it and take off . . .

Adam About what? The 'wuss' part, I mean . . .

Evelyn I was going to deface the statue.

Adam Oh. Oh . . . (*Pointing*) Is that paint?

Evelyn Yes.

Adam Great . . . From across the room, I thought you were maybe one of the cleaning people, I was hoping that was lemon Pledge or something . . .

They share a smile.

Paint's not really a great thing to have in a museum. People'll definitely take that the wrong way . . .

Evelyn How do they know which way to take it?

Adam I'm thinking outside would be the general direction they'd steer you with spray paint . . . Why do you have that?

Evelyn I was going to do something to the nude. Mess it up or . . .

Adam What, you mean, like, colour it or something?

Evelyn I was thinking more of painting a big dick on it, but whatever . . .

Adam Well, you could still colour it in . . . The dick.

Evelyn smiles at this.

Evelyn True. It might look kinda weird . . .

Adam Oh, I think a graffiti penis is gonna be plenty odd already . . . (*Beat.*) So, right over the leaves there, or just a free-floating number?

Evelyn Probably anatomically correct. I mean, if you're gonna do it, why not –

Adam – do it right? Absolutely. And, would 'why' be completely out of the question here?

Evelyn Why the 'dick'?

Adam Uh-huh. I mean, since I basically have to jump you now if you lift that can up, it'd help with my report . . .

Evelyn Because I don't like art that isn't true.

Adam 'True'. What do you mean?

Evelyn False art. I hate it . . .

Other patrons drift past. They watch them go.

Adam No, I understand the words you've used there, although they're both pretty subjective. 'Art'. 'Truth'.

Evelyn Exactly! That's the beauty of art . . . It's subjective.

Adam Right, but see, I don't know what you're referring to then. I mean, specifically . . . (*Beat.*) Didn't Oscar Wilde say something like, 'In art there is no such thing as a universal truth . . .' or whatever?

Evelyn Yes . . . Very good. 'A truth in art is that whose contradictory is also true.' Right, but that's an *aesthetic*. I'm talking about practicalities. Censorship. (*She points.*) This sculpture. It's fake, it's not real. Therefore, false art . . .

Adam No, it's a Fornecelli, it definitely is. I read the little thingie there one time . . .

Evelyn Yes, but the leaf cluster isn't.

Adam It's not? / What is it, a pastie or something, like strippers have?

Evelyn No. / It's plaster . . . It was added by a committee who had complaints from local townspeople. / Uh-huh. / They made a petition and got that put on, thereby removing its subjectivity as art.

Adam Really? / I didn't know that . . . / When did they do this?

Evelyn Seven or eight years ago now, I think. Before I got here, anyway. / See, they objected to his 'thing', the shape of it. Said it was too *life-like*. (*Beat.*) It's supposed to be 'God', you know . . . That's what pisses 'em off.

Adam Huh. / Yeah . . . He's not really supposed to have one of those, is he?

Evelyn No, and I don't know why . . . We're always calling him 'The Creator'. (*Beat.*) Look at it, you can see the . . . See right behind the grapes there, you can just see his . . .

Adam . . . Grapes. Yes. You're absolutely, huh. Didn't even cover him properly. Shoddy craftsmanship!

Evelyn I mean, if you're gonna do it, at least . . .

Adam . . . Exactly. Do it right. (*Beat.*) But why deface the thing? I mean, just out of curiosity. Why not, say, knock the plaster off and expose his . . . you know . . . cluster . . . If you're trying to . . .

Evelyn Because. That's so . . . Expected.

Adam Ahh . . . So, you're a student, then, or is this just basic anarchy?

Evelyn Yep. Student.

Adam Me too.

Evelyn Yeah? What's your emphasis?

Adam Umm . . . Taking out school loans, primarily, but I do sit in on a few English classes. You're in art?

Evelyn Mmm-hmm. M.F.A. / Applied Theory and Crit.

Adam Oh. / So, is this, like, a project?

Evelyn No, I'm just getting started on my thesis project now. A big sorta installation . . . 'thingie'.

Adam That's a good word, huh? 'Thingie'.

Evelyn It is . . . (*Points.*) Anyway, *this* is only a pet peeve . . .

Adam Thesis? You're graduating . . .

Evelyn In May.

Adam 'Kay. I'm only a junior . . .

Evelyn Huh. You seem older.

Adam Well, I am. I mean, older than twenty, anyhow . . . I worked for a couple years. Made money.

Evelyn Not enough, though. Still got two jobs . . .

Adam Don't forget the school loans . . .

Evelyn Right. So, basically, you're . . . fucked.

Adam Yep. But at least I'm educated, so I *comprehend* that I'm fucked . . .

They stand there for a moment. Adam checks his watch. Evelyn shakes her spray can.

Evelyn You're cute. I don't like the way you wear your hair . . .

Adam Thank you. I think . . .

Evelyn No, you're definitely cute, but you shouldn't style it so much. Your hair. Just let it go . . .

Adam 'Kay. I'll try that . . .

Evelyn Your relief's late . . .

Adam Yeah. Typical . . .

Evelyn So, do you have to stay at your station until they spell you, or . . . ?

Adam No, at punch-out time, I'm supposed to get down there and do it. They can really be pricks about that . . .

Evelyn You should go then . . .

Adam Right. Yeah, I . . . Can I call you?

Evelyn What do you wanna call me?

Adam Up. Just up, right now. Talk, maybe get crazy, take you to dinner . . .

Evelyn Okay. Ahh . . . Sure. (*Beat.*) Do they allow you to do that here?

Adam What, eat dinner?

Evelyn I meant hit on the patrons . . .

Adam . . . Umm, no, they've got a pretty strict policy about that, too, actually. But . . .

Evelyn . . . Ahh, the great equaliser. 'But.'

Adam Exactly. I'll take the risk . . .

Evelyn . . . Good answer, grasshopper.

Adam Huh?

Evelyn *Kung Fu* on TV. Remember when he was a kid? The old guy with the fakey contact lenses, and the . . .

Adam Oh, right . . . Sure. 'Grasshopper.' I don't really watch much television . . .

Evelyn My brothers loved that show. (*Beat.*) So, do you want a number?

Adam Absolutely! (*Checks.*) Damn, I don't have a pen.

Evelyn Me either. (*Thinks.*) Here . . .

Adam What?

Evelyn The jacket. Take it off for a second.

Adam Oh, that's, umm . . .

Evelyn What?

Adam It's my own . . . 'S not part of the uniform. It's mine.

Evelyn Good. Then you'll always have it on you . . . From the looks of it.

Adam follows her orders. Evelyn lays the coat open on the floor, looks around, then uncaps the paint and sprays a phone number inside.

. . . Don't worry, it dries quick.

Adam Thanks. Okay, so, I'll . . . Yeah. (*He glances back.*) Good luck with the . . . Nice to meet you. Again.

Evelyn You too.

Adam smiles at her, looks back again, walks off. Evelyn is left alone. She turns back to the statue and starts shaking her paint can. The little ball bearings inside rattle loudly.

A RESTAURANT LOBBY

Adam standing with Evelyn. He looks a bit different, not as bulky, and he's letting his hair go. Same jacket under his arm.

Evelyn . . . No, seriously. You have.

Adam Yeah?

Evelyn No question.

Adam I dunno. I think I still look . . .

Evelyn You can definitely tell. You can.

Adam Really?

Evelyn Definitely. Plus, the hair . . . / I bet you your friends say something. Twenty bucks . . .

Adam Well, I'm glad . . . / I mean, I can't tell and so I figured . . . Twenty bucks?

Evelyn Yes. That's because you see 'you' every day. Shower, getting dressed, that kind of thing. But . . .

Adam So do you.

Evelyn I don't see you shower. Or getting dressed . . .

Adam No, I meant every day. So far, anyway, since we first went to . . .

Evelyn I know, I'm kidding.

Adam Oh. Okay . . . (*Beat.*) I'd like that, though. If you would . . .

Evelyn Which?

Adam Both if you want. Either. Anything, any moment I can get with you . . . That's what I'd like.

Evelyn Ask and you shall receive . . .

Adam So, I'm asking, then.

Evelyn So you shall be receiving then . . .

They share a brief kiss; he looks around self-consciously.

Adam P.D.A. Public display of affection. I'm not used to that . . .

Evelyn No? I don't mind . . .

Adam Really?

Evelyn Nah, whose business is it? Ours, right? Kiss if we want to, make love in the bathroom stall . . . Who cares?

Adam I'd start with the management . . .

Evelyn Yeah, but why should they? I mean . . . We're two adults, we . . .

Adam I think this is a bigger discussion than before Jenny and Phillip get here . . . / I mean, no, I'd love to have it with you, the discussion, and I agree, somewhat, but . . .

Evelyn Whatever. / I understand . . .

Adam Another time, we'll definitely discuss it.

Evelyn Another time . . . I'd rather do it.

Adam Lemme go check the men's room . . . (*He laughs.*) . . . You amaze me.

Evelyn I'm glad. (*Beat.*) And *you* amaze *me*, you do. Look at you!

Adam . . . It's just a little jogging.

Evelyn No, it's not. It's not just that . . . You're running, you're eating better, are you still lifting?

Adam Yeah . . . I mean, I didn't today, but . . .

Evelyn That's okay.

Adam No, I'm gonna . . . So, yeah, alright, it's a whole routine thing. You're right . . .

Evelyn Do you like doing it?

Adam Honestly . . . No. I totally hate it!

They laugh.

Evelyn So why would you . . . ?

Adam Because you suggested it. Which is kinda pathetic, but true . . .

Evelyn You shouldn't do something you don't wanna do.

Adam Yeah, you should, why not? If it's for someone . . . I mean, I'm doing it for you.

Evelyn It's a life change. Really . . .

Adam Right.

Evelyn I gave you a couple ideas and you're changing your entire life. I'm very proud of you.

Adam Thank you . . . (*Cockney.*) 'Enry 'Iggins.

Evelyn What's that? Who's . . .

Adam Nothing. From a book. Play, actually.

Evelyn Oh. (*Beat.*) Are you keeping your journal? It really does help . . .

Adam Yes.

Evelyn Will you let me read it?

Adam . . . Some time.

Evelyn Good.

They stand for a moment. Evelyn checks her watch.

Adam And what about you?

Evelyn What about me?

Adam That's what I mean . . . I don't know.

Evelyn What?

Adam Nothing. I don't really know anything about you . . .

Evelyn Yes, you do!

Adam I don't. Not really . . .

Evelyn What's my name?

Adam Evelyn.

Evelyn Where am I from?

Adam Illinois. Near Chicago?

Evelyn Yes. How old am I?

Adam Ummm . . . Twenty-five, maybe.

Evelyn That's exactly right. Almost twenty-six. Sign?

Adam Gemini, I think . . .

Evelyn The twins, yes.

Adam Does that mean you have a split personality?

Evelyn No, it means I was born in June.

Adam Oh. (*Beat.*) And you're, what, a sculptress, right? an artist . . .

Evelyn Yep. Anything else you wanna know?

Adam Yes . . . Everything!

Evelyn So ask then . . .

Adam Well . . . Why are you always asking me questions if it's no big deal.

Evelyn Because you make me curious . . . I'm a curious person.

Adam I'm curious, too, though!

Evelyn Like I said . . . So ask then.

Adam . . . Why do you like me?

Evelyn What?

Adam Me . . . Why would you like me? I'm not anything, I mean . . . And you're so . . .

Evelyn Don't do that, okay? That's the only thing about you I don't like . . . What you see in yourself. Or don't see. Your insecurities. (*Beat.*) Do you like me?

Adam Of course, you know I do . . .

Evelyn Do I appear to like you? Hmm?

Adam Yes . . . It seems like it, yeah.

Evelyn I *do* like you. Do you think I'm smart?

Adam I think you're amazing . . . And you have a *great* ass. Just thought you should know . . .

Evelyn Not part of my query, but thank you.

Adam Welcome . . .

Evelyn And do I seem to know my own mind? I mean, generally . . .

Adam No question.

Evelyn So, don't you trust me, then, to know how I feel?

Adam Yeah. No, you're right . . .

Evelyn Don't worry about *why* when *what* is right in front of you.

Adam Those're very wise words from someone with such a great ass . . .

Evelyn (*playfully*) Kiss me, grasshopper . . .

They start to kiss again as a young couple approaches.

Jenny Ah, ah, ah . . . P.D.A.

Phillip I don't think anybody wants to watch you kiss, Adam . . . We'll be eating soon.

Adam Hey, Phillip, hello! Evelyn, this is Phillip, and his fiancée, Jenny . . .

'Hellos' all round.

Phillip So, we should grab a table, and . . . (*Stopping to look.*) Adam, what's up with you? D'you lost weight?

Adam . . . A little, maybe.

Jenny No, he cut his hair . . . Or something. That's it, right?

Adam Umm, yeah. I mean, both, sort of.

Phillip Huh. Okay, so, let's . . . Come on.

Jenny and Phillip lead the way. Evelyn stares at Adam as they follow; he pulls a twenty out of his pocket and places it in her hand.

A LIVING ROOM

Adam and Evelyn sitting on a couch. Jenny and Phillip in opposing chairs. Everyone holds a drink.

Adam . . . So, tell me this again, you're going to what?

Phillip Underwater. We're going to get married underwater . . .

Adam You've gotta be kidding me!

Phillip . . . Like those *Life* magazine photos you see or whatever. Seriously.

Jenny We wanted to try something bold . . .

Evelyn That oughta do it.

Adam This is crazy, really. And, so, if we want to attend we have to . . .

Phillip . . . Get in the tank with us. You bet.

Jenny No, honey, I thought we said . . .

Phillip . . . We haven't, okay, no, we haven't settled that part completely, but . . .

Jenny My dad could never do that. I mean, my mom would try, she would, but Dad . . .

Phillip Maybe people can watch from the glass window things or whatever, but I'd prefer if they came in with us . . .

He drains his glass, looking at Adam.

Adam That is nuts . . .

Evelyn I applaud you. I think it's very . . .

Phillip (*to Evelyn*) Yeah, well, don't expect my buddy here to follow in our footsteps. He's the least adventurous person I know . . .

Evelyn Really?

Phillip Absolutely! And the marriage thing? Uh-uh, not gonna happen, sorry. I don't know how many nights I listened to this guy say, 'Not me, man, I'm never getting hooked, no way, man . . .'

Evelyn Is that right? Well, well . . .

Adam Listen, don't encourage him. My room-mate doesn't need any –

Phillip Former room-mate . . .

Adam – more encouragement. (*Beat.*) I'm gonna look stupid in one of those wet suits.

Phillip Hey, let's not be a party-pooper here, my friend . . . This could've been you.

Adam laughs thinly; Evelyn doesn't understand.

Adam I know, I know . . .

Phillip Right?

Evelyn I'm lost. What's . . . ?

Phillip I stole Jenny away from Adam . . .

Adam Come on . . .

Phillip I did! (*To Jenny.*) Didn't I?

Jenny No, you didn't, stop being . . . (*To Evelyn.*) Adam and I had a class together, but he never got up the nerve to ask me out.

Evelyn Is that true?

Adam Something like that . . .

Jenny Four months we sat next to each other – I'm borrowing his pen, like, all the time, hint-hint – and he's this total monk the whole semester . . . Anyway, Phil picks him up from class one day, sees me, and we went to the movies that same night.

Phillip I cannot tell a lie . . . I've got the moves, God help me.

Adam God help all of us . . .

A collective laugh.

Evelyn Well, like I said, I think it's great. It's really amazing, it is, to find anybody willing to take a risk today. To look a little silly or different or anything. Bravo! (*Toasts.*) To people with balls . . .

They all toast, even Phillip with his empty glass, but he looks over at Adam. Adam blushes.

Phillip 'Balls', huh? Yep, that's my Jenny . . .

Jenny slaps him on the shoulder and blushes again.

Evelyn You know what I mean. Guts. That kinda thing . . .

Jenny Right. I got it.

Phillip (*toasting*) 'To balls, long may they wave . . .'

They all smile and mock-drink again.

I'll tell you what took some balls, the museum thing, a few weeks back, with the . . . balls. You guys read about that?! I mean, Adam, of course you did, you work there, but – Evelyn, you hear about it?

Jenny (*whispering*) The penis . . .

Evelyn (*whispering*) Yes, I did. Why are we whispering?

Phillip Because you don't say 'penis' in Jenny's house. But we're at my place now, and so we sing it from the eaves! 'Penis!! Pe-nis!!!'

Adam Okay, bar's closing, last call . . .

Evelyn I'm an artist, so I didn't . . .

Phillip No, seriously, do you believe that shit? Somebody with the gall to do that kinda bullshit on our campus?! That fucking burns me up . . .

Adam We should probably get, umm . . .

Phillip . . . What does that mean, anyway? 'I'm an artist'?

Evelyn It means nothing, really, just that I understand the impulse . . .

Phillip You what?!

Adam Evelyn, maybe we should . . .

Phillip No, wait Adam, I wanna hear . . . What 'impulse?' it's called 'vandalism'.

Jenny Does anyone want dessert?

Phillip holds up a hand to hush the group. He turns back to Evelyn.

Phillip No, hold on, this is rich. Go ahead . . .

Evelyn Just that . . . I don't think it was just kids playing. I think it was a sort of statement, a kind of . . .

Phillip . . . A statement?

Evelyn Yeah, I do . . .

Jenny What kind of statement would that be? It was pornography . . .

Evelyn No, it wasn't.

Jenny Yes, it was . . .

Evelyn Pornography is meant to titillate, to excite you. Did you see a picture of what happened?

Phillip We did, yeah . . .

Evelyn Does a penis excite you? I mean, just any ol' penis?

Phillip You're funny. And that's not the point.

Evelyn It's totally the point . . . How about you, Jenny, did you like what you saw? Did it get you hot?

Phillip This is, like, uncalled for, okay? All she said was . . .

Evelyn I know what she said, why don't you let her speak? (*To Jenny.*) Did you wanna say anything else? Huh? Okay, then . . . All I'm saying is that, in my *opinion*, it wasn't pornography, it was a statement. Of course, that's the beauty of statements, like art, they're subjective. You and I can think completely different things and we can both be right . . . Unless, and this seems quite probable, you just can't stand to lose an argument.

Quiet for a moment from the group.

Phillip Wow. The postgraduate mind at work . . .

Adam I'll help you get dessert, Jenny, if you want to . . .

Jenny . . . I still don't think that makes it a statement. It's graffiti . . .

Evelyn What do you mean, it would be a huge statement . . . Especially for a town like this.

Phillip Hey, some of us are from 'a town like this', so maybe you should watch it.

Evelyn Well, we've all gotta be from somewhere . . .

Phillip What do you mean by that?

Evelyn I mean, it's a little college town in the middle of nowhere and . . .

Phillip One you chose, presumably . . .

Evelyn No, it chose me, actually. *Full* scholarship. So, as I was saying . . .

Phillip You've got a real winning way, you know that?

Adam Look, Phil, it's no big deal, let's just . . .

Phillip Which 'Take Back the Night' rally did you find her at, Adam?

Evelyn . . . Can I finish, please?! Jesus, you're really the obnoxious type, you know that? (*To Adam.*) How long did you have to stomach this guy?

Everyone except Evelyn sort of freezes on that one.

Adam Evelyn.

Evelyn Anyhow, who knows what the person was saying by it, we don't, but I think it was a gesture. A kind of manifesto, if you will . . .

Phillip (*drily*) I don't think a person's dick can be a manifesto. Uh-uh. You can write a manifesto on your thing, but your thing can't be one . . . I'm sure I read that somewhere.

Evelyn See? You're just trying to be . . .

Phillip I'm not trying to be anything! Who the hell do you think you are, a few double dates and telling me anything about who I am? Un-fucking-believable!

Jenny This is getting a little, ahh . . .

Phillip . . . Adam, you can really pick 'em. Wow, man!

Adam Look, it's not, let's just forget the . . .

Evelyn You're not gonna take his side in this, are you?

Adam I'm not taking sides, I'm trying to get outta here with just a touch of dignity, okay? Jesus . . .

Jenny I've got a test tomorrow, anyway . . .

Phillip 'Statement', she says!

Evelyn Shut the fuck up, alright? Just fuck right off . . . How would you know? I think she was making one, so that's my opinion . . .

Adam Jenny, thanks for everything. Phillip, I'll call ya, or whatever, but we're gonna . . .

Phillip Yeah? How do you know it was a girl?

Evelyn . . . I don't. I didn't say it was a woman.

Phillip Girl, woman, whatever. You said 'she', how do you know that?

Evelyn I don't, I just said. It's a guess. What it was, where it was placed. An *educated* guess . . .

Phillip You are not . . . She's not trying to take a poke at my being an undergrad, is she? Adam, tell me she didn't just . . .

Jenny Can we stop, now, please?! You guys . . .

Adam Evelyn, let's go . . .

Phillip Hey, artiste . . . How'd you know it was a woman who painted the cock, huh? Very, very suspicious there . . .

Evelyn You are such a prick, man, how do you go on, day after day? (*To Adam.*) Let's go . . .

She rises, snatches up her things and moves toward the door.

Adam? Are you coming?

Adam I'm . . . Yeah, but, just go. I'll meet you downstairs, I just wanna . . . Go ahead.

Evelyn 'Kay. (*To Jenny.*) You're very sweet. Good luck . . . I don't think that's gonna be enough, but I still wish it on you.

She heads for the door and exits.

Phillip 'Good luck.' Hey, fuck you! (*To Adam.*) Where in hell did you meet that bitch?! / What'd she do, give you a haircut and a blow job and now you're her puppy?!! / You don't have to go . . .

Adam . . . At the museum. / No, I'm not her . . . / (*To Jenny.*) The wedding sounds great. Really . . . It sounds . . . Yeah.

He wanders off. Phillip and Jenny sit in silence.

Phillip . . . What?

A BEDROOM

Adam and Evelyn in bed. Holding each other, staring off. A video camera on a tripod nearby.

Evelyn . . . Umm, nice.

Adam Very. Yes.

Evelyn Our bodies are beginning to understand one another . . .

Adam You're right, I mean . . .

Evelyn Getting a rhythm. And less inhibited.

Adam Yep.

He leans over and whispers something in her ear. A huge smile across her face. She turns and whispers back to him. They laugh and kiss for a moment. They hold one another.

Evelyn (*quietly*) Were you always like this before? So . . . You know . . .

Adam . . . Shy? Just about the fact that no one would sleep with me. That's all.

Evelyn Come on . . .

Adam Seriously. You're only, like, I dunno, the third person I've ever . . .

Evelyn . . . No . . .

Adam Yes, I mean it. And they were both young. I mean, I was too, I wasn't, like, hanging out at a *daycare* or anything, but . . . It was during high school mostly. So . . . You're sort of in uncharted waters here.

Evelyn I don't wanna blow your cover but . . . I could kinda tell.

Adam (*smiling*) Yeah? Well, that's okay . . .

Evelyn And nobody here at school?

Adam Nothing serious. Dates. Some close calls. But not anyone . . . You know.

Evelyn . . . Like Jenny.

Adam No.

Evelyn You sorry you didn't ask her out? I mean, if I wasn't in the equation . . .

Adam Not really. We just never got the right . . . Whatever. I sorta blew that one. Anyway, it's kind of weird talking about . . .

Evelyn It's okay. That's nice to see, every so often. Someone gallant . . .

Adam Which is medieval for 'loser' . . . (*Beat.*) I wanna tell you something – and this is not because we've been sleeping together or because you mentioned another girl, it's not – I can't stop thinking about you. I can't. I mean, it's not like a stalker situation . . . Yet . . . But I'm finding myself hanging out by your classes. Following you . . .

Evelyn I've noticed . . .

Adam I figured, yeah. And taking my jacket off, like, thirty times a day and looking at your number. Staring at it. Wondering if you're looking at my number. And writing your name on anything! All over my books. In my *food*. Seriously, tracing your name in whatever I'm eating. I'm so whipped . . . You are dangerously close to owning me.

Evelyn Wow . . .

Adam I just signed my relationship death warrant, didn't I? What a dork . . .

Evelyn . . . No, it's sweet. (*Beat.*) Were you nervous tonight? I mean, about us with the . . .

Adam Nah. Not really. A bit.

Evelyn Sure?

Adam Yeah. It's just . . . Let's not watch it, okay? Do we have to do that?

Evelyn Not if you don't want to . . .

Adam Good. I don't think I could get into that, actually.

Evelyn Why not? It'd be fun . . .

Adam I don't really need to see myself doing that. Doing . . . stuff.

Evelyn See, I'm totally different. I think everyone should see themselves doing it, and their friends should see it, too.

Adam And that's why the tape's gonna stay at my place . . .

She smiles at this, kissing him.

Evelyn Don't be so frightened of everything.

Adam I'm not. Not frightened, anyway. I just don't think that's a thing other people need to see. Ever. My ass . . .

Evelyn People like who . . . Phillip?

Adam No, that's fine, you can show it to him . . . (*Beat.*) Are you nuts?!

Evelyn Why is he your friend?

Adam Do you really wanna go over that . . . ?

Evelyn I just don't get it.

Adam What's to get? We were room-mates, we occasionally see each other, have a drink . . .

Evelyn I just don't think you need that kind of person in your life. No one does.

Adam (*mock-serious*) . . . It may be a touch early to start dictating who my friends are.

Evelyn (*with charm*) Yeah . . . I s'pose.

Adam Geez, he really got under your skin, didn't he?

Evelyn Under. Over. Around. I hate that kind of guy . . .

Adam What kind?

Evelyn That kind. Whatever he is, that's what I hate . . .

Adam I'll let him know.

Evelyn No, God, no, don't give him the satisfaction. And he'd take it, too, believe me . . .

Adam Nah, maybe it'd help him, you know, be better . . . Or something.

Evelyn The only thing that would help him is a fucking knife through his throat . . .

They grow quiet for a moment. Adam studies Evelyn.

Adam Okay, I'm glad I don't have a pet rabbit or anything right now . . .

Evelyn (*laughing*) You know what I mean.

Adam Umm, no, not really.

Evelyn I've just been around his type, that's all. And I don't like 'em.

Adam Yeah, I got that part . . .

Evelyn No big deal.

Adam Right, no, it was the 'knife through the throat' part that was the big deal, I thought . . .

Evelyn Oh, that's just an expression.

Adam . . . From where, Transylvania?

She kisses him.

Evelyn No . . . From the 'Scorned Girl's Handbook'.

Adam Ahhh. Right . . . Page 666.

Evelyn (*smiling*) You've been peeking. You know what happens to peekers, don't you?

Adam Well, if they're DJs, they usually get asked to play 'Misty' on the radio all the time . . .

Evelyn Close. No, I'll show you . . . But you have to do me a favour.

Adam What's that?

She starts to slip under the covers.

Evelyn . . . Just smile. Smile into the camera. For as long as you can . . .

A PARK

Jenny waiting on a bench. Sitting by herself. After a moment, Adam appears.

Adam . . . Hey.

Jenny Adam, hi, hello.

Adam Hi.

Jenny Thanks for coming, I appreciate it.

Adam Of course. How's it going?

Jenny You know . . . Okay.

Adam Right.

Jenny Lots to do for a wedding.

Adam I'll bet . . .

Jenny Invitations to get out, arrangements to make . . .

Adam . . . Air tanks to fill . . .

Jenny laughs lightly.

Jenny That too.

Adam So, you guys're still going through with that?

Jenny That's what we're saying . . .

Adam What do you mean, 'saying'?

Jenny No, we are, it's what we're doing, I'm just . . .

Adam . . . Jenny, what?

Jenny I don't know. I'm, you know, worried.

Adam Why? About what?

Jenny What do you think? Phillip. He's just . . . I dunno, being funny.

Adam Funny, how? Like 'telling jokes' funny or 'making letter bombs' funny?

Jenny No, no bombs yet, but kind of . . . Just funny. Odd. (*Beat.*) Like, nice . . .

Adam 'Nice'?

Jenny Yeah, you know . . . Sweet. Now, I love him and all, I do, you know that, but that's not the way I'd describe him to people. 'Sweet.' Would you?

Adam thinks for a moment.

Adam No, I wouldn't exactly use his name and 'sweet' in the same short story . . .

Jenny And that's what's bugging me.

Adam Why, though? Maybe he's just . . .

Jenny I've only seen him like this once before, maybe twice. Definitely once, when we were first going out and he was seeing somebody else, too. It was over, mostly, but he was still seeing her. Remember that?

Adam . . . Yeah. I do. The 'other' one.

Jenny The other Jenny, exactly. I'd call and I could hear him freeze up, stop for a moment if he answered and I said, 'Hey, it's Jenny.' He didn't know what to do, so he'd get all sort of sweet and fish around slowly until he figured out if it was her or me . . . God, I used to hate that!

Adam So, do you know anyone else named 'Jenny' right now?

Jenny No, I don't mean that, not the name so much as the feeling . . . That sense that there's someone else.

Adam Nah . . .

Jenny Maybe I'm making it up, you know, my own insecurities and looking for a reason to not . . .

Adam (*smiling*) . . . Dive in? Take the plunge? Jump off the deep end? Stop me before I . . .

Jenny Cute . . . But yes. And that might be it, but I don't think so. I want to get married, I do, and I love the guy, whether he's sweet or not. It's just that I don't believe him now that he is . . .

Adam Well, you got me . . .

Jenny Really? You don't know anything, haven't felt that or . . .

Adam I only see him, like, once a week in our survey course, so it's not like I'm in the inner circle any more . . .

Jenny I know, I just thought that . . .

Adam . . . But I would tell you, Jenny, I would, seriously.

Jenny Really?

Adam I think so . . . I mean, that's a lousy thing to pass on to a person, and if I did, you know, know something and then told you, you'd more likely hate me forever than be grateful . . .

Jenny Yeah, that's probably true . . .

Adam Umm, you could lie, you know, feel free.

Jenny No, you're probably right . . .

Adam So, that doesn't exactly make me want to come clean here – which I don't have anything to come clean about, okay, honestly, I just mean, whatever – But I feel I would. I do, because I think you're pretty amazing, if the truth be known, and you're almost married so why shouldn't it be? The truth, I mean.

Jenny . . . Thank you.

Adam Not a problem. Anyway, that's all I know. Which is, nothing . . .

Jenny 'Kay. I'm just being stupid.

Adam Look, if you feel it, it's not stupid . . .

Jenny studies him hard.

Jenny You're a lovely person, you know that?

Adam 'Lovely'? Jesus, why don't you just call me 'gay' and get it over with?

Jenny Hey, 'lovely' is nice . . . I wish there were a few more 'lovely' people in the world. I mean it, you are. (*Looks at him again.*) And getting cuter by the day. What is that girl doing to you?

Adam Lots . . . She's amazing, really.

Jenny What happened to your . . . Are you wearing . . . Adam, are those contacts?

Adam Yeah. Contacts.

Jenny My God, this from the former 'tape around the nose thingie' champion . . .

Adam That was only for a week, that one time!

Jenny Still, you've gotta admit . . .

Adam I do, it's amazing. I feel better . . .

Jenny Better? You're, like, this totally hot guy now . . . (*Beat.*) I always thought you were handsome, anyway, but I didn't think you'd go in for the makeover thing.

Adam Me either. Who knew?

Jenny Well, apparently she did . . . (*Beat.*) You are still seeing her, aren't you?

Adam Oh yeah. She's . . . You don't hold a grudge, all she said that night at your . . . God, I couldn't believe that!

Jenny It was great. No, truthfully, it was, Phil needed to hear every word of that and he did, too. Hear it, I mean. Even said something after you guys left that night. Not an admittance of guilt, exactly, but as close to one as we're likely to hear from the guy . . .

Adam Really, what'd he say? I'm amazed . . .

Jenny As was I . . . He put on quite the show . . .

Adam (*sarcastically*) Yeah, I remember vaguely . . . They both did.

Jenny Right, but later he said something like, 'He could do worse.'

Adam Not exactly a seal of approval . . .

Jenny No, but a lot. For him. And after what she said . . .

Adam You're right. Huh.

Jenny Hey . . . Her middle name's not 'Jenny' or anything, is it?

Adam laughs at this.

Adam Nah, no such luck. It's 'Ann.' Evelyn Ann Thompson. Nice, right?

Jenny Eat.

Adam Huh?

Jenny 'EAT'. those're her initials, the acronym of her names. E-A-T.

Adam Hey, that's cute . . .

Jenny Oh God, you're a goner.

Adam I know, it's pathetic, isn't it?

Jenny Yeah, somewhat . . . But lovely.

Adam Not that again . . .

He puts a hand up to hide his face. Jenny grabs one of his hands, studying it.

Jenny What the heck is this? What is this?!

Adam What . . . ?

Jenny Did you stop biting your nails?

Adam Yeah, for, like, a month now . . .

Jenny Don't tell me . . .

Adam It's true. She put some crap on them, slapped 'em out of my mouth a few times and that was it. I stopped . . .

Jenny You have nails! This is crazy . . .

Adam It's no big . . .

Jenny Ever since I've known you, three years now, your fingers've looked like raw meat . . . Anyway, awful. And now you just quit?! This girl is the Messiah.

Adam I've quit before . . .

Jenny For, like, an hour! (*Beat.*) I love this woman . . .

Adam Me too.

Jenny Yeah, I see that. Wow . . .

She looks over at Adam again.

And you'd really tell me if you knew something?

Adam . . . I would. Yes.

Jenny 'Kay. Damn, when did you get so cute?

She kisses him lightly on the cheek. They look at each other for a long moment. Suddenly, they kiss. A real kiss, not a 'Great to see you, aren't we the best of friends' kiss. After a moment, they shudder to a halt.

Adam . . . Shit.

Jenny Yeah. Huh.

Adam What was that all about?

Jenny I dunno. I just . . . I'm not sure.

Adam Look, I'm sorry.

Jenny No, don't be. I am. I'm the one with the ring on . . .

Adam Yeah, good point. My friend's ring. Thanks for reminding me . . .

Jenny Welcome.

Adam Oh, God . . . Damn it!

Jenny . . . No, listen. It wasn't because of, you know, my worries or whatever. How I feel about Phillip right now. It wasn't . . .

Adam Okay.

Jenny It just –

Adam – happened.

Jenny Right. I've wanted to do that for a long time . . . Three years . . .

Adam . . . Me too. (*Beat.*) And now we take it out in the woods and bury it . . . Don't we?

Jenny Yeah. I mean, yes, definitely. I guess . . .

Adam Don't you think? We have to . . . Jesus, what're we even talking about?!

Jenny No, we do. Course. Don't you want to?

Adam Bury it?

Jenny Yes . . . Or . . .

Adam No, we can't talk about . . . Don't even say the . . . Do you have a shovel in your car?

Jenny I don't, no . . . But I have my car.

Adam . . . My bike's right over there.

Jenny Is it locked up?

Adam Uh-huh.

Jenny Then it should be fine . . .

Adam I suppose so. It's a small town, after all.

Jenny That's what people say . . .

Adam Good people. People we know and care about . . .

Jenny Right. (*Beat.*) Come on, we should go bury this. In the woods . . .

They kiss again, then stand up slowly and walk off. She puts an arm through his.

A DOCTOR'S LOUNGE

Adam and Evelyn sit on opposing couches, flipping through magazines. After a moment, he glances up and checks his watch.

Adam What time did they say?

Evelyn Like, ten-thirty . . .

Adam And it's ten-fifty now . . .

Evelyn No big deal, you always wait at the doctor's office.

Adam I know, I just have to be at work by twelve.

Evelyn Today?

Adam Yeah, I told you that . . .

Evelyn No, you didn't.

Adam I did . . . I always work Wednesdays.

Evelyn Really?

Adam Yeah, every Wednesday.

Evelyn Damn. I hope they . . .

Adam It's okay. I guess I could be a little late if I have to . . .

Evelyn Sure?

Adam Uh-huh. It's alright . . . I mean, they hate it but I can make something up.

Evelyn We can go.

Adam No, I wanna do this. I do . . . (*Beat.*) Who wouldn't want to get their nose chopped off?

Evelyn Come on! It's not . . .

Adam I'm kidding. No, I think you're right about it . . .

Evelyn It's just shaving it . . .

Adam Yeah, that's much better. 'Shaving' your nose off . . . That settles the nerves.

Evelyn You're only talking to them, anyway, that's all.

Adam I know, it's just weird to think . . .

Evelyn People do it all the time.

Adam Right, no, you're right, I just never imagined myself one of those people . . .

Evelyn I'm one of those people. Would you ever've guessed that?

Adam What? You are not . . .

Evelyn Bullshit. Take a look . . .

Adam Where . . . ?

He moves over to her, studies her nose.

I don't see anything.

Evelyn Exactly.

Adam You had your nose done? Honestly?

Evelyn At sixteen. My parents' birthday present . . .

Adam Thoughtful . . .

Evelyn No, I asked for it. I had this terrible hook. 'The Jewish slope' we called it in Lake Forest . . . The only ski run for miles around!

Adam (*smiling*) I can't believe it . . . I can't tell . . .

Evelyn That's the idea, isn't it?

Adam Yeah, but . . . You could be lying to me.

Evelyn And what would be the point of that?

Adam To get me in here. To watch chunks of my flesh get torn away . . . You could be a sadist, for all I know . . .

Evelyn Hey, quit sweet-talking me . . .

Adam Well, they did an amazing job. (*Beat.*) Wait a minute, your name's 'Thompson', that's not Jewish . . .

Evelyn On my mother's side, you dope. That's what makes me Jewish . . . Her maiden name is 'Tessman'.

Adam Oh.

Evelyn We don't have to stay here, Adam . . .

Adam No, it's alright, it just makes me a little jumpy . . .

Evelyn It's cosmetic, not corrective . . . It's no big deal. I promise . . .

Adam If it's cosmetic, why can't I just put some powder on it or something, or shade it in on the side like they do for Richard Gere in photos . . .

Evelyn You mean, before?

Adam . . . He had it done?!

Evelyn Take a look at *American Gigolo* and then at any picture of him today. I'm serious. Lots of guys do it . . . Joel Grey.

Adam Okay, that's it, let's go . . .

Evelyn (*laughing*) Kidding! What about Sting?

Adam Yeah, I knew he did. Looked totally different in *Quadrophenia*. I used to rent that video all the time, my 'mod' phase . . .

Evelyn That must've been cute . . . (*Beat.*) Does he look better now? Sting, I mean?

Adam I suppose so . . . Maybe it's just all that yoga, though.

Evelyn I think you'll look great. You have a good face, a nice shape to your nose, actually, but it's just got that bit of . . .

Adam What?

Evelyn . . . Bulb . . . At the end. Not a bulb, exactly, but . . .

Adam No, I got it, sort of the 'Rudolph' effect. At least I can guide your sleigh tonight . . .

Evelyn You can guide my sleigh any night.

They look at one another, kiss.

Adam P.D.A.

Evelyn Indeed . . .

Adam Shall I check the men's room?

Evelyn I dare you . . .

Adam Shut up!

Evelyn I'm serious . . .

Adam You're crazy . . .

Evelyn Quite possibly. I still dare you . . .

Adam What if they call us?

Evelyn Then they'll just have to wait, won't they?

Adam I suppose they would . . .

Evelyn Can you afford to be late, that's the question. Will you take the risk . . . ?

Adam Is this, like, my last meal or something? A conjugal visit before I'm drawn and quartered . . .

Evelyn Stop being so morbid . . . It's just flesh.

Adam Yeah, I see what you mean . . . 'It's just flesh,' that's not morbid at all.

Evelyn It isn't. It's one of the most perfect substances on earth. Natural, beautiful. Think about it . . .

Adam I'd rather not.

Evelyn Oh come on . . . You've bitten more skin off from around your fingernails than a doctor would ever trim off your nose. It's true . . .

Adam Yeah, but that's just . . .

Evelyn . . . What? It's the same thing. Now, that grows back and this wouldn't, but that's about the only difference. (*Beat.*) How did you get that scar on your back?

Adam Which, the . . . ?

Evelyn Yes. The raised one . . .

Adam A kid, umm, threw a stick at me . . . First grade.

Evelyn Stitches?

Adam Yeah. Thirty-three . . .

Evelyn And is that terrible? Are you disfigured because of it . . . ?

Adam Well, I don't like to wear tanktops . . .

Evelyn . . . And you should be respected for that.

Adam (*giggling*) I'm serious . . . It bugs me . . .

Evelyn Okay, but why? Because it looks ugly or because you think other people will think it looks bad? Which?

Adam I dunno . . .

Evelyn What's the matter with scars? Not a thing . . . (*Pulls up sleeve.*) Look at these, see there?

Adam What're those?

Evelyn They're scars . . . Lots of little scars. You didn't notice them before?

Adam Yeah, I guess I did, but I didn't think anything . . .

Evelyn Sure, you did. Of course you would, they're on my wrist. You know what they are . . .

Adam . . . Did you try to . . . ?

Evelyn No, not really. I mean, I cut on myself a little, tried to get attention when I was a teenager, but I didn't want to slit my veins open. Or I would have . . .

Adam Oh.

Evelyn I'm a very straightforward person.

Adam Yeah, I'm getting that . . .

Evelyn It's the only way to be. Why lie?

Adam You're right.

Evelyn Exactly. (*Beat.*) So, is my arm unattractive to you, then, because of those, or not? Tell me . . .

Adam No . . .

Evelyn Are you lying?

Adam No, not at all, I love your arm.

Evelyn 'Love' is a big word . . .

Adam I know that. That's why I used it. I don't throw it around, believe me . . .

Evelyn Either do I.

Adam I love your arm. It's beautiful . . .

He takes hold of her wrist gently, kisses it.

Evelyn They're like rings on a tree. They signify experience . . . Make us unique.

Adam I can see that.

Evelyn And that's all this is, the idea of you having some surgery. It's an experience . . .

Adam I know, it just makes me . . .

Evelyn . . . What, nervous? Of course you should be nervous, why not? It's something you've never done . . . But that's the adventure.

Adam 'It's a far, far better thing I do than I have ever done . . .'

Evelyn Something like that. Is that from a book?

Adam Yeah, Dickens . . .

Evelyn Huh. Well, I don't know about better, but at least different.

Another quick kiss.

So, are you gonna go check?

Adam What? . . . You mean, the rest room?

Evelyn Uh-huh.

Adam Umm . . . Okay. What if they call my name, though? Seriously . . .

Evelyn What if they do?

Adam (*smiling*) I smell trouble . . . Which I may not be able to do after this.

Evelyn Just go . . .

Adam (*standing*) Okay, why not? Then I can show you something . . .

Evelyn What?

Adam Just a little thing I had done. For you.

Evelyn Wait, what . . . Show me now.

He looks around, can't wait. He pulls open his pants and lets her glance inside.

Adam Look . . . A big religious no-no. (*Pulls at his waistband.*) Nice, huh?

Evelyn 'Eat.' Lemme guess . . . You couldn't afford the 'me'.

Adam No, you goof! Your *initials*. Like it?

Evelyn (*touching it*) I do, I like it. And I love the gesture.

Adam 'Love' is a big word.

Evelyn I know that. That's why I used it . . . (*Beat.*) Go check the 'handicapped' stall. I'm suddenly very hungry . . .

He slips off, out of the waiting room. Evelyn goes back to reading her magazine, when a voice calls out.

Voice Mr Sorenson. Adam Sorenson, please . . .

Evelyn looks up, glances toward where Adam has disappeared but says nothing. She smiles.

A LAWN

Phillip and Adam sitting on their jackets between classes, talking. Adam has a bandage across his nose.

Phillip I'm serious, it looks good . . .

Adam Just shut up . . . Don't get here late and then make fun of me.

Phillip No, you look distinguished.

Adam Phil, I look like a hockey player . . .

Phillip Yeah, but a distinguished one.

They chuckle.

What'd you do, anyway?

Adam . . . I fell.

Phillip Come on . . .

Adam Seriously, I did . . .

Phillip You sound like a battered wife. 'I fell . . .'

Adam That's not funny.

Phillip Yeah, it is . . . It's very funny. I mean, it's not that funny that wives get beat up, but the fact that you look like one, that I find hilarious . . .

Adam Well, anyway, that's what happened. I tripped, I fell . . . No big deal.

Phillip Sure it wasn't the bathroom door? That's the usual excuse . . .

Adam For who?

Phillip Abused women . . .

Adam You're sick.

Phillip Somewhat, yeah. But I'm nice-looking, which makes up for a lot.

Adam Not as much as you think . . .

Phillip 'Don't hate me because I'm beautiful.'

Adam I don't . . . I just hate you.

Phillip See, I knew you did, all these years . . . (*Beat.*) You really fell?

Adam Yeah. I tripped on the stairs going into my apartment and caught my face on the . . . You know . . . The . . .

Phillip No, what?

Adam Oh, come on! It's not that fascinating . . .

Phillip It is, too. It's completely fascinating. So, you don't wanna tell me then, right?

Adam Tell you what?!

Phillip What happened to your . . .

Adam I told you. I tripped going up the . . . And hit the edge of the . . .

Phillip Yeah, it's the 'edge of' that I'm a little hazy on here . . .

Adam Edge of the knob. My door knob.

Phillip She clocked you one, didn't she?

Adam Who?

Phillip 'Who?' The artist, formerly known as Evelyn, or whatever her name is . . .

Adam Are you nuts?

Phillip Well, I've gotta hand it to her, she certainly made a 'statement' . . .

Adam You are such an idiot . . .

Phillip Did she hit you?

Adam Stop!

Phillip I don't care if she did, I'm just asking . . .

Adam Yeah, well . . . You can be annoying.

Phillip It's one of my best qualities, actually . . .

Adam And there aren't many of them.

Phillip You really tripped? Truthfully . . .

Adam Yes.

Phillip . . . Huh. Okay.

Adam Why do you say that? 'Huh.' you don't believe me?

Phillip No, I just . . . Nothing.

Adam What? Don't do that, come on now. What?

Phillip It's no big . . . (*Beat.*) I saw your girlfriend the other day, maybe, what, last Thursday? You weren't in class, and I said to her, I asked her if you were okay, that's all . . .

Adam Yeah, so?

Phillip And she said 'yes', but you were recovering from an operation or something . . .

Adam What?!

Phillip That's what I said, 'He didn't tell me about anything,' and she said it wasn't really an operation *per se*, just some thing you had done. A procedure. And that was it . . . So I just thought . . .

Adam No, it's not . . .

Phillip Hey, you don't have to tell me, we're not on intimate terms or anything . . .

Adam I hurt it. Really . . .

Phillip Whatever.

Adam No, not 'whatever', Phil . . . I did. I hit it and, you know . . . I banged it pretty bad at home and so I had the doctor look at it. But he didn't . . . *operate* or anything. The bandage is from that. The door.

Phillip After you tripped on the stairs . . . Yeah, you told me.

Adam She must've just gotten confused.

Phillip Maybe. That doesn't seem to happen to her very often, though . . . She's pretty sharp.

Adam No, she is . . . I'm sure it's just the way I explained it. I mean, to her . . .

Phillip Right.

Adam . . . And where did you see her?

Phillip Evelyn? I don't know . . . Starbucks or somewhere. The mall, maybe.

Adam She doesn't drink coffee.

Phillip So, it was downtown then, Record City, I think . . . (*Beat.*) What, you worried I'm gonna steal her? Believe me . . .

Adam No, God . . . Don't be so . . . (*Touches nose.*) Anyway, it's gonna be fine . . .

Phillip Well, that's good to hear.

Adam Yep.

Phillip . . . So you're okay, though?

Adam No. I mean, yeah, I'm great . . . Absolutely.

Phillip Then good . . . (*Beat.*) And you'd tell me if there was anything seriously wrong?

Adam . . . Of course! Hey, what's up?

Phillip I mean, we're friends, right? You'd come to me . . .

Adam . . . About what? (*Beat.*) Phil, what's . . . ?

Phillip Jenny told me.

Adam What?

Adam looks at his friend. For the first time, Phillip seems less than in control.

Phillip She kissed you.

Adam Oh.

Phillip She felt shitty, I guess. I could tell for, like, a week that something was going on and finally she told me about it. How you guys met and talked about us – why do girls always have to talk about everything? – and later she leaned over and kissed you. That's what she told me.

Adam She did . . . I mean, she did do that but it was nothing.

Phillip Hey, it wasn't nothing, she's a good kisser. Hell of a kisser.

Adam I don't mean 'nothing', but it meant nothing. It didn't hold meaning for us . . . It just happened.

Phillip Okay. So, you can speak for her, then?

Adam For me . . . It didn't for *me*. It was just a . . . That's all she said?

Phillip Don't tell me there's more . . .

Adam No, God, not at all . . . I just . . .

Phillip It's alright, I'd been acting weird lately, this whole marriage idea is just . . . freaky . . . So, it's my fault.

Adam Right . . .

Phillip I mean, who gets married at *twenty-two* these days? Right? it's not the Middle Ages, for chrissakes . . . (*Beat.*) I just feel bad . . . You know, for her.

Adam Why?

Phillip Kissing you . . . That's hideous! It's what those new-age dumbshits would call 'a desperate cry for help' . . .

They laugh, catching each other's eye.

Adam Sorry . . .

Phillip 'S alright. It's better than me having to kiss you . . .

Adam Good point.

Phillip No tongue, right?

Adam Jesus . . .

Phillip I'm just asking . . .

Adam No! Please . . .

Phillip looks at his watch.

Phillip Well, I got a three-ten. You?

Adam Nah . . . I'm free. Gonna go work out.

Phillip You and the . . . What is going on with the 'metamorphosis' thing here? You're like Frankenstein . . .

Adam You mean, Frankenstein's monster. Frankenstein was the doctor . . .

Phillip Ahh, don't be such an English Lit prick . . .

Adam I am an English Lit prick.

Phillip I know, but you don't have to sound like one, do you? Doctor, monster, whatever! What's up with that?

Adam Nothing. It feels good.

Phillip How much weight have you lost?

Adam Not that much, maybe ten pounds or . . .

Phillip I'd say more like fifteen.

Adam Yeah, maybe.

Phillip And the hair thing going, no glasses now . . .

Adam It's just a few little . . .

Phillip Hey, it's the 'new you'. Plus, the nails. Jenny told me that, which is the one that I just cannot believe!

Adam It's a life change . . .

Phillip Please, don't make me throw up with the Oprah-talk, alright? I'm trying to compliment you here . . .

Adam . . . Thanks.

Phillip I used to find blood on our *phone*, okay, so it's not just this casual thing, quitting . . .

Adam I know. I know that . . .

Phillip Alright, then. (*Beat.*) No, you look good. I can see why she kissed you . . . Hell, I might even kiss you, with a few drinks in me.

Adam (*laughing*) I'll run home and hide the liquor . . .

Phillip Please, I'll help you! (*Beat.*) And nothing else happened, right, I mean, between you and Jenny?

Adam stops cold. Walked right into a trap.

Adam . . . What?

Phillip I'm just asking.

Adam Phil . . .

Phillip Not really looking for a speech or anything. Just an answer. She said 'no', just so you don't think I'm laying a trap here or whatever . . .

Adam I don't.

Phillip . . . Nobody saw you on campus or anything. A ranger out in the woods. You know, so . . .

Adam . . . What's that supposed to mean?

Phillip I'm just *saying*, I'll believe you, whatever you tell me. I've got no witnesses. So . . .

Adam Nothing happened, Phil. Truthfully.

Phillip . . . That's not what she said.

Adam freezes but doesn't falter.

Adam That's not true.

Phillip You sure?

Adam Yes.

Phillip You're right, it's not true. Hey, a man's gotta try . . .

Adam Uh-huh . . .

Phillip Not that I want out of this or anything. I love scuba-diving . . .

Adam Of course. As we all do . . .

Phillip Exactly. I'm just not sure I wanna share my air tank with the same person the rest of my life . . .

Adam says nothing, just smiles.

. . . But that's my problem. (*Beat.*) I gotta get to class . . .

Adam Alright. Take care.

Phillip Sorry for the, you know, crazy shit.

Adam It's okay . . .

Phillip . . . Don't kiss my girlfriend any more, alright?

Adam You got it.

Phillip See you . . . We should do something again one of these days, all of us, I mean . . .

Adam . . . Yeah . . .

Phillip If you guys wanna. Let us know. So long, Romeo!

Adam (*pulling on a coat*) Knock it off!

Phillip starts off but stops dead. He turns back and studies Adam.

Phillip . . . Where's your jacket?

Adam What?

Phillip Okay, this is too much. The cord jacket, the lumberjacky-looking thing . . .

Adam I dunno . . .

Phillip And this, umm, Tommy Hilfiger-ish job, where'd you come up with that?

Adam . . . The mall. I bought it.

Phillip *You* bought some clothes? You, like, went out to the mall on your bike and actually . . .

Adam No, Evelyn drove me. So? What's the big . . . ?

Phillip The deal is this . . . You've had that frumpy-looking fucker for three years, probably more, and I've never seen you out of it. *Ever*. Winter, the dead of summer, whatever, you've got that coat on. And now you're just like, 'Hey, whatever. (*Yawns.*) Yeah, I bought the ol' stars and stripes here with Evelyn.' That's like a sailing slicker!

Adam It's their yachtsman line . . .

Phillip I am gonna puke here, I swear to God! I did not just hear you use the word 'yachtsman' . . .

Adam Hey, she likes it . . .

Phillip Well, isn't that just neat? And peachy keen and whatever other *Little House on the Prairie* shit you wanna spout . . . What I wanna know is, do you like it?

Adam . . . It's okay.

Phillip Not what I said. I asked, 'Do-you-like-it?'

Adam It's fine. It's a coat . . .

Phillip And lemme ask you . . . Did you keep the cord job or did she make you toss it?

Adam . . . Who cares? This is . . . I threw it out, okay? Goodwill, actually.

Phillip 'Goodwill, actually.'

Adam It's really no big deal . . .

Phillip Dude, don't just say 'no big deal'. I begged you to throw out the farm coat our freshman year, I mean, you've lost *both* of us a lot of dates with that thing on! You've had it since, like, birth, okay, so do me a little favour and let's not pretend that the jacket and the, ahh, weight and the Jon Bon Jovi hair are no big deal. Because when it comes to routine, you used to be like Mister goddamn *Rogers*!

Adam Phil, it's a fucking jacket, so just lay off. Go to class . . .

Phillip Uh-huh. Fine . . .

Adam Fine.

Phillip I just hope next time we pass each other I recognise who the hell you are . . .

Adam Well, if not, you and Evelyn can always head over to Record City and have a chat . . .

Phillip Hey, I wouldn't get too deep into the moral issues during this particular conversation . . . Okay, Romeo? I may have a big fucking mouth, but at least I keep it to myself . . .

They stare at each other, a nearly visible wall going up between them. Adam blinks first and walks off. Phillip watches him go.

So long, matey!

A COFFEE SHOP

Evelyn stands with Jenny at a high table, sipping hot drinks.

Evelyn ... And you, everything's good?

Jenny Yeah, you know. Okay.

Evelyn Huh. Well, that's nice to hear ...

Jenny You?

Evelyn Oh, you know, pretty great. Just studying, working on my art ...

Jenny Right, you've got a big thing you're doing, or ... what do you call it?

Evelyn Thesis project. For my degree ...

Jenny That's terrific.

Evelyn Yeah. The showing's in a couple weeks ...

Jenny And it's going well? What is it again?

Evelyn I never said ...

Jenny Oh, well, that's why.

Evelyn Right. (*Beat.*) It's this sculpture thingie ...

Jenny Nice. Mmm, I love the arts.

Evelyn Really?

Jenny Yeah, you know, going to movies and stuff. We don't get so many here, we have to drive into the city for any of the newer releases, but I see a lot of videos. Phil watches 'em constantly.

Evelyn Yeah, and what kind does he like?

Jenny Oh, a bunch, but more artsy ones than I do . . . *Aliens. Blade Runner. Twelve Monkeys.* Is that right, or were there ten of 'em?

Evelyn No, it was twelve . . . A dozen monkeys, I think, all together.

Jenny Anyway, that kind. Sci-fi, but with some meaning, too. And action.

Evelyn Huh. That's great . . . I hate sci-fi. (*Beat.*) And you? What kind do you like, Jenny?

Jenny Umm, any, I don't mind . . . But I usually like at least some romance in them. That's always nice.

Evelyn studies her for a moment.

Evelyn Yes . . . Romance's good. Especially when you least expect it.

Jenny Uh-huh . . .

Jenny looks over, sees that Evelyn is watching her, looks away quickly.

 . . . You know, I was gonna say, I think what you've done with Adam, it's really great.

Evelyn And what've I done?

Jenny You know, just . . . He's changed.

Evelyn That's right. *He's* changed.

Jenny That's what I mean.

Evelyn He's done the work . . .

Jenny Of course, I didn't mean that you . . .

Evelyn I know. I'm just saying, he did it.

Jenny Right. That's always what they say, though, isn't it?

Evelyn What? And who are they?

Jenny You know, like in *Cosmo*, when they have those tests, asking what you'd like to change about your guy . . .

Evelyn Ahhh. Now you're gonna get all scientific on me . . .

Jenny It's true, though, right? Almost everybody I've gone out with, if you could alter just one thing, or even get them to stop wearing sunglasses up on their head all the time . . . Then they'd be perfect. It's that sort of deal, isn't it?

Evelyn Something like that . . . Or it could just be that I care about him.

Jenny Phil's got, like, six of those 'one things', but it's the same idea . . .

Evelyn Right. And how is ol' Phil?

Jenny He's . . . Phil. Six 'things' away from being amazing . . .

Adam arrives at the table, obviously unprepared to find both women waiting for him. He wears no bandage.

Adam . . . Hey, Evelyn. Hi, Jenny, hello.

Evelyn / Jenny Hi, Adam. Hello.

Adam I didn't know you guys were . . .

Evelyn I invited her.

Adam That's alright, then . . .

Jenny I like your new jacket! Phil told me about it . . .

Adam Oh, right. Yeah. It's . . . new.

Jenny And your nose! God, you okay?

Adam Yep. Course . . . It was nothing.

Jenny Falling down's not nothing. (*Studies him.*) Looks okay, though . . .

An uncomfortable pause. Evelyn looks over at Adam, who clears his throat.

Evelyn You *fell*?

Adam . . . Yeah. Anyway . . .

Evelyn Anyway, pull up some floor . . . We got you a cocoa.

He moves warily to them, squeezing in next to Evelyn.

Adam Thanks. (*To Evelyn.*) You don't drink coffee . . .

Evelyn It's not. It's decaf . . .

Adam That's still coffee.

Evelyn Good point. So I drink coffee, then, I just don't like the caffeine . . .

Jenny Me either.

Evelyn Really? You don't like caffeine either, Jenny? Did you know that, too, Adam, that Jenny doesn't like caffeine?

Adam No. I didn't know that . . .

Evelyn See? There's lots you don't know . . .

They all sip their drinks silently for a moment.

Jenny was just saying that she thinks you're great . . . I mean, doing great things with yourself.

Adam Yeah? Thanks, Jenny . . .

Jenny You're welcome. I just . . .

Evelyn She thinks you're just about perfect now, don't you, Jen?

Jenny I didn't say that.

Evelyn So, he's not perfect, then? Obviously his motor control's a bit off, if he fell, but . . .

Jenny I said that you guys are . . .

Adam Forget about it.

Evelyn It's true, I'm exaggerating. She said, and I paraphrase, 'He's changed.' but she implied for the better . . .

Adam Well, I agree. I have. And again, thank you.

Jenny Welcome . . .

Evelyn I think you've changed, too, Adam. A lot.

Adam Yeah? How's that?

Evelyn Well, I mean, it's obvious, all the minor things are pretty obvious, but in subtler ways as well . . . You've gotten cuter. And stronger. More confident. And craftier . . .

Adam 'Craftier', huh?

Evelyn Apparently so . . . That spill you took must've done it.

Jenny I'm sorry, am I missing something?

Adam I'm not sure . . . (*To Evelyn.*) Evelyn, what's up?

Evelyn Nothing. Not a thing . . .

Jenny I mean, you knew about him hurting himself, didn't you? (*To Adam.*) Phil said you had a big bandage on, so I just figured . . .

Evelyn No, Jenny, I saw it. I'm kidding . . .

Jenny Ahh. I couldn't tell . . .

Evelyn Sometimes it's hard to read me. Know when I'm joking . . .

Adam Very hard.

Evelyn It is. But I am . . . Joking, I mean. Adam took a bad fall and smashed his nose, but he's okay now . . . See?

She grabs Adam's face and holds it out for Jenny to look. Adam pulls away, a bit too quickly.

. . . It healed well, don't you think?

Jenny Yes.

Adam Do you guys wanna salad or something? I'm hungry . . .

Evelyn I'm fine. Jenny . . . Hungry?

Jenny I'm okay. (*To Adam.*) Your nose looks . . . How much weight have you lost?

Adam Not that much, really.

Evelyn Twenty-one pounds. (*To Adam.*) I peeked, is that alright?

He glares at her; Jenny tries to keep up.

Jenny 'Peeked'?

Evelyn His journal . . . A record of his progress that he's keeping. Twenty-one pounds as of –

Adam – last Friday. Yeah.

Jenny Really? That's so cool . . .

Evelyn *Cosmo* story in the making, huh?

Jenny Yep.

Adam It's good, yeah, I've been keeping at it . . .

Evelyn She knows, Adam, she already said you've 'changed'. And I already agreed. We're past that . . .

Adam Okay, I'm, like, totally lost here . . .

Evelyn You're mentioned in there, too, Jenny.

Jenny Where?

Evelyn Adam's journal. I mean, it's a veiled entry but I think it's you . . .

Adam Evelyn . . .

Evelyn I peeked twice. (*To Jenny.*) You're right next to someone known as 'cute waitress'.

Jenny (*cautiously*) . . . Why's that? I mean . . . Adam?

Adam You're not. It's . . . She's . . .

Evelyn Something about a meeting . . . And a drive after, in your cute little V-Dub . . .

Adam What're you saying?! Jenny, there's not any . . .

Jenny picks up her purse and smiles thinly.

Jenny You know what? It's pretty late, I should get . . .

Adam No, don't go . . . (*To Evelyn.*) Why are you doing this?

Evelyn I'm just having coffee. Decaf.

Jenny I need to go.

Evelyn I just wanna talk about the kiss. Why can't we do that?

The moment hangs. Jenny stops short.

We should just put it out there . . . I'm very open, and I just feel that . . .

Adam This is inappropriate, okay?

Jenny (*to Adam*) Did you tell her about the . . . ?

Evelyn No, no, he didn't . . . Phillip did. Days ago. We met and he told me all about it, Jenny. What you told him, anyway. The rest I got from loverboy's diary . . .

Jenny . . . Adam?

Adam She's making that up . . . She's . . .

Evelyn Am I?

Adam Yes!

Evelyn Then set the record straight . . .

Adam I don't wanna do this right now.

Evelyn Seems a touch late for that.

Jenny (*to Evelyn*) Phillip told you about our talk? When? (*Beat.*) What else did he tell you?

Evelyn Lots of things . . . He's a very chatty guy, when you wind him up.

Jenny . . . I can't believe it . . .

Evelyn Then you're never gonna believe the rest of this . . .

Adam Evelyn, let's just drop it, okay? If you're angry with me, alright, but this is not . . .

Evelyn We're just talking. People need to share more, that's how this stuff happens, this covert stuff, because we hide it . . .

Jenny Fine . . . You want to . . . Go ahead. Adam wrote something in his journal, obviously, and I told Phil about . . .

Adam Jenny, I didn't . . .

Jenny What do you wanna hear? We kissed.

Evelyn No, I knew that . . . I'm sorry, I've confused you. I meant about my kiss. With Phillip. That's the part I wanted to talk about with you guys . . . I didn't make that clear?

Jenny . . . What?

Adam That's bullshit . . .

Evelyn No, that's getting even. (*Beat.*) Unless you guys have something else to tell me about. Meaning, 'the drive' . . .

Adam We didn't go on any . . .

Jenny That's not true. You didn't meet Phil . . .

Evelyn Ask him.

Jenny . . . Or he would've told me . . . He . . .

Evelyn Apparently not.

Jenny . . . I'm going. I'm going now, 'Kay?

Evelyn Fine, then we'll just let that one hang for a bit . . . The woods, I mean.

Jenny I'll . . . see you. Adam, I'm . . .

Evelyn (*calling to her*) You guys are still coming to my showing, right? Phillip said you would!

She is gone. Adam takes a careful sip before speaking. He turns to Evelyn, about to speak, when Jenny returns.

Jenny (*directly at Evelyn*) Hey . . . Look, I don't know why I'm here, I guess I came back to say 'I'm sorry'. Sorry if I've offended you in some way, or done something to make you so indifferent to me, cold or whatever. And I don't mean what's happened, I don't, because I think you've been this way the whole time

I've known you. So . . . Sorry I'm not an artsy person or cool enough or, you know, I'm not super-smart, sorry about that. But as far as just *being* a person, like, an average-type person . . . I'm pretty okay. I am. (*Beat.*) That kinda came out bad, I mean, dumb, so I'm just gonna . . . Yeah.

She wanders off.

Adam . . . Okay, that was horrible.

Evelyn Oh, I dunno . . . I could've told her about the blow job I gave him. (*Beat.*) Kidding . . .

Adam No, listen, what you did was shitty, and awful and just plain wrong . . .

Evelyn As opposed to you two sneaking off and making out? Where would that fall on the 'bad behaviour' list . . . ?

Adam You had no right to do that.

Evelyn True.

Adam Make her feel that way . . .

Evelyn She's got a boyfriend who's shit. Now she knows. Hell, she already knew . . .

Adam It was still wrong to treat her like that! And me.

Evelyn Yeah, let's talk about you . . .

Adam Go ahead. You seem raring to go.

Evelyn You wanna tell me about the rest of your date, or should I . . . ?

Adam She called me, okay, asked if I could get together and talk, you know, about Phil. And them.

Evelyn And then you made out. Most natural thing in the world . . .

Adam It just happened. Look, I was going to say something . . .

Evelyn That was Hitler's excuse. Try another one . . .

Adam It was a mistake! Okay? I know that . . .

Evelyn And how *big* was that mistake? (*Beat.*) I don't care about what happened. I don't. I just want the truth . . . I told you about what I did – you think I wanted to kiss that guy? – I only did it for the effect. But I'm asking you . . . What else went on? I deserve to know.

Adam . . . Nothing.

Evelyn You're sticking with that?

Adam Yes.

Evelyn Even if I tell you I know something else went on.

Adam How could you? It didn't . . . And I did not put any 'drive' in my journal. That was a lie.

Evelyn No, it was a *bluff*. Because I could sense it . . . (*Beat.*) And the waitress *was* there . . .

Adam I'm telling you the truth. About Jenny, I mean . . .

Evelyn I don't believe you.

Adam . . . I am!

Evelyn Then we'll have to leave it at that. Won't we?

They stare at one another. She touches her nose.

Oh, and glad to hear about your trip . . . See you next fall.

Adam That's a bad joke . . .

Evelyn It's a worse lie . . .

Adam What was I gonna tell them? Huh?

Evelyn The truth?

Adam Come on . . . I took shit about my new jacket! That's all people say to me any more, 'What's up with you? What's going on?' I can't exactly spread it around about what I've done . . .

Evelyn What? You *fell* . . .

Adam What're we doing here?

Evelyn I dunno. You tell me . . .

Adam I don't know. I really don't . . .

Evelyn Are you tired of me? 'S that it?

Adam God, no! Are you nuts?!

Evelyn Then I don't get it . . . I don't wanna sound ol'-fashioned here, but you're a step away from fucking around on me . . .

Adam I would never do that . . .

Evelyn No, you would never do that with *her*, and mostly because she wouldn't. I know the type, she needed a shoulder, well, what the hell, why not a kiss while she's at it, and maybe a quick hand job. Who knows? But she's not gonna screw you and you probably wouldn't be able to get it up, anyway, because he's your best 'bud'. (*Beat.*) But lemme ask you, Adam, if it hadn't been her, if it'd been, oh, say that 'cute waitress' the other night . . .

Adam looks away; Evelyn doesn't let up.

. . . Didn't think I caught that, did you? The chatty-chat and the extra three bucks on the tip.

Adam . . . That was nothing.

Evelyn It's never anything. Until it's something . . . (*Beat.*) If it'd been her instead . . . Out on that drive . . .

Adam . . . We-didn't-go-for-a . . .

Evelyn . . . Whatever. But if she'd been there instead, then what? Just ask yourself.

Adam Jesus, next you're gonna tell me the handkerchief with the strawberries on it is missing . . .

Evelyn I don't know that reference.

Adam Don't worry about it. (*Pleads.*) Evelyn, please . . .

She smiles and begins more gently.

Evelyn I just wanna know where we stand . . . I thought I could trust you.

Adam You can!

Evelyn She's your friend's fiancée, Adam. I'm your girlfriend . . . Where's the trust in that?

He takes her hand suddenly.

Adam I'll do anything you want. Okay? I know what I did was wrong, I do, I messed up but I've never done that before. Lied to a person I was going out with . . . Shit, I haven't even gone out with someone for the two years before we met! So, tell me what to do and I'll do it . . . I just, I just don't wanna lose you.

Evelyn You're sure . . . ?

Adam I am so sure. I love you . . .

Evelyn I told you, that's a big word . . .

Adam . . . And I'm using it. I do, completely.

Evelyn Anything I say?

Adam Anything.

Evelyn (*without emotion*) Give them up. As friends, both of them. No explanation. Don't see them or speak to them again. Not ever.

Adam . . . Huh?

Evelyn That's what I want. That's the proof to me about how you feel . . .

Adam Evelyn . . . That's . . .

Evelyn One should always be careful when asking to be put to a test . . .

Adam . . . Jesus Christ . . .

Evelyn So, what's it gonna be, Adam?

Adam And if I don't . . .?

Evelyn Pretty much like these things end. I mean, in life, at least . . . If this was a movie, I'd see the light eventually, but no such luck. Final answer?

Adam stares at her for a long moment.

Adam . . . I choose you.

She pulls him close and kisses him for a long time.

Evelyn You choose well, grasshopper . . .

AN AUDITORIUM

Phillip standing around, dressed up. Adam enters, holding a glass of punch, tries to go the other way but Phillip stops him.

Phillip . . . Adam, dude, what's up?!

Adam (*looking around*) Hey, Phil. How's it going?

Phillip You know, okay. So, what, you don't take my calls now?

Adam No, I've been . . . I mean . . .

Phillip 'S okay, I understand. The whole . . . thing . . .

Adam Nah, it's just been busy lately. At work and stuff . . .

Phillip Yeah. Whatever.

Adam Seriously. (*Beat.*) I need to get a seat . . .

Phillip Hold on, hey . . . Where's the fire?

Adam (*nervously*) I just wanna . . . Good spot. (*Beat.*) Where's Jenny?

Phillip Funny.

Adam What?

Phillip Man, come on . . . We broke up. Broke it off, whatever. You knew that.

Adam What? No, I, when . . . ?

Phillip Like, two weeks ago . . . Right after . . . You know. And I'm sorry about that. I was pissed off, but, I mean . . . No call for that 'eye for an eye' shit.

Adam . . . It's okay. But you and Jenny're . . . ? I can't believe that.

Phillip Believe it. (*Beat.*) She came over one day, after seeing you guys, I guess, and that was it. The ring off, and gone.

Adam . . . I'm sorry.

Phillip Listen, no hard feelings . . . I was looking to get out, you know that. But once you start making those plans, you know, like picking out *napkins* and shit, it's almost easier to just do the thing! (*Beat.*) You did me a favour, really . . . Too young to get hitched.

Adam I don't know what to say . . .

Phillip Don't worry about it. (*Beat.*) You haven't seen her lately, have you? Jenny, I mean . . .

Adam No . . .

Phillip 'Kay. Anyway, this oughta be good, huh?!

They share a light laugh. Jenny walks up the aisle, sees them and goes for a seat.

Adam Jenny, hi . . .

Jenny Oh, Adam . . . Hello. Hi, Phil.

Phillip Hey.

Adam I'm sorry about . . . you guys . . .

Jenny (*glaring at Phil*) Boy, you just can't keep anything to yourself, can you?

Phillip What?

Jenny You never change . . . That's what.

She turns and walks off, taking a place in the auditorium.

Adam What's she . . . ?

Phillip It's not, like, totally *official* yet . . . Ahh, fuck, what're you gonna do?

The lights flicker twice. Adam looks up.

Adam We should find a place to . . .

Phillip (*looking*) There's two over there.

Adam Umm . . . Maybe we shouldn't . . .

Phillip . . . Got it. Okay, whatever. Take care, man.

He wanders off. Adam watches him go, then finds a place to sit.

Lights go down, theatrical lights up. After a moment, Evelyn (dressed up for her presentation) enters crisply and smiles.

Evelyn Good evening. Thank you for coming out tonight – it's very cold and rainy and I'm sure this is not how most of you would choose to spend your time away from campus . . . *On* campus. So, I promise to make this presentation as quick and painless as possible, for most of you at least, and get you back home as swiftly as I can. The accompanying visual portion of this graduate thesis project is currently under review but will hopefully be available in the exhibition gallery down the hall for your perusal next week, so if you don't stay tonight for punch and cookies, umm, please stop by and take a look at your convenience. (*Smiles.*) Okay, that's the boring stuff . . .

She turns over a note card.

My task here tonight is to unveil my semester's work, explain it and then smile and shake hands, leaving a few of you to examine it, grade it, etc. In essence, be at your mercy. Which is fine, since I realise I have been my entire academic life – at someone's mercy, that is – which reaches back to when I was five. So be it . . . That's the system and one person can't change it . . . But perhaps they can make you question that system and your values just a little bit. Thus, my rather, ahh, dramatic presentation at this time. (*Looks over card.*) Blah-blah-blah . . .

Evelyn starts to move but steps back into the light, as if she's forgotten something.

Oh, I almost forgot . . . And this is fairly personal, probably shouldn't even do it but it really is the capper to my time here at Clarkson, so please indulge me. (*Beat.*) I was given an engagement ring two days ago and I haven't answered the guy yet . . . So I wanted to do it this evening. Here goes. This is a beautiful stone and an amazing gesture on your part, for many reasons. By the time I'm through here, I promise that you'll have your answer . . .

She shows the ring off to the audience.

My graduate advisor gave me this advice five months ago . . . 'Strive to make art, but change the world.' Pretty wise words, I thought, at the time, and so, being a good little student, that's what I set out to do. As you know, every journey begins with a single step – boy, the 'coffee cup slogans' are coming hard and fast tonight – and so I set out to . . .

She appears almost nervous, but not quite. She looks at the audience for a moment.

As I looked around my world for something to change, I knew I'd been given a tall order. 'Change the world.' So, I decided to do the next best thing, which was change someone's world. I mean, that's a start, right? One person changes, and then another, and then, well, you get it . . . Crude but effective. With that in mind, I present to you this, my newest work. It is a *human* sculpture on which I've worked these past eighteen weeks, and of whom I'm very proud. I cannot legally name him tonight as he hasn't yet signed a waiver for the various items on display in the visual portion, but it's a small college, and a smaller town. (*Laughs.*) So you've got a pretty decent chance at guessing who it is. In fact, I've done all I could to be as visible as possible with him this year – I'm more of a stay-at-home person myself – since I thought that was an important aspect of his unique transformation. The piece itself – him – is untitled since I think, I hope, that it will mean something different to each of you and, frankly, anyone who sees it. His own name, however, is quite apropos.

She turns over a large photograph from a nearby easel. The face has been blurred out.

I did the MTV thing here on the face . . . This is a 'before' picture that I had a classmate take of us near the Pizza Hut out by the highway. That was our first official encounter after he asked me out – at his place of work, a big no-no, or so I was told – and it was here that I coaxed him into eating his first vegetarian meal. Well, as vegetarian as a spinach-and-mushroom calzone can be! He also had a salad . . . Anyway, he told me that, for him, it was a huge deal and it does mark the beginning of my systematic makeover, or 'sculpting', if you will, of my two very pliable materials of choice: the human flesh and the human will. (*Beat.*) I first spotted my chosen base material . . . It's so funny not to use names! Sorry, but a lawyer actually told me I had to say that, 'base material' . . . On January 9th, the fifth day of winter semester, as I was actively pursuing another set of 'base material'. (*Grins.*) Obviously, my current creation appeared much more right for my work and so I created a scenario that would allow for our eventual, yet seemingly random, connection.

She scans the audience.

Still with me? You're very quiet . . . Okay. The exhibit itself will give you many first-hand examples of my efforts, some hands-on such as video tapes or sound recordings of our conversations and others more scientific in nature, as in growth charts, X-rays and accompanying data. As you can see from this photo, however, the hair, the glasses, the excessive amount of weight, offered a number of physical areas that made him unique and perfect for this project. A short list of alterations I've induced would include eating better and losing weight – some twenty-five pounds or more – an exercise regimen that included both cardiovascular work and weight training, the purchase of contact lenses, a complete change in hairstyles and significant wardrobe alterations as well. He even tattooed his body for me, without asking . . . In a highly questionable place. These are surface items, to be sure, but if I, in fact, tell you that I'm going through with it and marrying the guy, you'd probably all shake my hand and say, 'Wow, how the hell can I do that to my boyfriend?' but this, I'm afraid, was not done out of love or caring or concern . . . This was a simple matter of can I instil 'x' amount of change in this creature, using only manipulation as my palette knife? I made sure that nothing was ever forced during our sessions or 'sittings' together – I can't really say they were dates, not on my part, although the illusion of 'dating' was imperative – and that his free will was always at the forefront of each decision. I coaxed, made suggestions, created the illusion of interest and desire, but never said, 'Please do this.' Not once. Any questions yet?

She scans the crowd.

Umm . . . You may be asking yourselves, 'Well, did she at least tell him?' Of course not, no, I couldn't. Not until tonight, or he really wouldn't be a piece of art. He would be a jilted lover, a spurned fiancé, etc. But he is more than that . . . He's my creation. Now, it'll be easy for many of you to condemn my actions as harsh, inhumane or unrealistic as you drive or walk home tonight, but remember this, like so many of you when pursuing your personal best in relationships and at work . . . I was interested in humanity, yes, but insistent on results above all else. How many here can say that they have never looked at their significant other and/or a business associate and said, 'They're perfect, they're great, except for just *one* thing . . .' Well, I too have taken my base materials and honed them into something new, something unique and, in the eyes and standards of society, something arguably improved. But, with the artist's ruthless pursuit of truth and historical disregard for rule and law . . . I've gone a step further. I found that, with the right coaxing of my material – yes, 'coaxing' often of a sexual nature, I'll admit – I could hone the inside of my sculpture as well as the surface. I found myself suddenly creating strong moral ambiguity where I could detect only the slightest traces before, often in direct proportion to the amount of external change. This means, as my subject became handsomer and firmer and more confident, his actions became more and more, ahh, *questionable*. Against medical advice, he had work done to his face, cosmetic surgery at age twenty-two, and insisted to those around him that he had merely fallen down. He also started to deceive his friends and myself with greater abandon during this period while showing increased interest in other women. Indeed, he had relations with his best friend's fiancée and continues to harbour details from us about the incident to this day. Moreover, he was willing to give those friends up when asked, walk away from them without any further contact, after said encounter, leading me to an assumption of further wrongdoing with the young woman in question. And, as stated earlier, these universal corrections culminated in an offer of marriage to me, this coming from a confirmed, albeit young, bachelor. I call this act 'morally questionable' because it seems to be motivated, in my mind at least, as much out of guilt as genuine feelings for me. He has then, as I see it, been utterly and totally refashioned as a person. (*Beat.*) As my grandfather used to say, 'He's a real piece of work . . .'

She holds up a large 'after' photo for all to see.

And yet open any fashion magazine, turn on any television programme, and the world will tell you . . . He's only gotten more interesting, more desirable, more normal. In a word, *better*. He is a living, breathing example of our obsession with the surface of things, the shape of them. (*Beat.*) Now, my work will fade, to be sure. Like chipping marble or crazing paint, it will succumb to a can of Pringles, a late morning in bed. To time itself. But for this one glorious moment, it is perfect. As perfect as I made it . . . (*To photo.*) Not bad, huh? And ladies, he is available. (*To Adam.*) This was a startling and unexpected gesture, but obviously, I can't accept . . .

She takes off the ring and places it on an easel.

You can examine the stone and setting further when it's placed in the exhibit. (*Beat.*) As for me, I have no regrets or feelings of remorse for my actions, the manufactured emotions . . . None of it. I have always stood by the single and simple conceit that I am an artist. Only that. I follow in a long tradition of artists who believe that there is no such concept as religion, or government, community or even family. There is only art. Art that must be created. Whatever the cost. (*Beat.*) With that in mind, I present you with my untitled sculpture and supporting materials tonight. Thank you.

She takes a short bow and steps out of the light.

AN EXHIBITION GALLERY

Several podiums scattered about with various 'supporting data' on them. Evelyn standing all alone, punch in one hand, cookie in the other. After a moment, she takes a nibble. She crosses to a box of photos and browses. Adam enters and stares at her.

Adam . . . Not a big 'modern art' crowd, I guess, huh?

Evelyn Hey. (*Beat.*) Glad you stopped by . . .

Adam Yeah, well, I didn't really have anything to do . . . Plus, I can't show my face in the streets, so it seemed logical.

Evelyn Look, Adam . . .

Adam Please don't 'Look, Adam' me now, okay, or I might not make it through this . . . (*Beat.*) Just refer to me as 'it' or 'untitled', it'll help me keep some perspective here . . .

He wanders over and pours some punch. Stuffs a few cookies in his pocket. Shoves three in his mouth and chews them down.

. . . That's gonna shoot some piece of data all to shit, isn't it?

Evelyn Doesn't matter now, do what you want . . . You're finished.

Adam 'You're finished.' Wow. (*Considers.*) Most people just say, 'Hey, sorry, can't marry you.' And they say it in private . . .

Evelyn . . . Yeah, that might've been a bit too far.

Adam Oh shit, Evelyn, you are so beyond 'far' that you're in danger of hitting Uranus. And I mean the planet . . .

Evelyn (*smiling*) See, you're still funny . . .

Adam Just stop, alright? I was never funny, ever, or good-looking or clever. I was nothing until you started dicking around with me. I admit it. No-thing. But you know what? I was absolutely fine with that . . .

Evelyn I know this is a lot for you to take in and everything . . .

Adam Uh-huh . . . I got a little Gregor Samsa thing going right now, so . . .

Evelyn I don't get that . . .

Adam Doesn't matter. I do . . . I get it.

A moment of dead silence.

Evelyn . . . Listen, I know my work relied on not telling you what was going on, but I . . .

Adam Here in a 'small town' we just call it lying . . .

Evelyn I did lie to you, yes . . .

Adam Yeah, just a little. (*Beat.*) 'I'm a very straightforward person . . .'

Evelyn I had to say that. Sorry.

Adam You're sorry? Well, that's good . . . I figured I was gonna have to really work to get that one out of you.

Evelyn I'm not sorry. I mean, not for what I've done. I just feel bad that you're so upset . . .

Adam Oh, I see . . .

Evelyn I even thought maybe you could handle it. I did, really . . . Otherwise I wouldn't have invited you tonight.

Adam Yeah, just me and two hundred of my closest friends.

Evelyn Adam, you don't have any friends. (*Beat.*) You gave up the only ones I've known you to have. Gave 'em up pretty easily . . .

Adam shivers at this one; she's turned out to be a cool little number.

Adam Geez . . . Don't hold back at all, please. Call it exactly how you see it.

Evelyn I just want to keep it as truthful as possible.

Adam (*laughing*) That'll be different . . .

Evelyn ... You're *so* angry ...

Adam Well, you know, Evelyn, what do you want me to say?! You messed with my life and you put it under fucking glass ... That might make anyone a touch cross.

Evelyn What'd I do wrong? (*Beat.*) Seriously, tell me ...

Adam Screw you ...

Evelyn You have screwed me. A lot. You wanna watch it? There's a cassette over there somewhere.

Adam You are seriously twisted up. I mean it ...

Evelyn Yeah ... What was so bad? I wanna know, tell me ... From your perspective.

Adam I'm not gonna give you a last little thrill. Fuck that.

Evelyn Listen to your mouth, Adam ... You never used to talk like that.

Adam You're gonna take credit for that, too, huh?

Evelyn Nope, you picked that up all on your own. Cute guys always have potty mouths. They think it makes 'em cuter ...

Adam Yeah, well, tell me how 'cute' this one is, then ... Up yours, you heartless cunt.

Evelyn So, tell me then. Go ahead, you feel that way about me, you can tell me what I did wrong. *If* I did something wrong ...

Adam You don't see this as wrong?!

Evelyn I said, you tell me. I wanna know what you think I did ...

He stops for a moment, taking a deep breath. Not really wanting to engage.

Adam You honestly have no concept here . . .

Evelyn Just say it . . .

Adam Aww, shit. Look . . . I don't have time, okay? I'm not gonna stand here and . . .

Evelyn The exercising? Or was it the new clothes that really bugged you?

Adam That is not the . . .

Evelyn Everything I did made you a more desirable person, Adam. People began to notice you . . . Take interest in you. I watched them . . .

Adam Well, lucky me. I got to be part of your installation 'thingie'.

Evelyn You *are* my installation thingie . . . (*Beat.*) Look, if you hadn't been here tonight, hadn't heard all this stuff . . . wouldn't you still be happy? Waiting at home for me, hoping this went well, wanting to make love . . .

Adam That's not the point . . .

Evelyn Yes, it is! It's the *total* point. All that stuff we did was real for you, therefore it was real. It wasn't for me, therefore it wasn't. It's all subjective, Adam. Everything.

Adam Not love. Not cruelty.

Evelyn Of course they are . . .

Adam (*reaching*) I'll tell you something 'real', I should sue your ass.

Evelyn You could . . . I did take that risk.

Adam That's right, you did, and you're crazy if you think I'm gonna let you put all this shit on display. Our time together. (*Points.*) Those're our video tapes, aren't they? The . . . sex ones. They are! You are nuts . . .

Evelyn There's a lot of stuff here. I haven't even put it all out yet . . .

Adam Well, you might as well keep it packed up, then.

Evelyn You should be proud of it . . . most of it . . .

Adam Just save it, 'kay?

Evelyn Well, what about your jacket? Where should I put that?

Adam . . . What?

Evelyn Your old jacket. The one I sprayed my number in, at the museum. (*Beat.*) It was only four bucks at the Goodwill . . .

Adam . . . Why would you buy that?

Evelyn Just so I'd have it. In case . . .

Adam So, blackmail, too, huh? Ohh, shit . . . (*Beat.*) Which page of the 'Scorned Girls' Handbook' is that on?

Evelyn I dunno, but I bet it's in there . . .

Adam I do not doubt it.

Evelyn Just wanted you to know, that's all . . .

He scans the room, then throws his hands up. He wanders about.

Adam . . . Fine.

Evelyn What?

Adam It's fine, forget it . . .

Evelyn What is?

Adam What the hell . . . It can't get any worse. You get off on showing people my old socks and scuzzy sheets, go for it . . .

Evelyn I don't 'get off' on it . . .

Adam It means so much to you, have a field day . . .

Evelyn . . . Adam, this is my work. (*Beat.*) I'll give back whatever you want, soon as I get my grade.

Adam Whatever . . .

Evelyn I will.

Adam The ring'd be nice. It was my grandma's.

Evelyn I'll take care of it.

Adam Thanks. Good . . .

Evelyn (*honestly*) . . . Hard feelings?

Adam Me? Nah . . . We had some fun, right?

Evelyn Yeah.

Adam But, hey, that's subjective.

Evelyn Exactly.

Adam Then I had some fun, fell in love and all that . . . And you got yourself a grade and a column inch or two in the college paper. Congrats. Seriously . . . But do me a favour, don't fool yourself and think that this is 'art'. 'Kay? It's a sick fucking joke, but it is not 'art'.

Evelyn Is that right?

Adam Pretty much, yeah. (*Beat.*) You know, when Picasso took a shit, he didn't call it a 'sculpture'. He knew the difference. That's what made him Picasso. And if I'm wrong about that, I mean, if I totally miss the point here and somehow puking up your own little shitty neuroses all over people's laps *is* actually art, then you oughta at least realise there's a price to it all . . . You know? Somebody pays for your two minutes on CNN. Someone always pays for people like you. And if you don't get that, if you can't see at least *that* much . . . Then you're about two inches away from using babies to make lamp shades and calling it 'furniture'. (*Beat.*) Look, I know they call it the 'art scene', but that's not all it should make. A scene. It should be more than that. Anybody can be provocative, or shocking. Stand up in class, or at the mall, wherever, and take a piss, paint yourself blue and run naked through a church screaming out the names of people you've slept with. Is that art, or did you just forget to take your Ritalin? There's gotta be a line. For art to exist, there has to be a line out there somewhere. A line between really saying something and just . . . needing attention. (*Beat.*) . . . I guess I'm done.

Evelyn Wow. Okay . . . So, you're saying I should be a 'better person'. Is that it?

Adam That's the nutshell, yeah.

Evelyn Better like . . . you?

Adam No. Just better . . .

Evelyn Well, we'll just have to agree to disagree, then, won't we?

Adam Yes, we will. We will definitely do that. (*Beat.*) Don't forget what Oscar Wilde said . . .

Evelyn He always had something to say, didn't he?

Adam Yeah . . . 'All art is quite useless.' He said that.

Evelyn Huh. I thought you were gonna go with 'Insincerity and treachery somehow seem inseparable from the artistic temperament.' That's a good one, too . . .

Adam It is, yeah. Damn, wish I'd said that.

Evelyn Don't worry about it . . . Look how he ended up.

Adam Yep . . . Alone, penniless and in prison. Everything I wish for you . . . (*He smiles.*) Tell me, though. One thing.

Evelyn Yes?

Adam Was any of it true?

Evelyn What do you mean?

Adam Not the things we did, or the kind words or whatever . . . But any of it?

Evelyn . . . No. Not really.

Adam I mean about you. The nose-job or Lake Forest or your mother's maiden name? One thing you ever said to me?

Evelyn My mom's name is Anderson . . .

Adam Oh. Are you twenty-five?

Evelyn Twenty-two. Just . . . I skipped third grade.

Adam Okay . . . (*Beat.*) And the scars are . . .

Evelyn I made it all up.

Adam Got it. I got it . . . Gemini at least?

Evelyn No, Pisces. Sorry.

Adam Don't be. Hey, it's . . . *art*.

A moment of silence. They look at each other for a bit.

Evelyn (*checking watch*) I should probably get going, I gotta hook up with some guys from my department . . .

Adam Alright.

Evelyn . . . and I think the Dean wants 'a word' with me, too. (*Ricky Ricardo voice.*) 'I got some 'splaining to do.'

Adam What's that from?

Evelyn Nothing. *I Love Lucy.*

Adam Ahh, TV. That other great art form . . .

Evelyn Uh-huh. You coming?

Adam Nah, not yet . . . (*Holds up hands.*) Don't worry, I'm not gonna do anything to your stuff. No spray paint. I just . . .

Evelyn I understand. Go ahead.

Adam Thanks . . .

Evelyn The door locks if you just close it.

Adam Great.

Evelyn smiles at him once more, but says nothing. What's to say? She heads for the door but stops.

Evelyn . . . That one time.

Adam Huh?

Evelyn In your bed, one night, when you leaned over and whispered in my ear . . . Remember?

Adam Course. I remember everything about us.

Evelyn And I whispered back to you, I said . . .

Adam I remember.

Evelyn I meant that. I did.

Adam Yeah?

Evelyn Yes.

Adam . . . Oh.

She starts to say something else but catches herself. She goes out. Adam stands alone in the quiet room, looking about. He takes a few more cookies, eating them as he wanders around and picks up items from his recent life with Evelyn. He finally stops near the TV/VCR. Suddenly, he pops in a tape and settles back on the floor. He finds the moment he is looking for . . . The exchange of whispers.

He presses 'play' and watches it. He rewinds and does it again. And again. He scoots over and pulls on his old jacket, huddling there on the ground. He watches the picture intently, but what is being said remains elusive. Unheard. He continues.

Silence. Darkness.

FAT PIG

Fat Pig was first produced at the Lucille Lortel Theatre, New York, on 23 November 2004 in an MCC Theater production with the following cast:

Tom Jeremy Piven
Helen Ashlie Atkinson
Carter Andrew McCarthy
Jeannie Keri Russell

Director Jo Bonney
Design Louisa Thompson
Lighting Matt Frey
Sound Robert Kaplowitz

Fat Pig was first produced in London at the Trafalgar Studios on 27 May 2008. The cast was as follows:

Tom Robert Webb
Helen Ella Smith
Carter Kris Marshall
Jeannie Joanna Page

Director Neil LaBute
Design Christopher Oram
Lighting Johanna Town
Sound Fergus O'Hare

This production transferred to the Comedy Theatre, London, on 11 September 2008 with the following cast:

Tom Nicholas Burns
Helen Katie Kerr
Carter Kevin Bishop
Jeannie Kelly Brook

Characters

Tom
Helen
Carter
Jeannie

Act One

THAT FIRST MEETING WITH HER

A Woman in a crowded restaurant. Standing at one of those tall tables. A bunch of food in front of her and she is quietly eating it. By the way, she's a plus size. Very.

After a moment, a Man enters juggling a lunch tray. He glances around, then moves toward her.

Man . . . Pretty big.

Woman Excuse me?

Man I'm sorry, I was just sort of, you know, speaking out loud. Pretty big in here. That's what I was saying . . .

Woman Oh. Right.

Man Lot of room for, you know, people.

Woman Yes. It's popular.

The Man looks around, trying to see if there's a spot for him yet.

Man And yet nowhere to . . . actually . . .

Woman You can eat here if you want.

Man No, I don't need to, umm . . .

Woman What?

Man I dunno, I hadn't really thought the rest of that one through! Ahh, 'intrude', I guess.

Woman You're not. I'll make some room for you.

Man You sure?

Woman Of course.

Man Thanks.

She slides some of her food to one side, allowing him a space if he wants it. He takes the spot. Silence.

Woman . . . I thought you meant me. Before.

Man I'm sorry?

Woman When you said that, 'pretty big', I thought you were saying that to me. *About* me.

Man Oh, no, God no! I wouldn't . . . You did?

Woman For a second.

Man No, that'd be . . . you know. Rude.

Woman Still . . .

Man I mean, why would I do that? A thing like that? I'm not . . .

Woman You'd be surprised. People say all kinds of things here.

Man In this place?

Woman No, not just *here*, this restaurant or anything, I mean in the city.

Man So . . . you mean, people actually . . . what? Say things to your face?

Woman Of course. All the time.

Man About what?

She looks over at him without saying anything. Silence.

Woman . . . My *hair colour*. (*Beat.*) What do you think?

Man Oh, I see. (*Smiles.*)

Woman It's not a huge deal – I was just mentioning it.

Man Yeah, but . . .

Woman You get used to it. I guess they think that, I don't know, after a certain size or whatever . . .

Man Geez, that's hard to . . .

Woman I shouldn't have all this stuff for lunch, anyway, but . . . I'm hungry.

Man Sure . . . hey, it's lunchtime, right?

Woman Yeah.

Man I mean, look at me . . . Look how much *chicken* they put on my salad!

Woman That's not exactly comforting . . .

Man I just meant . . . whatever. Sorry.

Woman I had three pieces of pizza, the garlic bread *and* a salad. Plus dessert . . .

Man Hey, you know . . . it's your . . .

Woman How does that sentence end?

Man Badly, I'm sure! Hell, it's your body, you do what you want. That's what I think . . .

Woman Really?

Man Of course. I mean . . .

Woman So, do you really like *sprouts* or does that only hold true for me? Your little theory there . . .

Man No, I'm just . . . I had a really big breakfast, so I'm . . .

Woman That's a lie.

Man Ahh, yeah. Yes, it was. You saw through that one . . . Damn, you seem pretty good at this!

Woman What, the truth?

Man Yeah, that.

Woman I'm not bad, actually . . . not too bad at all.

A moment between them, then they both get down to some serious eating.

You work nearby?

Man No . . . I'm just up here for this meeting. Usually I eat downtown. (*Beat.*) And you?

Woman Yes, I'm over at the library. I was at an interview, actually, for a different branch . . . that's why I have the, you know, 'Miss Kitty' hair today. All *dolled* up.

The Man nods and points at a plastic bag on the table.

Man Ahh, cool . . . I get it. *Gunsmoke*. You look nice. (*Grins.*) Yeah, I saw the library bag earlier.
Wow. (*Points.*) That's a *lot* of videos there.

Woman . . . It was a long weekend . . .

Man Right. (*Smiles.*) So, lemme guess . . . *When Harry Met Sally*, *Sleepless in Seattle*, probably, umm . . . *The Notebook* . . .

Woman Wrong! Take a look.

She smiles at him as he reaches over and glances in the bag. Pulls a few out. Library emblem on each case.

Man *The Guns of Navarone*, *Where Eagles Dare* . . . *Ice Station Zebra*?

Woman I threw myself a little Alistair MacLean festival.

Man Huh. Don't get me wrong because I love that stuff, but . . . that's not very 'girlie' of you.

Woman . . . You're probably just dating the wrong *kinds* of girls.

They share a grin and a chuckle. The Man reappraises her.

Man No doubt about that – I can't even call 'em 'girls' without getting hit by a *lawsuit*, so . . . (*Smiles.*) You're a librarian?

Woman Yeah. Well, we don't really use that term any more, but, ahh . . .

Man Sure, of course! It's probably, like, 'printed word specialist' or something now, I suppose . . .

Woman Exactly. (*Beat.*) They're always coming up with new names for stuff, something to make that person feel better . . . a 'refuse technician' or what-have-you.

Man That's so true . . .

Woman Right? Problem is, you still find yourself picking *shit* up off the street, no matter what they call you! I mean . . . you know . . .

He laughs at this and she joins in. She makes a lovely sound as she goes at it. The Man studies her.

Man . . . You have a terrific laugh.

Woman Thanks.

Man You're welcome. A *potty mouth*, but a really cute laugh . . .

Woman That's sweet, thank you! (*Laughs.*) . . . Now that I'm so self-conscious that I'll never do it again.

Man Exactly!

They laugh together again and then don't know what to say next. They decide to take a bite of their meals instead.

How's that *spinach* coming along?

Man Mmm . . . so darn good!

Woman Looks great.

Man Yeah. Yummy.

Woman The pizza's terrific here. I come by all the time for it . . .

Man I'll bet. (*Looks over at her.*) I just mean . . . you know. If it's so good, I would understand. That. (*Beat.*) Please-help-me . . .

Woman I get what you meant.

Man Great.

Woman You shouldn't be so nervous . . . I mean, if we're gonna start dating.

Man *What?*

Woman It's a joke.

Man Oh, right. Got it. Little slow!

They laugh together. He looks around, self-consciously.

Woman I'm sorry. You should've seen your face . . .

Man What? No . . .

Woman I thought you were gonna choke on your *avocado* there . . .

Man That's not true, come on . . .

Woman Pretty close.

Man No, that's not . . . why would you say that? You just caught me off guard is all. Seriously.

Woman Anyway, I was just playing. Big people are *jolly*, remember?

Man Umm-hmm . . .

Woman It's one of our best qualities.

Man Well, at least you've got one.

Woman And you don't?

Man Ahhh . . . open for debate.

Woman Really?

Man I mean . . . you know, if I really had to come up with one, for, say, the big guy upstairs or whatever, I'd probably do something like, 'does not run with scissors' or one of those . . . 'plays well with others'.

Woman Really? Handsome guy like you and that's all you're good for . . . to look at?

Man Pretty much.

Woman Good to know. (*Opens a pudding.*) You want one?

Man Nah, I shouldn't . . .

Woman Why?

Man Excellent question. Okay.

He takes a tub of rice pudding from her and digs in.

Woman Good?

Man Mmm . . . wonderful. Haven't done that in ages.

Woman What?

Man Enjoyed myself. Like that. Put something in my mouth without reading the back label like some *Bible scholar* . . .

He gives an example – holding the pudding up to the light as if it was an antiquity and squinting at it. Examining it from all angles. This makes her laugh again. A lot.

Alright, OK, we're gonna have to ask you to leave . . . you're actually *enjoying* yourself during the work week.

Woman Right! Sorry . . .

Man No, It's, I told you, I love your laugh.

Woman Thanks. Again.

Man You're welcome . . . again.

Woman So . . . no other good qualities, huh?

Man Ahh, I suppose. Faithful friend and co-worker, dependable, takes directions well.

Woman What about good lover? Not on the list?

The Man stares at her, glances around. She keeps looking right at him.

Man That's very direct . . .

Woman Librarians are funny people.

Man I *guess* . . . I shouldn't've let my card lapse!

Woman So?

Man Umm . . . I'm OK. I mean, no reports of absolute dissatisfaction, but I don't think I'm, like, Valentino or anything.

Woman He died really unhappy, though. I've read his biography.

Man One of the perks of the job . . .

Woman Right! I've read just about every biography in the place, actually. Real people interest me. I don't really have much time for fiction. 'Fiction is for the weak and faint of heart.' Somebody said that, a Frenchman, I think.

Man Cool . . .

Woman Anyway, you don't have to answer the question. It was rude.

Man No, I . . . I mean, I sort of did.

Woman And you're what? Just OK?

Man Something like that . . . I do fine! Wow. I've never . . . been asked that before. In *that* way.

Woman No?

Man Not at lunch, anyhow! (*Beat.*) It's kind of invigorating, actually. You seem like a really . . . I don't know. An interesting person, I guess.

They laugh together again. Really enjoying themselves.

Woman You should swing by the library some time. See what you've been missing . . .

Man Yeah. Listen, I'm . . . I need to get back to the office. Downtown. So I should finish up my, ahhh . . .

Woman Course. (*Beat.*) Sorry if I was . . .

Man No, no, it was . . . but could we . . . I don't know what I'm asking here. Should we see each other again?

Woman Why?

Man I dunno . . . I mean, I'm just, it'd be good, I think. You seem really nice and I'm . . . what can I say, I'm just asking . . . sort of outta the blue. So, could we? (*Beat.*) I'm not trying to pick you up or anything, I just . . .

Woman Too bad. (*Smiles.*) Yes. We should.

Man For lunch? Or, umm, dinner . . . ?

Woman I don't *only* eat. I can be coaxed into doing other stuff, too . . .

Man Of course! I didn't mean . . .

Woman I know. It's a joke.

Man Right, sure . . . I'm really striking out on the humor part here!

Woman You're doing fine . . . (*Beat.*) So when?

Man Any time.

Woman How about Friday? I'm good for Fridays, my day off.

Man Umm, yeah. Evening.

Woman Great.

She reaches over and takes a pen out of his shirt pocket and writes her number down on the edge of a napkin.

Now when you wipe your mouth you'll think of me.

Man Good plan. (*Beat.*) So, OK, library lady, I'll call you . . .

Woman Helen. My name's 'Helen'.

Man As in 'of Troy?' (*Groans.*) That was so lame, sorry . . .

Woman Right, the thousand ships and all. But that was just so they could carry me back –

He stands there, thinking about this. Doesn't get it.

– because it would take that many to *lift* me . . . don't worry about it.

Man Oh, I see. (*Laughs.*) I got it!

Woman Yeah. Just trying to be cute.

Man No, yes, I get it now . . . but you shouldn't do that, though. Make fun of yourself so much.

Woman Why not?

Man Umm . . . I'm sure there's a very good reason. I'll get back to you.

Woman You do that. You've got my number there . . .

Man Right. I'll call you. And I'm Tom, by the way.

Woman I'll see you. Tom.

She wanders off with her tray and her bag. The Man stands alone. After a moment, she returns. Walks right up to the Man and gets close.

So, look, I figure there's every reason why I'll never hear from you again, and that's why I came back here . . . just to say that I don't do this, come after guys or anything, not like some regular habit or whatever, so I thought you should know that. I think you're really cute and nice and that sort of thing . . . you might have a girlfriend already or not be attracted to me, I would just totally understand that, I would, but I really do hope you call me. Just even to talk on the phone would be fine, because I'd like that, if we were only these phone buddies . . . I think I would. Just . . . don't be afraid, Tom, I guess that' s why I came back here to say that. Please do not let yourself be afraid of me or of taking some kind of blind chance, or what people think . . . because this could be so great.

She smiles at him and does what she promised: wanders out of the joint. He watches her go, waves when she nears the door.
The Man goes back to eating the pudding and then looks up, off in the direction that she left in. He slowly folds the napkin up and pockets it.

BACK TO BUSINESS AND UNDER SUSPICION

Tom at his place of work. Busy doing something. Another guy enters, carrying some files and a cup of coffee. He throws himself down in a chair. His name is Carter.

Carter . . . So you're not gonna tell me, right? Anything else, I mean.

Tom No, I'll . . . you know . . .

Carter Uh-uh, no you won't. I know you.

Tom That's not true, I always tell you crap! All kinds of crap about me.

Carter Yeah, but not the good stuff that I wanna hear. The dirt.

Tom I don't have *dirt* . . .

Carter Everybody's got dirt, my friend! We're dirty, us folks. Very dirty.

Tom Who's 'us folks'?

Carter People. You-and-me type people.

Tom It's not . . . this is not some nasty thing that I'm trying to keep from you. Seriously.

Carter . . . OK then, so?

Tom This is just . . . it's new, that's all. I don't know what it is yet, so . . .

Carter So, like I said, you're not gonna tell me shit.

Tom Kinda. Yeah.

Carter Fine. I don't care.

Tom Bull . . . you're dying to hear.

Carter Yes, but I'll wait. I'll hire some private eye or whatnot, get the scoop that way. Whatever it takes.

Tom Come on! I just wanna see what it is first, if it's worth talking to anyone about or not. What I will say right now is that I am very happy . . .

Carter OK, now you're frightening me . . .

Tom What?

Carter I don't like it when you get all upbeat! Then it's like *girlfriend city*, and that's scary.

Tom It's not scary . . .

Carter This is when we lose you for weeks at a time. Tom gets a lady friend and he drops off the map, I know how this one works . . .

Tom I'm not at all like that!

Carter Yes, you are . . .

Tom No, uh-uh. If anybody is, you are.

Carter Yeah, but that's for good reason. I'm actually having sex with them.

Tom Very funny.

Carter Seriously.

Tom Shut the hell up! I have sex . . .

Carter Uh-uh, 'oral' doesn't count . . . and especially for someone who thinks it means *talking* a person to death.

Tom Hooo . . . funny! (*Beat.*) Are you in here for an actual reason?

Carter I'm sure I had one when I started down the hall.

Tom Perfect . . .

Carter Oh, yeah, now I recall. Because I was bored in my office . . . (*Beat.*) Plus, you have nicer windows.

Tom Feel free to open one and jump . . .

Carter Tommy, you are so clever!

Tom Seriously, though, I've got work.

Carter I've got work, too. We've all got work, Tom, that's why they call it that. 'Work'. Because that's what we do here.

Tom I agree. And I want to get back to mine . . .

Carter Fine. (*Picks up a ball.*) Dollar a point?

Tom nods and the two men break into a lazy game of Nerf 'pig'. The hoop hangs on the back of Tom's door.
A female co-worker walks in, carrying a stack of reports – ruins the game. She stops at Tom's desk and drops a few. Smiles. Carter eyes her, then speaks.

Co-Worker Hello. Morning, Tom . . .

Tom Hey, Jeannie.

Jeannie Hi. (*Drops off muffin.*) Snagged you the last muffin . . .

Tom Oh, wow. (*Glances at Carter.*) Thanks.

Jeannie No prob.

Carter I'm sure mine's being *toasted*. (*Waits.*) Kidding. Guess what?

Jeannie What?

Carter I said *guess*.

Jeannie Ummm . . . you're an asshole?

Tom giggles out loud at this one. Carter blushes, then regroups. The girl smiles over at Tom.

Tom Aaah, you cheated! Somebody gave you the answers . . .

Jeannie Exactly!

Carter You guys are hilarious.

Jeannie What is it? I need to get back.

Carter OK, then don't worry about it.

Jeannie Just tell me. *What?*

Carter Need-to-know basis. Tom's got a gal.

Tom Would you shut up!

Carter Word on the street . . .

Tom Carter, seriously . . .

Jeannie Really? (*To Tom.*) That's not true, right?

Tom No . . . he's just being a dick.

Carter Am not! I mean, yes, I am a dick sometimes, but not at the moment.

Jeannie Tom . . . ?

Carter He does.

Tom I do *not*.

Carter It's what I heard . . .

Tom Carter, knock it off. Jeannie, he's just trying to . . .

Jeannie stands there for a bit longer, looking back and forth between the men. Finally she saunters out.

You prick.

Carter *What?*

Tom That's not funny.

Carter It was pretty damn funny from over here . . .

Tom I'm serious.

Carter Me, too. Try sitting on the couch and see if it's any funnier. (*He moves over.*) Plenty of room.

Tom You know we've been dating . . .

Carter Of course. I-know-all.

Tom I mean it. You know how she gets.

Carter Yes, I *know* . . . (*Beat.*) Why do you think I said something? I'm not gonna tell the *snack shop guy* out front . . . I mean, why the fuck would he care?

Tom You are a piece of work, you know that?

Carter I try. (*Beat.*) Anyway, that's what you can expect, by the way. Mean-spirited shit like that until you tell me who she is.

Tom I'm not gonna say a damn thing now . . .

Carter Your choice. But I'll find out, I promise . . .

Tom Yeah, yeah . . .

Carter And then up goes her Polaroid in the break room.

Tom Fucker.

Carter Maybe. After you're through with her, of course . . .

Tom Shut up and go back to your *lair*, Satan. Begone.

Carter Okay. (*Beat.*) Hey, seriously though . . . does Jeannie look kind of soft to you?

Tom What?

Carter A minute ago . . . doesn't she look a bit sloppy or something? In her ass, I'm saying. A couple of pounds.

Tom . . . *No* . . .

Carter Come on, I'm just talking. It's not a judgement on you.

Tom I know, but . . . I'm not obsessed by bodies the way you are. I'm not.

Carter I don't know what it is, but I was noticing yesterday. She came in to my office with her suit jacket off and had on one of those, you know, flimsy pair of slacks, with no seam up the rear and . . . I seriously think her backside isn't as taut as it used to be.

Tom Dude, you need some help . . .

Carter What? It's an observation, that's all . . . Her ass is right *there*. I can't help it if I observe things.

Tom No, but you can keep it to yourself! And your therapist, who I hope you're still seeing . . .

Carter Nah, that shit was too expensive. Plus, she was a total bitch.

Tom Nice.

Carter It's not, like, some derogatory thing I'm saying about her – not the therapist cunt, but Jeannie – it's just an idle thought. That's the problem with winter: chicks don't get out much and they bloat up . . .

Tom OK, I really can't deal with you right now, so . . . go.

Carter Whatever. We on for basketball tomorrow? Chad can't make it any other time . . .

Tom Ahh, yeah. But after nine, OK? I've got a dinner thing. (*Off Carter's look.*) For *work*, dumb-shit.

Carter Sure.

Tom It is! I've got those folks from the, ahhh . . . you know . . .

Carter No, what?

Tom The Chicago group is coming into town. (*Beat.*) They *are* . . .

Carter Cool. I'll email the other guys and meet you at the Y. See ya.

He finally gets up and saunters over to Tom – a quick 'high-five' and Carter exits. Tom returns to his work as Carter looks back inside the room.

I'm swinging past the restaurant to check, so you better be telling the truth . . .

Tom Asshole.

Carter That's me. But when I get my PhD it'll be Dr Asshole, so, hey. Something to look forward to . . .

He is gone. Tom shakes his head and gets back to the files that Jeannie has left. A minute later he looks up to see her standing in his doorway.

Jeannie Hey. (*Smiles.*)

Tom Oh, hi. There.

Jeannie Got a minute?

Tom Sure.

Jeannie I forgot some . . .

She holds up an extra file.

Forgot this one.

Tom Ah. Thanks.

Jeannie Oh, I, umm, I went on Ticketmaster and they still have those Coldplay seats, so . . .

Tom Really? Orchestra?

Jeannie Uh-huh, yeah. A few pairs . . .

Tom Huh. I thought I checked all the . . . Maybe they . . . Hmm. (*Beat.*) Cool. I'll . . .

He gets up and crosses to her, reaching for the folder. She holds it a moment and they both tug on it.

Jeannie So . . . is it true, what he said?

Tom Who, Carter?

Jeannie Yeah.

Tom Umm . . .

Jeannie Oh. (*Beat.*) So where does that put us, then? I mean, I thought . . .

Tom No, I'm not saying it's . . . He's an idiot, so, you know, you have to make some allowances.

Jeannie Right. (*Grins.*) That's true . . .

Tom But . . . I don't know what I'm doing. You know that. I'm . . .

Jeannie Yes, I do. All while we've been going out I could tell that, but I still liked you. Gave you a million or so chances, but . . . hey. Whatever.

Tom I know that, Jeannie, I know, I'm just . . . It's complicated.

Jeannie I'm not saying that I'm some, you know, *beauty queen*, but guys do like me. They really, really do.

Tom I know, come on . . . *please*. I like you. Don't say it like that.

Jeannie Yeah, well . . . I wish you'd fire up a signal flare every now and then. (*Smiles.*) Could use it over here . . .

Tom Sorry. I *do*, though . . .

Jeannie Doesn't seem like it. I mean, I've tried sweet and forceful and, you know, *nonchalant*. *Every*thing. I don't get it. What do you want me to do here?

Tom *Nothing*. I'm . . .

Jeannie *What*? (*Beat.*) So, just tell me. Is he lying or not?

Tom Carter is . . . I mean, by nature he's a liar. You know that. He likes to provoke people. Get 'em riled up.

Jeannie Which says nothing.

Tom Jeannie, come on . . .

Jeannie So you are.

Tom I'm not . . . no. I'm not 'seeing' any other person, alright? Promise.

Jeannie Look, I'm just asking, so don't make it seem like I'm pulling on your eye teeth or something. If you don't wanna tell me, then OK.

Tom I'm saying it, to you, right now.

Jeannie Yeah, but . . .

Tom Carter's an ass. He's . . .

Jeannie . . . So why do you hang out with him then? Huh? All those guys down in Development. (*Beat.*) Why?

Tom Because . . . I'm needy and shallow. (*Smiles.*) Hell, I dunno! Because we all started out here together and it's, you know, it's easier to go along sometimes, to just hang out and not make, like, some big *tsunami* or that kinda thing. I know it's dumb, but . . . he's *funny*. He doesn't bug me that much.

Jeannie Obviously.

Tom Jeannie, come on, don't be . . . He's just playing around.

Jeannie So, nobody then?

Tom I didn't . . . because . . . I'm not saying that I'm . . . What?

Jeannie Don't do your circles thing, OK? Do not do that . . .

Tom What're you even . . . ?

Jeannie Talking around shit, that's what I'm saying. I hate that! Are–you–dating–someone?

Tom No. Kind of. Hell, I dunno! I'm . . . It's not some big thing.

Jeannie I see.

Tom Look, we agreed that we should be able to . . . I'm not doing anything, like, *wrong*.

Jeannie But you're pretty defensive about it.

Tom Yeah, because . . . because you get all . . . You know how you are.

Jeannie I'm not *anything*. Except confused. By a guy who tells me that he's interested in me. 'Very', in fact, was the word he used. 'I am very interested in you.' And we date and then we stop and then he sends me stuff, like flowers and letters and keeps calling and wants to do it again, to try one more time, he tells me . . . But then we do not go out. We see each other at work but he keeps putting off the next date because of . . . God, I couldn't begin to list all of the excuses because it's Monday afternoon and I would probably be here, like, through the *weekend*. But now I hear he's met someone, a someone that he has managed – even with his many work obligations and boys' nights out and all his other related *juvenile* crap – he has somehow squeezed yet another person on to his social calendar.

Jeannie edges a bit closer to Tom now. Tom steps back.

Tom . . . See? This is what I was talking about.

Jeannie No, this is what *I'm* talking about right now! The bullshit you do to me and expect me to keep crawling back in here and taking it.

Tom . . . I don't . . . want you to . . .

Jeannie Oh, so now you don't want me here? Is that it? Go ahead, then, say it. Go on. Say it.

Tom No, Jeannie, Jesus, can we just . . . I'd like to talk about this, but not in public. Alright? (*Off Jeannie's look.*) I mean, can we . . . maybe . . .

Jeannie You can 'maybe' kiss my ass, Tom, and that's a *definite* maybe. You can *pencil* that one in your planner right now, OK?

Jeannie turns abruptly and walks out. Before Tom can even react she is back. Standing in the doorway.

Tom Jeannie, please. Let's . . .

Jeannie I can't *wait* to meet her. Really, I can't. (*Holds out file.*) Here. I forgot to give you this . . .

Tom moves apprehensively toward the door. Jeannie drops the file on to the floor and stalks off.

A SURPRISING NIGHT OUT TOGETHER

Tom and Helen sitting at a table in a cosy restaurant. A meal spread out before them. Tom is chowing down on exotic cuisine; Helen is a bit more hesitant.

Tom . . . Go on, jump in there! (*Prompts her.*) Be brave.

Helen You're absolutely sure it's dead, right? Because if it's just holding its breath, then I'm . . .

Tom Yeah! (*Laughs.*) Definitely . . .

Helen OK. (*Looks again.*) Positive?

Tom Well, I wasn't back there watching 'em fix it but, yeah, in theory.

Helen I mean, I'm pretty *adventurous*, but, you know . . .

Tom No, I'm the same way. It's . . . I'm not big on swallowing anything I saw on Discovery Channel either, believe me . . . (*Smiles.*) It's good. Promise.

Helen smiles and nods, gobbles something down with her eyes closed. Happy with the results. Tom smiles as he eats something, too. Lets a moment of silence hang.

. . . Can I ask you something?

Helen No. I'm kidding. Sure, what?

Tom I meant to ask you this the other night . . . I mean, when we went to that martini bar . . . (*Beat.*) You love war movies?

Helen smiles over at him and nods. Says nothing else.

Okay, first obvious question. *Why?*

Helen Just because.

Tom Not fair! That's not an answer . . .

Helen Yes, it is.

Tom But not a good one. One that tells me anything about you . . .

Helen Ohh, I see. You're gonna dig deep now, is that it?

Tom Something like that . . . little *Freud* action.

Helen Oh, Freud, huh?

Tom I figured you read his biography.

Helen Yes, I have. (*Beat.*) I like war movies because of all the big . . . *long* gun barrels.

This makes Tom laugh and he reaches out for Helen's hand. He grabs it and squeezes, holding on to it. She notices.

Tom Come on! Seriously . . .

Helen OK, OK . . . I'm . . . (*Beat.*) You have my hand there, you know.

Tom Yeah, I . . . Is that not . . . ?

Helen It's fine. Just wanted to ask and see if it was an accident or not.

Tom Umm . . . no. It wasn't, no. But . . . now you're making me self-conscious.

He looks around the restaurant. Helen notices this too.

I want to . . . hold it, I mean, if that's OK.

Helen Of course.

Tom Good.

They sit and stare at one another for a moment. Silence.

Helen I would like to have a bit more of my tuna later . . . but I can wait.

Tom Sorry! Shit . . .

Helen I'm kidding you.

Tom looks at her, then pulls away. Embarrassed. He points at her food.

Tom No, you should . . . that's fine. We can do that after, or walking back to the car or something. We should eat. Yes.

Helen Tom . . . I really was joking.

Tom I know, but . . . (*He eats.*) I'm ready for some of mine, too.

They both take a bite or two, laughing across the table.

So, seriously . . . what's the deal on the war flicks? You know way too many of those things to've just been reading the *TV Guide* or that kind of thing . . .

Helen Please, I'm a professional.

Tom Oh, yeah? Prove it.

Helen Let's see if you can keep up. *Von Ryan's* . . . Come on, little quiz . . . *Von Ryan's* . . .

Tom . . . Train . . . no, wait . . . *Express*!

Helen Lonely are the . . .

Tom *Brave.*

Helen *Porkchop* . . .

Tom . . . *Hill.*

Helen *Kelly's* . . .

Tom . . . *Heroes.*

Helen *Aces* . . .

Tom . . . *High*.

Helen Alright, a little bonus round here. *Heaven Knows, Mr* . . .

Tom Magoo!

Helen No, *Allison*.

Tom Jesus . . . and most of those are obscure, too!

Helen I know. (*Beat.*) I work in Audio/Visual.

Tom Well, you're very . . . Except that one.

Helen Which?

Tom *Lonely are the Brave*.

Helen It's a . . . what?

Tom A western. Sort of. With Kirk Douglas.

Helen Oh, right, no, I mean . . . is it?

Tom Yeah. You know, with him on the horse and he's being chased by, like, guys in helicopters and stuff? It's that one. It's really good, but, yeah. Western.

Helen Huh. (*Considers.*) Oh, right, right, yes, I've seen it, black and white right? But I'm getting the name confused. I meant *None But the Brave*. The Frank Sinatra one. On that *atoll* in the Pacific . . .

Tom You're . . . *nobody's* seen that one! Alright, this is now, like, an officially *quirky* side of you. (*Grins.*) 'Atoll'?

Helen Hey, I'm a librarian . . .

Tom Uh-uh. 'Printed word specialist.'

Helen Right! (*Laughs.*) Anyway, I grew up with 'em, that's all. I have three brothers, plus my dad. They were on all the time, and so I watched a lot of them, or parts of 'em, anyway. All growing up.

Tom Yeah, me too. I mean, that same scenario. What is it about fathers and those movies? (*Beat.*) He also directed that one, too.

Helen Your father?

Tom No . . . Sinatra! You're funny.

Helen Thanks.

Tom I mean, *jolly*.

They both laugh again. Really enjoying each other now.

But, seriously, I wonder. Why?

Helen Well . . . most of them either fought in wars or wanted to, or had some relative who did or whatever. Or they just like watching other guys get *shot*, that could be it, too.

Tom Probably right!

Helen I'm not joking. I think guys today feel left out, like, guilty about not having to kill things, provide food. All that 'Early Man' stuff. (*Beat.*) But for me . . . I just enjoyed being around my family. Sitting on the couch, big bowl of popcorn. It felt good.

Tom Right . . .

Helen *And* it saved me the embarrassment of waiting around for boys to call me up.

Tom What do you mean?

Helen Ummm, you probably couldn't guess, but I didn't date a lot when I was in school.

Tom Oh.

Helen (*whispers*) . . . I used to be a little *heavy*.

Helen chuckles. Tom joins in half-heartedly, then stops.

Tom Huh. (*Beat.*) And is that . . . is it alright to talk about . . . I dunno, your weight and everything, or should I . . . ?

Helen No, go ahead. It's not a shame thing for me. Not any more.

Tom 'Any more'?

Helen Well . . . it's all shame when you're younger, isn't it? You hate how you look or sound or, you know, all that stuff that we go through. As kids. But I'm pretty alright with who I am now. The trick is getting other people to be OK with it!

Tom Right. And, so . . . have you always been, like . . . you know?

Helen No. What?

Tom Umm, big . . . boned, or whatever.

Helen laughs out loud at this one. Another beauty, which makes Tom giggle along. She takes his hand this time.

Helen That was kind of precious. One of my favourites, actually . . .

Tom What?

Helen 'Big-boned.' My dad used to throw that one around, too.

Tom Well . . . I'm just trying to be . . .

Helen Don't. Not for me. I just want you to be truthful, OK? Seriously.

Tom Alright.

Helen However things end up here – and I have high hopes, but – (*Smiles.*) I want you to be honest with me.

Tom . . . I can do that. Promise.

Helen Good. Great. Fair enough.

Tom So, then, ummm . . . I don't know what to say here exactly, but . . . (*Beat.*) Helen, I like your body . . . what I *imagine* your body to be. It's . . .

Helen Tom, it's OK . . . I'm not worried about it. I mean, you would not be here next to me, if you didn't want to be. Right?

Tom Sure. Yes.

Helen So, then . . . I'm good. Secure about it. Truthfully. I know that you're here because you like me. A little bit, anyway.

Tom That's true. I do, yes. Like you.

Helen Then good . . . (*Smiles.*) So, why don't we finish up our seafood . . . (*Thinks.*) *stuff.* What's this called again?

Tom Ahh . . . you got the, umm, 'Yellowfin Tartare' and I got their, I don't remember now. 'Spicy Kimchi', maybe? With crab . . .

Helen Yeah, that was it.

She smiles and touches his hand again, then goes back to eating. Tom watches her as she takes a few more bites.

Tom How's your meal? OK?

Helen Delicious, actually. Little bit of ginger and scallions, I like it . . .

Tom Good. (*Beat.*) You know, the yellow fin is traditionally the 'biggest boned' of the tuna family . . .

Helen Oh really? (*Giggles.*) Tell me more.

Tom Seriously – with a hearty, *heavy* flavour . . .

Helen and Tom laugh together, their heads coming in close contact. Suddenly, Helen notices that Tom is now staring off, behind her. She swings around and spots Carter, a drink in one hand. Tom awkwardly stands up.

Hey . . .

Carter Well, hello there.

Tom Carter, this is . . . Helen, I'd like you to meet my . . . this is Carter, who works with us. I mean, me.

Helen smiles and holds a hand up. Carter takes it and shakes it. Looks around.

Carter Where's the rest of 'em? Late?

An uncomfortable moment hangs in the air. Helen begins to stand.

Helen I'm going to use the little girl's room. Even though I hate the term.

Tom Right! (*Tries to laugh.*) Me, too.

Carter Well, it's better than 'shitter'.

Helen Very true. (*Beat.*) Great to meet you, Carter.

Carter Yeah, you too.

She walks off and Carter watches her go – all the way off. He then turns to Tom and gestures.

. . . I hope it's *twins*. (*Smiles.*) Bet you're glad you promised to play basketball tonight, huh?

Tom . . . Uh-huh.

Carter What the *hell* is that?

Tom I just told you. Her name's Helen and she's . . . you know . . .

Carter And how come the others aren't here?

Tom Because we're . . . I mean . . .

Carter reaches over and pokes at Tom's sweater. Giggles.

Carter Jesus . . . nice sweater there, bub. You join the PGA or something?

Tom Very funny! I'm not . . .

Carter . . . They didn't just send her, did they? Not that she couldn't eat for *five* . . .

Tom Carter, don't say stuff like that. It's not nice.

Carter I know that. I wasn't being nice. That was me being honest.

Tom Seriously, though . . .

Carter Hey, she's not here, OK, so can you ease up on the knights-of-the-round-table shit? She's off to the bathroom . . . (*Beat.*) With a basket of dinner rolls hidden under her skirt, if I'm not mistaken . . .

Tom Can you please . . . ? Jesus.

Carter OK, alright! God, you are really just not fun at all when you're out with a woman, you know that? Even some *beast* from work . . .

Tom She's not . . . just leave her alone.

Carter Fine. (*Beat.*) You gonna be there by nine? Howard's gotta hit the road by eleven-thirty . . .

Tom Yes, you know that . . . Yes. (*Looking around.*) Why are you here?

Carter I told you I was coming by.

Tom Yeah, but how'd you know where . . . ?

Carter Because you always come here! But Tom? This place is kinda out-of-the-loop, I hate to tell you. By, like, ahh, *three* years.

Tom Yeah, well, I like it. (*Beat.*) So, can I just finish up and . . . Do you mind?

Carter No, whatever. Just checking on ya.

Tom Fine.

Carter Thought I might catch you with . . . you know. *Her.*

Tom You really are an ass . . .

Carter Pretty much. But, surprisingly, it doesn't give me a big head . . .

Tom Will you just please go?! Come on.

Carter Fine, fine. See you at nine.

Tom Yeah. See you.

Carter takes another gulp from his drink, then stops. He starts off but leans in close to Tom.

Carter Dude . . . I so wish I would've caught you with her! Damn it. Anyway . . .

At that moment, Helen returns and stands next to Carter. He pulls out her chair and seats her.

Helen Thank you . . .

Carter Pleasure. (*To Helen.*) And don't let this cheapskate stiff you on the dessert! They've got a hell of a green tea ice cream here . . .

Helen . . . Good to know . . .

Tom See you later, Carter.

Helen Goodbye. Nice to meet you.

Carter You too, umm . . . what was it again?

Helen 'Helen'.

Carter Right. (*Over his shoulder.*) And say 'hello' to the Windy City for me!

Carter is gone. Tom watches him go and then turns back to Helen. Tries to smile.

Helen What does that mean?

Tom He's . . . you know, he's a . . .

Helen Why would he think I'm from Chicago?

Tom He doesn't. No. That was for me. *To* me. I'm . . . going there for work.

Helen You are?

Tom For, like, yeah. Just a day or two next week. Business.

Helen Oh. I see . . . *Really?*

Tom Yep. I was gonna tell you, but then we got to talking, is all.

Helen Right. (*Beat.*) He seems OK. Nice. And he works with you?

Tom Uh-huh. Down the hall. I mean, not *with* me, but . . . I see him around. (*Beat.*) He's not going to Chicago. Just me.

Helen Got it. (*Beat.*) Did I mention my second interview that I got? It's for that . . . I did, didn't I? Yeah.

They both return to eating their meals. Silence. A long one, in fact. Finally, Tom stops and looks at Helen.

Tom I know that you know. I mean, I can tell. That you do. I made a . . . he thinks that this is, like, a *business* dinner and I didn't say anything.

Helen OK.

Tom No, its not OK. So, I want you to know that I'm sorry. I am. He really just surprised me and I got all . . .

Helen I understand

Tom I did wanna say something but I'm, I . . . I didn't.

Helen At least you're honest.

Tom -ish.

Helen It's OK. It's something to work on then, right?

Tom . . . Yeah. That's true.

Helen reaches over and gives Tom a kiss on the mouth. He responds and the moment grows in intensity.

ON THE TRAIL AND OUT TO LUNCH

Jeannie is in Tom's office and rummaging through his desk drawers. Looking for something. She finds an address book and leafs through it. Stops on a scribbled phone number.
She glances over her shoulder then uses the office phone to call. Waits.

Jeannie Ah-ha! (*She dials.*) Hello? Hello?! Who's . . . Oh. Ticketmaster? I'm sorry, wrong number. (*To herself.*) Stupid . . .

She goes through a few more pages. Finds another number and tries this one, too.

Yes, hello? Who's this? What? I don't have to tell you who this is . . . I called you. Who is this?! Are you some – Susan who? Sullivan? (*Covers receiver with a hand.*) Shit! (*To receiver.*) Sorry, no, I had another call coming in . . . you're not related to 'Tom Sullivan', are you? Oh, his mother. Nice! Well, that's related. Absolutely! Great, good, I was, umm, hoping I might catch you – who? Oh, this is, ahhh, I'm a Susan, too. Isn't that a funny . . . Yeah. Same name, I mean, what're the chances, right? So, anyway, Tom and I work . . . out together – He does, yes, all the time – so some of us we're hoping we could get you to, ahhh, well, come to a little surprise birthday party for him that're we're planning. Yep. Excuse me? Oh, yeah, no, I realise it's not for . . . how long? Seven months. Sure. September, right? Oh. October. No, you're right . . . that's seven. I wasn't counting. I mean, I was but not correctly. Yes. I get it now – but that's why I called. We want to make sure we get a really good jump on it so that it's special. After all, this is a big year, right? Want it to be pretty exciting . . . ol' number . . . which? Right. Thirty-four. Well, that's kinda special. Just one more to thirty-five, after all! (*Beat.*) Anyway, I'll get back in touch with you again, say, around Labor Day . . . Yeah, and we'll make sure you get a good seat at our . . . big event. Good! Look forward to meeting you. What? Oh, my name is Susan . . . Eglasias. Yes, just like the singer. Uh-huh. Yes. It is different, isn't it? I get that a lot. Great, well, I'll be looking for you, too, and please, don't say anything to Tom. No, it's going to be a big . . . big surprise, so . . . yes. We might even have a clown. Or magic! Not sure yet but it's gonna be terrific. I'm sorry? Tom likes ponies? Oh, when he was a boy. Nice! OK, I'll remember that . . .

Carter walks in and stops cold. Sees Jeannie on the phone and with address book in hand. He smiles.

Sorry, gotta go, I've got another call coming in. (*Clicks a button.*) Yes, this is Tom Sullivan's phone. I'm sorry, no, he's not here right now. Can I take a message? Fine, try after lunch and I'm sure he'll be back. Thanks very much. Bye.

She turns and looks at Carter. Slips the address book on the desk as casually as possible.

I had to pick up some, you know –

Carter Sure.

Jeannie – and Tom's phone rang. It rang and so I took the call but then another one came in . . . a call . . . just as you were . . .

Carter That last one?

Jeannie Yes, the one that I just finished. With.

Carter Cool.

Jeannie Good.

Carter Just so you know, though, I mean, in case somebody else walks in on you as you're going through Tom's personal items in a jealous-like frenzy – these office phones? The little button there lights up when a call comes in. That's how I knew you were bullshitting at the end . . . no light. Your performance was actually pretty good.

Jeannie Oh . . . fuck off, Carter.

Carter I promise I won't tell him.

Jeannie His phone did ring and I answered it . . . the other thing was just because I got a little flustered when you walked in and so I . . . whatever. Don't worry about it.

Carter I'm not worried. I'm . . . what's the word?

Jeannie A 'douchebag'?

Carter No, thanks, good try but that's not it . . . it's more like . . . 'intrigued'. I am very much intrigued.

Jeannie Listen, I came in here and I had some . . . files to get . . . and that's why . . .

Carter And you thought they might be tucked in his desk or inside his address book, so naturally . . . No, I get it now . . .

Jeannie Carter, just leave it, OK? (*Beat.*) Please?

Carter Sure. Of course. (*Beat.*) Absolutely. If.

Jeannie 'If' what?

Carter Oh, I dunno, lemme think . . . keeping my big mouth shut for . . . you're talking about for all time, correct, not just today or like that but forever? Tom never knowing that you were in here and rifling through his things? Right?

Jeannie That's the idea. (*Beat.*) So come on! What?

Carter Okay, so that's lying to my friend and . . . suppressing evidence, aiding and abetting a known felon . . . Shit, that's a lot of bad stuff you're asking of me, Jeannie.

Jeannie Just go! I know you want something so say it. (*Beat.*) GO!

Carter I could prob'ly do it for – maybe – a kiss.

Jeannie What?!

Carter No tongue.

Jeannie Are you fucking nuts?!

Carter No, I just worry that a week from now I'm sitting with Tom and I have one too many Amstel Lights –

which are really good, by the way, don't know if you've had one but they're great, never bitter – I see me all shit-faced and I slip and say something. That would be bad, it really would, but I feel like I could keep my admittedly big mouth shut for the price of a single kiss from you. Open mouth, no cheating. But as promised, sans any tongue-age. *No* French action. At all. (*Beat.*) Do we have a deal?

Jeannie . . . You can't be serious . . .

Carter Totally. (*Beat.*) Anyway, what do you care? You guys aren't even officially going out any more – don't hit me, I didn't make it happen – just think of this as . . . some sort of community service. Or being drafted.

Jeannie I'd rather tell him myself!

Carter Yeah?

Jeannie Than kiss you?! Without question.

Carter Great. Lemme get a good seat for this –

He goes to the couch and gets comfy. Settles back. Smiles up at Jeannie.

– just act like I'm not here.

Jeannie You're not funny. You do know that, don't you? Carter?

Carter Yes. I am reminded of it on a fairly regular basis by various colleagues. Women that I date. My parents. People on the street, even . . . (*Beat.*) Children . . .

Jeannie Okay!

Carter So, yeah, I get it. Not funny.

Jeannie Good. Just so you know.

Carter 'Not funny at all.' Check.

It's a Mexican stand-off now. Jeannie tries to think of an alternative but finally lets out a screech and stomps her foot. Gestures to him.

Jeannie OK, OK, shit! AHH! Just hurry up!

Carter Awesome!

Jeannie Don't get all . . . God, just . . . eww . . .

Carter Wait . . .

Takes a hit of breath spray.

There.

Offers it to her.

Want a shot? It's even got retsin in it; it's nice. Minty.

Jeannie Just do it! He'll be back soon!

Carter Fine, so you wanna embrace or should we maybe just . . . sit and be casual . . . ?

Jeannie Fucking kiss me, you jackass! NOW!

Carter starts to say something else but she grabs him and gives him the real deal – there's no mistaking what just took place. Some kind of 'moment'.
They pull apart but remain close. Looking at each other.

There. Satisfied?

Carter My God . . . I'm blushing. You hussy.

Jeannie Oh, stop! Are we done here?

Carter I don't know . . . I suddenly feel all . . . dirty inside. (*Beat.*) Some people might call that an 'assault', you know.

Jeannie Shut up. You're such an asshole – and you loved it, by the way.

Carter OK, you've seen through my disguise. (*He smiles.*) So when do we send out the . . . you know? Whatdoyoucallems?

Jeannie What?

Carter Wedding announcements.

Jeannie Umm, let's see, today is Tuesday, so . . . three weeks would be . . . Ahh, never! Loser.

Carter Yeah? Well, I have two canker sores, so who's the loser now?

Jeannie I hate you . . .

Carter Sticks and stones, baby, sticks and . . .

Jeannie kicks him in the leg and walks out in a snit.

Oww! Why does bad shit happen any time I use that phrase?! Seriously. Any time!

He limps over to the couch and sits down. nursing his leg as Jeannie returns. She approaches him and grabs him up by his collar. Right in his face.

Jeannie And you say a word, I mean it, one fucking word about any of this – the call or the kiss, anything – and I will pull your ball sac up over your head like it was a hoodie. From behind. (*Right in his face.*) Do you get that? Do you?!

Carter Is that even possible? I mean, I get it but, come on . . . seriously?

Jeannie Try me.

Jeannie stomps off. Carter watches her go, then sits back on the couch. He mimes trying the idea of his balls being pulled over his face. Shakes his head. He's unconvinced.

A moment later Tom walks in. Whistling. Stops dead when he sees Carter.

Carter Can't do it. (*On Tom's entrance.*) Hey, buddy!

Tom Hi, Carter. Do you ever knock?

Carter Seems like a lot of wasted energy . . . (*Beat.*) Hope you don't mind, I was just camping out on the ol' couch here for a moment. Had a real scare earlier . . .

Tom Yeah, what happened?

Carter You wouldn't believe it – I was just in the hall, minding my own business, and –

He's about to say something when Jeannie pokes her head in the door. Looks right at Carter.

Jeannie Like-a-hoodie. Just so we're clear.

Carter Of course! Thanks!

Jeannie I'm not kidding.

Carter No, yeah, I mean, if you're going shopping then yes, I could use . . . that hoodie. That's very kind of you, Jeannie. Thanks.

Jeannie My pleasure. (*To Tom.*) Hey, Tom. Hope you had a good lunch. Whenever. With whomever you were wherever at. For however long . . . I hope it was yummy. So so yummy for you.

And with that she is gone again – Carter looks seriously frightened now.

Tom . . . What the hell was that?

Carter Dude, I think she's possessed. Seriously.

Tom Shut up . . .

Carter Yeah, well, if she comes in here and gets all pea-soup vomity on you later, do not say I didn't warn you . . .

Tom Idiot. (*About Jeannie.*) I didn't understand a single word she said just then.

Carter Me either.

Tom And what's all the 'hoodie' thing she was going on about? Hmm?

Carter . . . Oh that.

Tom Yeah, 'that'. What?

Carter Nothing, no, I just mentioned that I was in need of one and she said that she was gonna go shopping at lunch and so she'd grab me one while she was out . . . (*Beat.*) I hear the weather's gonna turn. Later today. (*Beat.*) Chilly.

Tom Oh.

Carter Yep. So that's all that was . . . Yeah.

Tom Are you lying to me? What is up with you two?

Carter Nothing! Dude, would I bullshit you?

Tom Of course. Any time, for no reason. Yes.

Carter OK, you got me. (*Beat.*) But I'm not!

Tom I do not believe you. Come on, man . . . what's going on?

Carter Nothing. Promise.

Tom Carter . . .

Carter Dude . . . Shhh . . . (*Holds up a finger.*) She's like a jackal! She just appears.

Carter sneaks over to the door and looks both ways. He seems satisfied and returns to Tom.

Tom What're you doing?

Carter OK, it's clear. So listen, earlier I was –

And like clockwork, Jeannie returns with some files. She clears her throat. Carter screams like a schoolgirl and jumps behind Tom.

(*Pointing at her.*) AWWW! You're a witch! Be gone with you!

Tom What is going on here?!

Carter Save me, Tom, save me . . . !

Jeannie I have files for you, I don't know what goes through the mind of your retarded colleague . . .

Carter I'm not retarded! I'm not! I was diagnosed as ADHD and I only rode on the short bus because of zoning patterns! (*Beat.*) I'm sorry . . . that might be more than either of you needed to know. I'm going back to my area now . . .

He finally steps out from behind Tom and moves cautiously toward Jeannie.

If you'll excuse me?

Jeannie Of course. (*She steps aside.*) Go on.

He moves toward Jeannie. She makes a sudden move at him and he jumps. She laughs.

Carter Stop that! You're only embarrassing yourself . . .

Jeannie Really? How?

Carter By being . . . Because . . . I don't know! I thought that phrase stood by itself!

Jeannie It doesn't.

Carter Then fine!

Jeannie Fine.

Carter You're . . . Tom, jump in here and help . . .

Tom Carter . . . Jeannie, I don't mean to put too fine a point on it, but . . . what the fuck's going on?!

Jeannie Carter?

Tom Please? Somebody.

Carter Jeannie's trying to . . . I mean . . . we were . . . nothing! It's just this sexual tensiony thing we've always got between us . . . Can't help it. Sorry. It's just a yoke that we both carry around! Forgive us!

With that Carter scoots out of the room and disappears. Tom watches him go, then turns to Jeannie.

Tom You guys have sexual tension? Really? I never realized that . . .

Jeannie Yeah, like Fred and Ethel.

Tom Ha! (*Smiles.*) *I Love Lucy*, right? Nice to see you joking around and actually acting like yourself again.

Jeannie Of course. No hard feelings here. About anything. Ever.

Tom Good.

Jeannie Just because you're dating somebody else and you didn't have the decency to even let me know. That's cool.

Tom Jeannie, that's not . . . Let's not do this again. Let's have lunch and talk . . . or . . .

Jeannie When?

Tom Soon.

Jeannie When soon? Tomorrow?

Tom Umm . . . can't tomorrow.

Jeannie The next day? Thursday?

Tom Some time. This week, maybe, or first of next. I promise.

Jeannie Yeah . . .

Tom I do! We will deal with it. 'Kay?

Jeannie Sure. Like Coldplay.

Tom I did call about that! I just . . . ahhh . . .

Jeannie Doesn't matter. I got the tickets. Do you still wanna go? (*Beat.*) Even as friends?

Tom Maybe.

Jeannie 'Maybe'? Maybe what? Why is it always a 'maybe' with you or a, a, a 'we'll see'? Hmm? Do you need to call Susan and ask permission? Just be a man, God!

Tom Who? Call who?

Jeannie What? (*Beat.*) Nothing. Susan. Your mom.

Tom Why're you . . . how'd you know my mom's name is Susan?

Jeannie What? (*Beat.*) Of course it is. It's Susan Sullivan. I mean, God, we only dated for, you know . . . however long . . . like I wouldn't know your mom's name! We girls ask about things like that because they matter to us, the little details in life, OK? That is how I know, because I care about you! That's how! (*Beat.*) Shit, I can't believe you'd even question me about something like that! How insensitive . . .

Tom OK, sorry, I just don't remember telling –

Jeannie You don't seem to remember a lot of crap, Tom. Like how great it was when it was . . . great. Between us. That's because you're a guy and you don't know things even if you think you do. You don't know when a concert is or, or, like, the first names of mothers because all that you care for is yourself whereas I know your favourite foods and your mother's name and, and . . . that you even liked ponies when you were a boy! I know that because I listen and because I care! Okay?! (*Gives him files.*) Take 'em! I carried them all the way down here from Word Processing to you and why? Because I care, Tom! That's why! I *care*!

She stomps off and out. Tom stands there dumbfounded. He hasn't understood anything from when he walked into his office. Suddenly she returns.

. . . They're playing next Thursday over at the Coliseum and the National is opening for them. We could go late and get some dinner or just eat there. I leave it up to you. I'm just putting it out there – putting myself out there once again. One more time because I am a beautiful and loving person and I don't hold a fucking grudge . . . (*Beat.*) Lemme know by the end of business today or I'm gonna ask somebody else!

Tom Alright, umm . . . when is it again?

Jeannie *God!* You know what?! Don't worry about it.

Tom Jeannie, that's not . . . I just didn't know the date of the . . . !

She's already gone.

Good talk. Thanks.

And off she goes again. Tom shakes his head and goes to his desk, very confused. Finds his address book out on his desk top. Looks around, checks his stuff. Puts it away. Looks up to see Helen in the doorway. Jumps up.

Helen . . . Geez, you even have windows.

Tom Helen!

Helen Hi there.

Tom Hey! This is . . . really . . . Come in, come in!

He ushers her into his office and sits her on the couch. Checks both ways out the door.

Helen Surprised?

Tom Very. Yes. A lot. So . . . they just let you right past security? I mean, usually . . .

Helen No, I asked for you. Somebody said your office was this way and I could go back if I wanted to.

Tom Good. Great. That's . . . very . . .

Helen You left your phone. So. I . . . I was gonna call and tell you but then . . . Hey. (*Holds up phone.*) I have it! Your phone, I mean, so that was a bad plan. And I don't know the number at your work. Here. Since you never gave it to me . . .

Tom Sorry. I just figured . . . with my cell . . .

Helen Of course! No biggie. You don't have the number to the library, either. I mean . . . do you?

Tom No . . .

Helen Good, 'cause that'd be weird. Sort of. Nobody has the number to libraries in their phones . . . except maybe the elderly.

They both smile at this – not sure what to do next.

Tom True! (*Checks his watch.*) Anyway . . . so I left it there? Gawd, that's so stupid!

Helen No, you were just in a hurry, said you had to get back and so that was . . . but I was getting ready to leave – I used the rest room before I left, probably way too much info for you there – and the waitress came over with it. Said she found it on the table next to us – I guess you put it there when we ate. That was nice, right?

Tom Very. So . . . cool. And then you came all the way over here to . . .? You're so sweet!

Helen Hey. That's me. 'Sweet.'

He sits with her for a minute, gives her a quick kiss on the mouth.

Tom I love your perfume.

Another peck on the cheek.

There. That's your reward.

Helen Thanks. I was hoping for a fifty but I suppose that'll do . . .

Tom And . . . I wasn't finished yet . . . I'm gonna throw caution to the wind and take you back out. Right now. For a, a . . . a bite!

Helen Tom, we just ate. Even I'm full . . .

Tom No, I know! But I felt bad that we didn't get a chance for any dessert so let's do that now. Okay? (*Beat.*) I hated having to leave you there before, and I wanna make it up to you – let's go over there to the, um, Cheescake Factory and get something tasty. Like . . . cheesecake. It'll be fun!

Helen You sure? I mean . . . I don't wanna . . .

Tom No, it's great! I hate being all cooped up here – Let's do it!

Helen OK, but . . . you wanna show me around first or anything? Lemme see how the other half lives?

Tom Ha! No, that's, it's just an office, anyhow. No

biggie. (*Points.*) See? My desk, a chair. And there? My stapler. Now you've pretty much seen it all . . .

Helen 'Kay. Maybe the rest some other time.

Tom Sure. You can come by and we'll . . . That's a good idea, meet some of my . . . Yeah.

A silent beat where Helen looks around the office, taking it all in. Tom watches her and the door in equal measure.

Helen I wouldn't say 'no' to a banana split if you twist my arm . . . or even if you don't.

Tom Great! Come on, we can . . . Sounds fun!

He quickly helps her gather her things and they go out into the hall. In a minute he's back – calls out to her:

No, go ahead, sure! Grab that elevator! I just need to make a quick call and then I'll . . . Yes. See you in the lobby! Great!

He smiles until she's gone. After he steps back inside his office he starts to breathe heavily. Looks around, then quickly dials the phone.

Hey, yeah, this is Tom . . . How're you? I'm good. Would you tell 'em I'm gonna be a little late for the 1:30 meeting. I know! Just make something up for me and I'll . . . I will hurry . . . yep. OK, thank you. (*Hangs up.*) . . . Shit.

He grabs his jacket off his chair, checks his watch and finally goes out.

Carter just misses him. Walks in and looks around. Looks surprised that the place is empty. He starts to turn as Jeannie appears behind him.

Jeannie Boo!

Carter Ahh!! (*Jumps.*) Fuck! Stop doing that!

Jeannie Where's – The hell did he go now?

Carter I dunno.

Jeannie Great . . .

Carter Yeah. Great.

Jeannie What is it with that guy?! Damnit.

Carter He's complex, you know? (*Off her look.*) I'm just saying . . .

Jeannie Whatever.

They stand there, looking at each other. After a moment, Carter moves closer – starts to make a move to kiss her.

Carter So Jeannie, maybe we should . . . continue our little . . .

She puts her hand in his face and pushes him away.

Jeannie Fat chance, dumbshit.

She exits with a turn of her high heels. Carter looks after her – when she's gone, he bravely calls out:

Carter YOU WISH!

He yawns and plops down on the couch. Grabs up a magazine and lays back to read. Notices the pillow under his head. Picks it up. Sniffs at it. Perfume. It seems familiar.

Carter ponders this for a moment. Lost in thought.

Act Two

THE WORK FRIENDS FIGURE IT OUT

Tom at his desk, working. Carter sprawled on a couch and reading a magazine. He holds up a photo for Tom to look at. They both smile.
  After a moment, Jeannie appears in the doorway. Silently staring over at Tom.

Carter Hey, Jeannie. What's up?

Jeannie Hi. (*To Carter.*) Gee, you're in here and not working. That comes as quite a shock . . .

Carter You so dig me.

Jeannie Oh God. Tom?

She is done with Carter and turns to Tom. Stares.

Tom What? Good morning, by the way . . .

Jeannie Good morning. How's things?

Tom You know. Okay.

Jeannie I'll bet. I will just bet. (*Beat.*) Carter, can you give us a minute?

Carter Not if this is gonna get good . . . (*To Tom.*) Do you want me to go?

Jeannie Please . . .

Tom I don't . . . I'm not afraid of us talking in front of him. He'll find out, anyway.

Carter Exactly! I promise not to say a word.

Jeannie Yeah, just print a story in the *newsletter* . . .

Carter Well, I gotta get it out somehow.

He laughs but no one joins in. He sputters out and sits back.

Jeannie Fine. Whatever.

Tom Seriously . . . Jeannie, if you wanna say something to me, go ahead. (*He stands up.*) That's fine.

Jeannie Then why're you standing?

Tom What? Oh, you know, just . . . I felt like stretching.

Carter laughs. Jeannie glances over at him – he smiles and mimes zipping his mouth shut. She turns back to Tom.

Jeannie You know I'm in Accounting, right? You do know that.

Tom Of course.

Jeannie So anything you turn in is going to come past me, I mean, over my desk. True?

Tom I guess . . .

Jeannie No, you *know* it. I know that you know because I've had you come in there, to my office, looking for stuff before. (*To Carter.*) Quit looking at my ass. An old receipt or some stack of files. I mean, it's how we first got to be . . .

Tom No, you're right. That's true . . .

Jeannie We met that way so I'm sure you realise just how these things go. The course they take. You turn in your expense reports, attach the receipts and write in the little explanations and we do the rest. You know all this.

Tom Yeah, Jeannie, I get it. I mean, I know how to do that. So . . . ?

Jeannie . . . I waited for your big Chicago dinner to come through, just so I could see. I heard Carter joking around about it and so I wanted to, you know, check out who you were with. (*Beat.*) But nothing has been turned in yet. Why's that? Because you've always been – how can I put this? – pretty damn *anal* about it before.

Tom doesn't say anything, glancing over at Carter.

Carter . . . One quick interjection? It was just an off-handed comment, that's all.

Jeannie Just shut up, OK?

Carter I'm done.

Jeannie (*turns*) So . . . Tom? What's up?

Tom *Nothing.* Jesus, I mean . . .

Jeannie I'm just curious. But it's also my business, so, you know . . .

Tom What, to, like, stalk me?

Jeannie Please, you *wish* . . . to keep up on how people are utilising their expense accounts, shit like that.

Tom So, what? You're busting me for not asking to be reimbursed?

Jeannie No . . . I'm keeping things straight. Alright? It's my job.

Tom Yeah, but I bet you're not . . . you know, down at everybody's office, going through all their . . .

Jeannie Yes, I am, as a matter of fact. I stay here late almost every night, digging through mountains of crap that you guys spend out there on the road and in restaurants and at your little luxury hotels, so it's not just you. Alright? Please do not flatter yourself . . .

Tom Whatever.

Jeannie Yeah, 'whatever'. That's exactly what I'm asking. 'Hey, "whatever" happened to that Chicago dinner that Tom supposedly went on?'

She finishes and waits. Carter sits up, interested.

Tom I . . . I guess I must've forgot.

Jeannie To what?

Tom To turn in the report! *God*. My receipts and stuff. I'll . . . I can staple it to next month's, right?

Jeannie You could. Or I can take it from you now, if you want.

Tom No, I'm . . . I've got it all back at my apartment, so . . . later's fine.

Jeannie It was a business dinner, right? With the guys from Chicago.

Tom . . . Yes.

Carter It's what he told me.

Tom Carter.

Carter (*holds up a hand*) Sorry . . .

Tom I mean, not with the 'guys', per se, but this woman. One woman who came in from . . . yeah. A woman.

Carter 'Helen', I believe. (*Looks at Tom.*) What? I'm just being helpful . . .

Tom Yeah, thanks. (*To Jeannie.*) She was in town and we sat down and had a meal and talked over the, I mean, some of the . . . accounts from there. Like AmTel and . . . others.

Jeannie I see. Fine.

Tom Alright? Can we put the hot tongs away now, or was there some more stuff that you wanted to . . .?

He tries to laugh and Carter joins in. Jeannie stares.

Jeannie Carter, can you please leave us alone for a second? *Please.*

Carter Tom?

Tom No, Jeannie, shit . . . this is my office and he can . . . *What* is up with you?!

Jeannie God, fine. Whatever you want . . . you scared or something?

Tom Umm . . . maybe. Yeah. I wouldn't exactly want you handling a *butcher* knife right now or anything . . .

Carter laughs again, which makes Tom giggle a bit.

Jeannie Chicago doesn't have a record of anybody coming here last month. No one. No employee – man, woman. Fat chick. *Nothing.* I verified.

Tom . . . You called Chicago?

Jeannie I did, yes.

Tom Jeannie, I mean, shit . . . that is . . . that's, like, so –

Jeannie – *within* my job description.

Tom No, that goes beyond your . . . I mean let's be honest here, you are . . . being a little nuts about this!

Jeannie If I am, you made me that way.

Tom I didn't do . . . (*To Carter.*) Dude, back me up here.

Carter Yeah, I gotta say . . .

He starts to speak but Jeannie cuts him off.

Jeannie Shh! So I found it odd – especially when I had

to manoeuvre around the weight issue, trying to describe her from what Carter had said – and I'm just drawing blanks from this woman over the phone who's probably thinking I'm some crazy person but I have all the right information and the clearances and so she's accessing a bunch of these personnel records but, uh-uh, nothing. Not a single flight booked here in over three months. *So –* I slapped one of those little Post-it flags on it and came down here to ask you about the thing. Maybe you can help me out.

Tom looks over at Carter, who holds up a finger.

Carter ... I never said 'fat'.

Jeannie Carter, you told me she was huge.

Carter Yeah, which is totally different. Shaq is huge, but nobody says the guy's fat . . .

Jeannie You said she was a pig!

Carter I don't think we should get off on a tangent here . . . (*To Tom.*) I mean, Tom, you're the one who said she was in from Chicago.

Tom No . . .

Carter You didn't?

Tom No, I was . . . You inferred that . . .

Carter Yeah, because you told me you were having dinner with the . . . So, was she or not?

Jeannie That's really the question, isn't it? (*Beat.*) Tom.

Tom She was . . . yes, I was having dinner with one of our, she's a colleague from Chicago, but from one of our subsidiary suppliers . . . I should've been clear about the . . . her . . .

Carter The name was 'Helen', I believe.

Tom Right, 'Helen'. About Helen's trip to . . . to see us.

Jeannie Tom.

Tom I mean, not 'see' us, no, she wasn't just dropping in, like checking up on us or anything, but she came here to explain some . . . several . . . new . . . options for our involvement in a, a, variety of . . . stuff.

Jeannie Tom . . . Tom, listen to yourself. *Stop!* You are, like, the worst liar ever. I mean it. In *history*.

Tom Fine. Whatever you say.

He sits again, frustrated. Jeannie approaches him.

What?

Jeannie Umm . . . just the obvious stuff. Who–was–it?

Tom She's a . . . just this girl.

Jeannie Excuse me?

Tom Woman, then! I dunno. You know I mean 'woman'. A woman I met. She's someone that I've . . . who I took out, just got talking to at lunch one time and I was . . . Yeah.

Jeannie is lost for words. Carter is connecting the dots.

Jeannie I see. And, so, she's . . . ?

Carter Oh . . . shit. Fuck! Are you fucking kidding me?! HOLY SHIT!!

Carter realises he is being loud and gets up, crosses to the door and shuts it. Smiling broadly.

Dude . . . (*To Tom.*) This is not her. You gotta tell me, tell me that much. This is not the . . . her her. Is it?

Tom . . . Yeah. (*Beat.*) *Yes*, Carter.

Carter OhmyGod. Ohmy . . .

Tom Just stop, OK?

Carter I mean . . . OHMYGOD! This is a . . . Jesus Christ! She's . . . I gotta tell somebody!

Tom Would you just get out of here?!

Jeannie Fine, Tom, I'll go.

Tom Not you, Jeannie.

Carter Yeah, I gotta go find my camera. 'Tommy Joins the Circus!'

Tom Asshole.

Carter Oh, come on, man! You'd be doing the same thing to me . . .

Tom Bullshit . . .

Carter That's a lie and you know it! You totally would . . .

Tom No, I wouldn't. Nope. (*Beat.*) We mess around a lot but I do not make fun of your . . . you know . . .

Jeannie So . . . you are seeing her, then.

Tom It's not, no, but why do I have to discuss this?! Come on, people we're at work here.

Jeannie Sure, fine, but if you wanna stop and talk about the Lakers for two hours with the guys, that'd be OK, right? Yeah, that's cool, but if I come in here because I'm trying to figure out just what the hell is going on in my relationship, well, that's something we better talk about later. Let's save that for some later time. Yeah, that's pretty fair!

Tom We don't *have* a relationship!

Jeannie Oh, really?!

Tom Newsflash: no, we don't . . . I'm sorry, but you keep saying that, and I'm . . . you know . . . I keep trying to tell you that I'm not . . . this isn't . . .

Jeannie You said you wanted to try again! *You* told me that!

Tom To keep you from nagging at me! Just to stop you from calling and going on and on and on about this all the time! That's why!

Jeannie . . . Oh.

Tom Okay? I mean, God . . .

Jeannie I see.

Tom I'm sorry, but . . . I just don't . . .

Jeannie Then fine. Good.

Shee suddenly reaches across the desk and smacks Tom across the face. Hard with an open palm. He stumbles back and hits his chair, which rolls out from under him.

Jeannie walks to the door, swings it open wide. Before she goes, however, she turns back to Carter and pushes him hard against the couch. Jeannie exits, slamming the door behind her.

Tom crosses to the door, opens it. Looks out. Holds up a hand to someone down the hall. Closes the door again.

Carter . . . I think she took that pretty well.

Tom You dick.

Carter Hey, don't blame this shit on me.

Tom I'm not, I just . . . damn it! Why do we even have to do this crap? Get all involved with people and . . . ?

Carter Because we're clingy. It's what makes us different than the rest of the animals . . .

Tom Yeah, thanks, that really helps.

Carter I do what I can . . .

Tom sits back down in his chair and Carter plops back on the couch. They sit in silence for a moment.

Hey . . .

Tom What?

Carter This isn't meant as a . . . you know, to make up for what I said or whatnot, but in the spirit of full disclosure . . . my mom was fat. *Is.* As we speak.

Tom . . . That's great.

Carter No, I'm just saying . . . I know what it's like, I mean, why you were so embarrassed or . . .

Tom I wasn't! I just . . . Hell. I dunno. I sorta froze and, and then . . .

Carter Dude, I understand. Like, totally. (*Beat.*) I used to walk ahead of her in the mall or, you know, not tell her about stuff at school so there wouldn't be, whatever. My own *mom*. I mean . . . I'm fifteen and worried about every little thing and I've got this fucking Sumo wrestler in a housecoat trailing around behind me. That's about as bad as it can get! I'm not kidding you. And the thing was, I blamed her for it. I mean, it wasn't a disease or like some people have, thyroid or that type of deal . . . she just shovelled shit into her mouth all the time, had a few kids and, bang, she's up there at three-fifty, maybe more. It used to seriously piss me off. My dad was always working late . . . golfing on weekends and I knew it was because of her. It had to be! How's he gonna love something that looks like that, get all fucking sexy with her? I'm just a kid at the time, but I can remember thinking that.

Tom God, that's . . .

Carter waves this off, drifting in his own thoughts for a moment.

Carter Yeah, it's whatever, but . . . this once, in the grocery store, we're at an Albertson's and pushing *four* baskets around – you wanna know how humiliating that shit is? – and I'm supposed to be at a game by seven, I'm on JV, and she's just farting around in the candy aisle, picking up bags of 'fun-size' Snickers and checking out the calories. Yeah. I mean, can you believe that?! So, I suddenly go off on her, like, this sophomore in high school but I'm all screaming in her face . . . 'Don't look at the package, take a look in the fucking mirror, you cow! *Put 'em down!*' Holy shit, there's stock boys – bunch of guys I know, even – running down the aisle. Manager stumbling out of his glass booth there, the works. (*Beat.*) But you know what? She doesn't say a word about it. Ever. About the swearing, the things I called her, nothing. Just this, like, one tear I see . . . as we're sitting at a stop-light on the way home. That's all.

Tom Wow. I'm, I mean . . .

Carter I did feel that way, though. Maybe I shouldn't've yelled or . . . but it was true, what I said. You don't like being fat, there's a pretty easy remedy, most times. Do-not-jam-so-much-food-down-your-fucking-gullet! (*Beat.*) It's not that hard.

Tom Right. I guess that's true. (*Beat.*) It's confusing, though, the . . .

Carter What?

Tom I dunno, I'm, like . . . I mean, that night, when you saw us? Why didn't I just come clean, say that I was having dinner, out with a friend even, instead of making all that shit up?

Carter . . . Because you're a pussy.

Tom . . . Man, come on . . .

Carter No, I say that in the best way. We all are – guys, I mean – if it comes right down to it. Very rare is the dude who stands up for the shit he believes in . . .

Tom I know! I wanna be better at that sorta stuff, but a lot of the time I'm just . . . yeah. A big wuss, and I hate that! Despise that about me, but God, it's . . . No. I'm gonna work on it, I'll . . . I'll . . .

Carter Dude, relax, take a breath, don't hurt yourself . . . we can't all be Thomas More. And anyway, look what happened to him! Poor bastard . . .

Tom True. (*Beat.*) No offence, but how the hell do *you* know about Thomas More?

Carter Hey . . . I *only* cheated off the top two percentile in my class.

Tom nods and drifts. Carter does the same. Silence.

Tom . . . Geez, I wish Jeannie wasn't so, you know. Damn.

Carter She's pissed. I mean, nobody likes getting screwed around.

Tom I didn't . . . (*Beat.*) You think this is how I wanted it to end up? Huh?

Carter No . . . but it's the way these things usually do.

Tom I guess.

Carter I *know*. The guy who first thought up the whole 'I hope we can still be friends' thing must be giggling his *dick* off somewhere . . .

Tom Probably. (*Beat.*) You think maybe I should go down there and talk to her? Just . . .

Carter Oh, yeah, that's a good idea. Meet her on her turf . . . with all those accounting chicks around. *Perfect*.

Tom I don't want her all mad, though. Maybe just an email . . .

Carter Yeah, with one of those smiley-faced icons or something. Come on, be serious!

Tom What?

Carter It's over. You are so done . . .

Tom I *know*. I'm not saying to try and salvage anything, but just so that we can . . . shit, I dunno! We have to work together, so . . .

Carter It's the way of the world. Break-ups are ugly. I mean, unless you get to watch 'em from over here. (*Laughs*.) She so nailed you!

Tom Come on, Carter, don't.

Carter I'm sorry, but it was awesome. I mean, I've seen you get tagged by some bad boys playing ball, never even budge – and this little girl walks in and takes you out like Sonny Liston . . . BAM! Pretty cool.

Tom Yeah, hilarious. (*Beat*.) Maybe I'll just send her a quick one . . .

Carter waves him off and picks up another magazine. Tom quickly types something on his computer and hits a button to send it off.

It can't hurt.

Carter Not as much as your face, anyway.

They sit and stare at one another for a moment. Silence.

You got a photo? Of her.

Tom You are not getting a picture. Not even a peek . . .

Carter I will not take it. I promise.

Tom Uh-huh. Sure.

Carter I won't! I just wanna see her one more time.

Tom Man, you are so . . . I don't even get why I like you.

Carter Because you're like me.

Tom No, I'm not.

Carter You so are! Absolutely.

Tom That's not true. (*Grins.*) No.

Carter *Right.* (*Beat.*) You do that little boy thing, 'Oh, I'm so innocent' trick that women eat up but you are so much like me it's not even funny. Seriously . . .

Tom Carter, that's not at all . . .

Carter Bullshit! You laugh at the same jokes and check out the same asses that I do, you date all these gals and act like you're Mr Sensitive but how does it always end up? The *exact* same way is does for me . . . you get bored or cornered or feel a touch nervous and you drop 'em like they were old produce. Every time. Dude, I'm not blind . . .

Tom Yeah, but that's because, I mean, with Jeannie it's been . . . you know.

Carter I'm not talking about just her. I mean with anybody. Since I've known you. There's no shame in it . . . It's not very nice, but I don't think we were put down here to be nice. Not exclusively, anyway. Every so often we sprinkle a little 'nice' in on top, just to keep 'em guessing, but . . . that's about it.

Tom You scare me a little . . . I mean it.

Carter Ahh, it's just Tuesday. Tuesdays suck . . .

They sit back down and contemplate this for a bit. Carter yawns and turns back to his friend.

Seriously . . . can I see her?

Tom No.

Carter Tom, that's not very . . . I said some stuff and I'm sorry. I didn't know you two were dating.

Tom Its . . . I just took her out a few . . . She's nice. OK?

Carter It's fine. (*Beat.*) So, lemme see.

Tom Jesus . . .

Pulls a snapshot out of his wallet.

I'm holding it.

Carter That's mature.

Goes over to look at it.

Oh, cool. It's one of those 'makeover deals' isn't it?

Tom I guess. Yes.

Carter Very nice. I like the boa.

Tom Don't be a prick.

Carter Kidding! She's sweet. I mean, from meeting her and everything, I could tell.

Tom Thanks.

Carter Does she . . . I mean, does her weight go up and down or . . . ? I only ask because she's got a nice face, so I'm curious.

Tom She's not worried about that kind of thing – buy into all of those diet fads . . . which is sort of refreshing, actually.

Carter Sure. I'm just saying . . . can't turn on CNN without some doctor talking about . . .

Tom Because, you know . . . Yeah, I think she's pretty as well, but we don't ever talk about that 'what if?' kinds of shit about her size. She's happy with who she is, and so . . . it's . . .

Carter Then great. (*Looks again.*) Can you please let me . . . I'm not six years old. I promise not to take it.

Tom 'Kay.

Tom very warily lets go of the photo. In stages. Finally it is in Carter's hands. He studies it.

Carter No, I can tell that she's a very genuine person, even from some photo. I like the starburst effect. (*He smiles.*) That's a *joke*.

Tom Here, just give it back.

Carter Wait . . . I'm serious, though. Could probably get on one of those reality shows if she lost, like, eighty pounds, she'd be kinda stunning.

Tom I know, but I just said . . . here.

Carter I mean, I'm only talking. I'm not an expert. Perhaps we should see what everybody in the cafeteria thinks . . .

Tom Carter! CARTER, YOU FUCKER!

But Tom is trapped behind his desk and Carter is off like a rocket – out the door and down the hall. Tom starts to follow but gives up after a second. Returns to his desk.

Bastard. Ahh, screw it. I don't care. I'm not gonna be . . . whatever.

A little bell goes off. Ding! Tom looks at his computer and sees an email has arrived. He clicks it and reads.

'DEAR TOM, FUK U AND UR FAT BITCH. ASSHOLE. LOL.'
(*Beat.*) That's charming . . .

He starts to type a response but it slowly dissolves as he begins to pound harder and harder on the keys. Finally he stops, exhausted. Pushes it away. Sits.

SOME OLD TERRITORY FOR THE NEW COUPLE

A bedroom. Tom and Helen are lying on top of the covers, watching a movie. Helen is concentrating, Tom is kissing her.

Tom Mmmm. God, you're so . . .

He continues to kiss her as Helen watches the TV.

Helen Tom . . . hold on . . . look . . .

Tom I am. At *you* . . .

Helen Remember this part? (*Pointing.*) I think he's just about to . . . they're gonna find the gold . . .

Sound of gunfire, shouts. Helen laughs. Tom looks at her.

Tom Pretty *funny*. He got shot.

Helen Yeah, but it's meant to be . . . you know. It's a comedy. Mostly.

Tom Uh-huh. (*Kisses her.*) Mmmm . . .

Helen Wait . . .

Tom I don't wanna *wait* . . . I wanna . . . well, *lots* of things. Kiss you. And . . . more kisses, and . . .

Helen But . . . this is due back tomorrow.

Tom Oh, OK . . . (*Laughs.*) Here . . .

Helen Umm, don't start with the good stuff . . .

Tom You love the good stuff . . .

Helen Yes, but we can't always . . . Ohh, yes, you can keep doing *that*, actually . . .

Tom See?

Helen But we should . . . Tom . . .

Tom Can't help it . . . I love your mouth. Each lip. Both.

Helen Thank you. (*Kissing him.*) Thanks.

Tom I really do like the way you kiss. So much.

Helen Me too. We fit, you know? Our mouths together. It's important.

Tom I, yeah . . . agree . . .

Helen and Tom begin to make out – the movie is forgotten. He reaches around, finds the remote and the sound drops out. After a moment, she gently pulls back, studies him.

Helen . . . So, you feel comfortable with me? I mean . . .

Tom I'm . . . yes. I am. I have honestly never been more relaxed around a person. (*Beat.*) Well, my *mother*, but that gets into a weird area . . .

Helen Ha-ha-ha. (*Beat.*)

Tom Seriously, I haven't felt this way for a long time. *Ever*, probably.

Helen I'm glad.

Tom No, I mean it. (*Kisses her.*) I *adore* you.

Helen Me, too. (*She kisses him.*) And I wasn't trying to get that out of you . . .

Helen punches him playfully on the shoulder, which leads to horseplay. After a moment, Tom lays back. Relaxed.

Tom God, this feels so damn good! You know? I mean . . . just laying around here, us together. All alone.

Helen I know.

Tom It's like . . . I feel like we're on a raft or something. Paddling along, all the time in the world . . . no one around to bug us. (*Mimes paddling.*) Ahhh, this is the life!

Helen Like the beginning of *Heaven Knows, Mr Allison*. Remember?

Tom Exactly! Yep . . . (*Smiles.*) And you could play the Deborah Kerr part. You'd make a very *saucy* nun . . .

Helen kisses him and Tom slips back into a comfortable position.

Helen . . . Sounds good. (*Beat.*) Sorta.

Tom What?

Helen I dunno, I just . . . I sense something. A kind of being . . . isolated. At times.

Tom Helen . . . haven't I been with you every day? I mean, my friends have even said things. Noticed it. I'm hardly with them any more.

Helen But . . . that's what I mean.

Tom What?

Helen Neither am I. You know? I mean, we've been going out for . . . however long, and I only met that one guy. Carter. At the restaurant.

Tom That's true, but . . . I mean, I've been waiting for the, maybe, a right time or something. One of those office parties or . . .

Helen Tom.

Tom No, truthfully! I thought maybe on the Fourth or . . . we do a big party at the beach. A cookout and stuff.

Helen Great . . . should I go with a *thong* or be a little more conventional?

Tom Very funny. I was being serious . . .

A sort of silence drops over them. Both of them staring off. Quiet.

Helen . . . It's just a little like we're, I dunno, hiding or whatever. From people.

Tom . . . No . . .

Helen You don't think?

Tom No, Helen, I really don't. At all. (*Beat.*) I mean, we're not exactly hanging out with all your pals, either. We've barely . . .

Helen That's not true – I ask you all the time if you'd want to, or if we –

Tom Yeah, but . . .

Helen I'm dying to show you off, Tom, if you'd let me . . . I've told you to pick me up at work, all kinds of things!

Tom I know, but . . . it's a *library*. Not supposed to talk in there . . . I'll be in trouble.

Helen Tom . . . *please*. (*She waits.*) Listen, I had a thing come up for me at the . . . this opportunity. Remember the interview that I . . . Yeah. That. It's only a couple towns over, but far enough away that . . . whatever. The *point* is, it's a great offer and the more I think about this – every time we end up ordering in or you run out to get videos – some little thing in my head, this warning buzzer says, 'Watch it. Just watch out.'

Tom Helen . . .

Helen I just hope you're not *embarrassed* by me in some way, because, well, I mean . . . I don't know what . . .

Tom No. Why would you say that? I'm not at all . . . What're you . . . ?

Helen Nothing. I'm not saying anything, except I need you to be honest with me here. *Today*, if possible.

Tom . . . Well, what am I supposed to say now? To that?

Helen Just the truth.

Tom I'm . . . I meant something easier.

Helen smiles at this as Tom scoots closer to her on the bed, holds her. A kiss.

Helen . . . you can't leave town, I need you around. You're like the sunrise to me. Like Vitamin C or something. My *oxygen*. (*Beat.*) I need you . . .

Helen I'm not looking for fairy tale or out-of-the-ballpark or anything . . . just a person who cares about me like I do them. Simple.

Tom . . . Love isn't simple. It's . . . *never having to say you're sorry.*

He starts to say more, but Helen stops him. Smiles.

Helen . . . I don't need you to be clever here! No jokes. Or *film quotes* . . . Just be very clear . . . and honest.

Tom kisses Helen, then sits her down on the bed. Joins her. Tries to get serious.

Fine. Look . . . I wanna be truthful now, so just let me . . . you know, bumble along. Alright?

Helen Please. Bumble on.

She smiles and Tom slowly returns it to her. He touches her face. Strokes her hair.

Tom Helen . . . I want you. Both mentally *and* physically. Each curve, every last inch of you . . . (*He kisses her.*) I'd hope you can see that by now . . .

She starts to speak but he holds up a finger to silence her.

So . . . I don't know how to do this. To say exactly how I'm feeling because, you know, I'm a guy and we're taught how to *kick* stuff, and tear the wings off shit – but, look . . . I can see that we've got something here, I'm not stupid, right? – do not answer that – and I need you to know. That *I* know. I'm really just so damn . . . *overcome* by this. Here. Us. I don't take it lightly or in some carefree manner at all. No. Helen, you are just, well, very important to me . . . *very* . . . (*Beat.*) Look, I've fallen for you, fallen *hard*, and . . . yeah, I love you and I hope . . .

Helen Sorry, what?

Tom I love you.

Helen What? I didn't . . .

Tom I love you.

Helen Wow.

Tom So I hope that you give me a chance to prove it in the near future, at the, aforementioned volleyball-slash-beach party or at some other to-be-determined public gathering. *And* if you take that other job, even a few towns over, it would be a real, you know. Bad thing. (*Grins.*) OK, that sort've sucked, but most the ingredients were in there . . .

Helen Yeah . . . and it was kind of lovely.

Tom Then, good. Thanks.

Helen No, thank you . . . Tom Sullivan.

Tom You're welcome . . . Helen . . . what's your last name again?

Helen smacks him playfully on the shoulder again. Twice.

I know it has, like, a 'B' in it.

Helen 'Bond.' (*Laughs.*) You ass . . .

Tom Right, 'Bond', sorry. 'Bond'.

Tom Mmm! (*Kisses her.*) You're awesome.

Helen You, too, Tom. You're a good man. (*Kisses him back.*) Good and strong and brave and . . . ummm . . . *lots* of nice things . . .

Tom . . . Mmmm! I love it when you talk *dirty*.

He begins to kiss her. More and more. Helen responds and, after a moment, lets him unfasten her bra. Tom starts to caress and kiss her there. Helen's eyes slowly close.
Her hand searches around, finds the remote again. Click! Up come the sounds of war and mayhem on the soundtrack. Loud.

TWISTS AND TURNS AT THE OFFICE

Tom at his desk again. Working. Jeannie standing nearby with a file in her hand. Waiting.

Jeannie So are you bringing her to the thing next month?

Tom Huh? (*Looks up.*) Oh, yeah. I think.

Jeannie Can't decide?

Tom Ummm, you know . . . she's gotta check if she can get off from work.

Jeannie Oh. I see. And what's she do?

Tom She's . . . she's a printed word specialist.

Jeannie Ahh. (*To herself.*) Perfect.

Tom What's that?

Jeannie Nothing. (*Points.*) Are you almost done there? I need to get those out by five . . .

Tom Yeah, hold on.

He goes back to work while Jeannie glances around. Takes in the space.

Jeannie No pictures of her up yet.

Tom Nah.

Jeannie How come?

Tom, frustrated, drops his pen and looks straight at her.

Tom . . . Wasn't the one that appeared on everybody's desktop this morning enough? (*Turns his monitor round.*) You need more laughs than this?

Jeannie I wouldn't mind.

Tom Great.

Jeannie Yeah, I'd be up for that.

Tom Jesus . . . you really are *awful*, you know that? I mean it.

Jeannie Just keep signing, OK? Your little sermon isn't needed.

Tom I'm not . . . whatever.

Jeannie That's exactly right. Whatever.

Tom ... Jeannie ... can't we just be ... ?

Jeannie Don't bother. *Sign.*

Tom is about to follow instructions but pulls the files from his desk and slips them in a drawer. Shuts it. Sits back as he checks his watch.

Tom No, uh-uh, you've got time. And I want you to tell me ... go on. What the hell I did to you that was so bad. Do it.

Jeannie Tom, don't be a prick, alright? I need to make Fed-Ex.

Tom You will ...

Jeannie No! I'm not obligated to talk with you about shit ... We're co-workers, we work together now and that is all. Give me the files.

Tom Nope.

Jeannie You're an asshole ...

Tom Maybe so. I dunno ... maybe I am. Or have been to you. That's what I'm saying! If I have, then tell me. Show me how ...

It's a stand-off for a moment, then Jeannie makes a move toward Tom. He stands up and holds his ground. She backs off and stands to one side, hands on her hips.

Jeannie I don't even wanna discuss your fat bitch, OK? She's ...

Tom Stop that.

Jeannie So, forget it. I'll just say about us, I mean, what we've ...

Tom No, let's do the whole ...

Jeannie Fuck you! Don't tell me what we'll do. At all.

Tom I'm *not*. I'm just saying we should probably, you know . . .

Jeannie We should've *probably* done a lot of things! We should probably be engaged now, if you weren't such a spineless shit, like every other guy . . . so . . .

Tom Your mouth is, like, I dunno. Wow.

Jeannie Yeah, exactly right. 'Wow.' I'm twenty-eight years old and I just keep hitting the booby prize and you know what? After a while, it really starts to get you down . . .

Tom But, I'm not . . . that's not my . . .

Jeannie What? Problem? I didn't say that. It's no one's problem, *me* included . . . It just sucks. That's what I'm saying. (*Beat.*) I thought maybe you were different, but you ended up being the same kind of lame guy that I perpetually date and it just freaks me out a little. That maybe you're the only type's out there. These baby boys who run around in nice clothes but all they really wanna do is breast feed for the rest of their days . . .

Tom I can't speak for other people, Jeannie, but I . . .

Jeannie I don't care any more. I don't.

Tom I'm just saying that . . . you and I didn't end up working out, but it doesn't mean . . . I like you. I did always like you, but . . . we're . . .

Jeannie Tom, I know that you think that means something to me, but it's really just drivel. OK? More of the same.

Tom Fine. I'm sorry.

Jeannie And that doesn't do shit, either.

Tom nods, then sits and pulls out the files. Signs his name in several more places and then holds them out. Jeannie goes over and grabs them. Hovers.

Tom Yes?

Jeannie Listen, Tom . . .

Tom Don't worry about it, Jeannie.

Jeannie You just get me so frustrated.

Tom It really is fine . . .

Jeannie No, I figure that I should just . . . I mean, who knows the next time we might see each other, like, in a *non*-professional way, and the thing of it is, the strange part of it is this – I'd take you back right now. I'm serious. I would, and I'm not sure why . . . because you are not really that . . . great, you weren't so nice to me, Tom. Not at all. You didn't hit me or anything, do something that the police might contact you about, but you really hurt me. A lot. By just being . . . you know. You. And yet when I'm standing here, looking at you I still have all these . . . whatevers toward you. *Feelings* and all that stuff, so, yeah. It really is a bit weird still. Tender, or . . .

Tom . . . I understand.

Jeannie No, you don't! I mean, no offence, but how could you? You're you and sitting over there – I'm a whole other person – so, you can't know how it felt for you to do all that crap to me, 'cause if you did know or could feel it then I, I, I just refuse to believe that you'd've done it, because that'd suck. That would actually suck shit if it were the truth, so no – I'm ruling that out as a possibility. I wanna at least *pretend* that I was going out with a better guy than that, even if it wasn't true – even if he was *secretly* thinking that I wasn't good enough or, or cute enough or, just, like, whatever . . . not *enough* of something – I'm gonna fool myself into buying that other story because it'd be just way too awful to know that the opposite is what was really going on . . . that we were out there having fun and being all intimate and whatever, but that you were never really gonna give us a shot at this, were you? . . . at being a couple. Us two.

Tom Jeannie, I'm . . . I *hear* you, I do, but maybe we shouldn't get into all this right now. 'Kay?

Jeannie . . . Fine. That's no surprise. (*Beat.*) Look, I know you're with her now – this *Helen* person – and I said I wasn't gonna . . . but I *really* do need to know.

Tom . . . Yes? What?

Jeannie Come on. *Tom.* (*Points at screen.*) What is the story with that one?

Tom Jeannie . . .

Jeannie I mean, I hope it's some sort of mothering thing or whatever, 'cause if not, it's just so off-the-charts gross that I don't know what to say.

Tom We should probably stop now.

Jeannie I mean, you know what everybody is saying around here, right? I know that you know. And it doesn't even faze you, huh? At all?

Tom I'm . . . I don't wanna do this. Here.

Jeannie It's not like she's . . . she's really *fat*, Tom! A fat sow and you know it. I can tell you're aware by the way you're acting, which is really the puzzling part . . .

Tom I–like–her. *End* of story.

Jeannie Yeah, but what the hell? Did you do something bad in some former life that you're making up for? Tell me, because . . . she's . . . well, you know what she's like better than the rest of us . . . I mean . . . is she a good cook, or . . . ?

Tom STOP IT! Jeannie, just stop this. I get that you're pissed at me and you needed to blow off some steam so that's why I, I . . . I allowed you to say stuff, but . . .

Jeannie You didn't 'allow' me shit, Tom! I can say whatever I want, *any* time I want. The whole company is, why should I be any different?

Tom Then talk if you want to! I–DO–NOT–CARE! I enjoy her because she's not you, *anything* like you . . . She is not obsessed with looks and money and clothes and useless bullshit like that! OKAY?! (*Beat.*) I like who I am when I'm with her, alright, so just . . . fuck, leave us alone.

Jeannie Ohhhh . . . 'us'. So it's 'us' now, huh?

Tom Yeah. It is.

Jeannie And, forgive me for saying it, but she seems a little obsessed with some things . . . like maybe Doritos.

Tom starts to come round his desk now, determined to put an end to this. Jeannie stares him down.

Tom I'm serious here . . . you need to go.

Jeannie I am going, I *am*, but not because you say so. Because I want to. I want to be as far away from you as I can be . . .

Tom Good.

Jeannie Yeah, 'good'. Nice retort.

Tom Just . . .

Jeannie What an *ass*. (*Beat.*) I'm sure you thought this would hurt me, right? Like, 'What's the worst thing I'd be able to do to her?' And this is what you came up with, some self-image killer like this one . . . Tom ditched me for fucking Momma Cass! Boo-hoo, woe is me! Is that what all this shit is about, getting back at me?! Huh?!

Tom Jeannie, get out of here! NOW!

Jeannie It doesn't hurt me at all! NOT ONE BIT! It just makes you look like some creepy fucker and a totally . . . AHHH! I don't care. I hate you. HATE YOU. So, so much.

Jeannie storms out of his office, leaving the door wide open. Tom doesn't have the strength to close it; crosses to his couch instead and sits. Rubs his eyes.
When he opens them, he sees Carter standing at the door.

Tom . . . Go away. Seriously.

Carter That's not very neighbourly.

Tom Neighbours don't treat neighbours like that. Enemies barely do . . .

Carter Dude, it's a joke. (*Beat.*) Think of it as payback for forwarding everybody my email about that one lady at lunch. And I *did* see the string of her tampon, by the way . . . when she crossed her legs.

Tom I'm not kidding, Carter . . .

Carter I thought Helen looked good blown up like that! Several people I talked to said they're gonna keep it . . .

Tom Come on, man. Really. Just leave me alone today.

Carter Fine.

But instead of leaving, Carter goes and drops into Tom's chair and starts playing with it. Swinging in circles and raising/lowering the seat mechanism.

Tom If Moses had needed, like, another plague . . . I would've given him your number.

Carter Bad day?

Tom I'm getting used to 'em.

Carter That's why I'm here. To be, like, a calming influence.

Tom Great. If you're my best chance, then I'm screwed.

Carter Nah. All will be fine, my friend. I promise.

Tom O–kay. (*Beat.*) I don't even need to ask you why you're here . . .

Carter Just chillin'.

Tom Uh-huh. Figured.

The men sit in their respective spots for a bit, staring up at the ceiling. Finally, Tom speaks.

So, lemme ask you something, then.

Carter Shoot.

Tom And honestly now . . . just an opinion is all, so no big deal.

Carter I'm ready.

Tom What do you actually think of her? Helen, I mean.

Carter Umm . . .

Tom Not for you, or, like, scoping her out down in Jamaica or that type of thing . . . just as a person.

Carter Oh. Like that.

Tom Yes.

Carter sits back in the chair, thinking for a moment.

Carter You're begging for trouble.

Tom That's . . . why do I even ask you?

Carter No, and I'll tell you why! I will. I know that I'm not super familiar with her or anything, like, her qualities – of which there may be many . . .

Tom There are –

Carter – and that's great. Terrific. But I'm just talking purely as an 'Is this a good deal for my pal here?' thing.

Tom Fine. And?

Carter *And* you got a long road ahead, that's all. Just being honest.

Tom Fine.

Carter I'm not saying I don't admire you – I do, actually, 'cause I know that I couldn't do it! – but she's gonna end up a weight around your neck. Forgive the pun . . .

Tom You're . . . doing that strictly on a 'physical' basis . . . which is . . .

Carter Of course! Fuck, what else can I go on? (*Beat.*) I don't wanna come off like some Elton John here, but you're a good-looking guy. You're successful, bit of a player in the industry . . . I don't understand you taking God's good gifts and then pissing on 'em . . .

Tom Carter . . .

Carter Dude, you're the one who evoked a biblical thing earlier . . . so take a glance at Noah and all that flood shit! He didn't pair up the apes with the antelope, right? It's one of the many laws of nature. 'Run with your own kind.'

Tom That is so . . . out of whack that I'm, like, completely lost now . . .

Carter Hey, it's a free country, and if this is how you really feel, then you are fucking Gunga Din. 'Better man than I am' and all that shit. Just do not be surprised when you turn a few heads down at the mall.

Tom But why can't we . . . I mean, shit! I dunno, man, I like her. A *lot*. She makes me happy, and I really wanna make her happy, too . . .

Carter I'm not saying she can't be happy. That she shouldn't meet somebody, but it oughta be a fat somebody, or a bald one. Whatever. Like her. A somebody that *fits* her . . .

Tom That's crazy . . . things aren't just based on *appearance*!

Carter Maybe you should snap on the TV once in a while. (*Beat.*) I'm not talking about what people deserve, I'm saying what they *get*. You look one way, you have access to all this . . . look some other way, all you get is that. Sorry, but it's true.

Tom . . . Yeah, well, it sucks . . .

Carter It's whatever. Truth. People are not comfortable with difference. Ya know? Fags, retards, cripples. Fat people. Old folks, even. They scare us or something.

Tom I don't think that's true. I mean, I'm not . . . No, Carter, I don't buy that. We're all . . .

Carter Come on, be honest! The thing they represent that's so scary is what we could be, how vulnerable we all are. I mean, *any* of us.

Tom Old people, though? Come *on*. We're all gonna age. It's . . .

Carter Not me. I hope I'm a goner before then. The elderly make me sick . . .

Tom This is . . . You're not helping me, Carter! That is the most depressing shit I've ever heard. (*Beat.*) Seriously.

Carter holds up his hands and shrugs. Tom sits up on the couch, thinking. A bit lost.

Carter All I'm saying is this . . . do what you want. If you like this girl, then don't listen to a goddamn word anybody says. Not one. (*Beat.*) However . . . if you're looking for my opinion, it's this – you've got your whole life to be a positive person, OK? To do some good in the community and be a big-hearted fellow or whatever. Overlook people's flaws and plant saplings and shit. But you're only young once. Handsome and youthful and vibrant. So don't fuck it up, that is all I'm telling you here. Don't take a complete dump on your one moment in the sun . . . (*Beat.*) Not for somebody like *her*.

Tom Carter . . . Fuck! You're not . . . God . . . You don't always have to say something. You know? Like, *every*thing that comes into your head. I mean . . . *shit*.

Tom catches himself, stops. Silence. After a minute, Carter yawns and slowly stands.

Carter Yeah, I should stuff an envelope or two. (*Laughs.*) So look . . . I wanna run this past you first, I mean, . . . I'm gonna ask Jeannie to that beach deal coming up. Is that cool?

Tom Umm . . . sure. No, of course.

Carter I mean, no weirdness for us?

Tom None. I think you two could . . . just might be perfect for each other.

Carter Yeah, me too! (*Beat.*) I heard she's started going to a gym, so that's something. I mean, you know her body, right? Obvious potential . . .

Tom Course.

Carter Anyway . . . as long as we're still . . .

Tom Sure. I think we'll remain exactly what we are. You and me.

Carter Friends, right?

Tom Sorta. (*Gestures with his fingers.*) About this much.

Carter Good enough for me. Oh I forgot.

He reaches into a shirt pocket and hands Tom the photo of Helen that he took before. Pats Tom on the shoulder.

I know you'll do the right thing.

He exits. Tom goes to the couch and sits down. Holds the picture in front of him. Brings it closer now. Staring at it. Hard.

ONE OF THOSE BLUSTERY DAYS AT THE BEACH

A stretch of sand. Tom, in a flowered swimsuit, sitting alone on a blanket. Trying to focus on a biography.
After a moment, Jeannie approaches. She is looking fit and is wearing a skimpy bikini. She towers over him.

Jeannie . . . Thought that was you.

Tom Yeah. Hey. (*Jumps up.*) . . . You look good. I mean, *nice*.

Jeannie Thanks. Yeah . . . I'm doing pilates now. (*Beat.*) How come you guys are sitting way down here?

Tom Oh, we're just . . . little privacy, I suppose. Edge of the group is all.

Jeannie Ah. Cool.

Tom So . . . (*Beat.*) You and Carter, huh?

Jeannie Yeah, how 'bout that?!

Tom It's good.

Jeannie I hope so. He's actually OK once you get him outta the office . . .

Tom Most people are. That's not, like, the best environment for a person. Those *cubicles* . . .

Jeannie Probably not. (*Smiles.*) Anyways . . .

Tom Right. Anyway. I hope you guys . . .

Jeannie . . . Thanks. You, too, I guess.

She leans toward him and Tom gives her a peck on the cheek. Tom responds briefly.

Well . . . come down and do a little volleyball later or something.

Tom Will do. Maybe.

Jeannie 'Kay. (*Beat.*) See that you're still wearing that swimsuit I got you . . .

Tom Yes. I like it.

Jeannie Looks good on you. I mean, nice. (*Grins.*) Alright, so I'll see you, then . . .

Tom OK. Take care.

Jeannie Same to you. (*Hangs on.*) And, look, about all that other stuff . . .

Tom Don't worry about it, Jeannie, it really is fine . . .

Jeannie OK, yeah, but I just want you to know that . . . that I'm . . .

Helen arrives on the scene juggling a large tray full of food. She is wearing a one-piece suit, with a beach wrap around her waist.

Hey. Get everything you need?

Helen Yes, thanks. (*To Jeannie.*) Hello.

Jeannie Hi, I'm Jeannie. Tom and I . . . work together.

Helen Oh, nice. I'm Helen.

Jeannie Yeah, I figured. (*Beat.*) I just mean, Tom mentioned you before.

Helen Oh. (*Hugs Tom.*) That was sweet.

Tom Hey.

Jeannie Anyhow, I came down to say 'hello' and invite you guys over for some games later . . .

Tom Cool. We'll, umm . . .

Helen I'm not too sporty, but . . . not that you could tell or anything!

The two women share a little laugh. Jeannie glances at Tom, who tries to smile but only grimaces.

Tom We'll see. Thanks, though.

Helen Yes, we appreciate it. And really great to meet you . . .

Jeannie You, too. So long, Tom.

Tom OK. Bye, Jeannie . . .

Jeannie throws one last look at Tom, then heads off down the beach toward the others. Tom sits down on the blanket with the food. Helen follows in a moment, out of breath.

So. That's Jeannie. She's in Accounting.

Helen That's *quite* a swimsuit she's got there. For an *accountant*. (*Recovers.*) Seems nice, though.

Tom Yeah. Pretty much.

Helen What's that mean?

Tom Oh, ya know . . . have our differences at work sometimes, that's all.

Helen Ahh.

They settle themselves on their blanket and begin to sort the food items into two stacks.

Tom Oh, good, I'm glad they had those kettle chips . . . (*He looks off.*) Is that Carter?

Helen Yeah, he said 'hi' when I was down there. He introduced me around.

Tom Good, that's – (*Yells.*) HEY, BUDDY! (*Laughs.*) Yeah, right! Sure!!

Helen You can go down there if you want.

Tom Huh? No, I wanna be here with you. We'll, you know . . . later.

Helen 'Kay. (*Looking up.*) Beautiful day.

Tom Uh-huh, yep. Super nice . . .

They sit for a moment, taking in the sun. The surf.

Helen How long do these things usually go? Any idea?

Tom Umm, no, but . . . we don't have to stay or anything. That's fine. I just need to, you know, make an appearance . . .

Helen No, I like it. Being here with you and all your . . . it's great. (*Beat.*) We just promised those guys that we'd . . . at some point drop off the cheque . . .

Tom Oh, right, the travel agent. Sure. (*Beat.*) We should maybe . . . later. Go.

Helen Hmm, weird vibe here. Tom are you sure . . . ?

Tom . . . Yeah. You kidding me? It's a . . . great place. I love Miami.

Helen I sorta meant about the part where we get to be together, but . . .

Tom Oh, that. (*Yawns.*) Yeah, that's OK.

Helen swats him on the arm. Tom reacts and sits back. She watches him as he turns away.

Helen So, are you excited about it? The trip, I mean?

Tom What? Of course. (*Beat.*) It's all set and everything.

Helen That's not really the same as just saying 'yes'.

Tom Jesus, fine . . . *Yes*. Better? (*Beat.*) Food looks good. Thanks for going down there . . .

Helen Figured we should grab some before it was gone.

Tom Right. Sorry, I should've . . .

Helen No, it felt nice, to walk through the surf like that. Fun.

Tom Cool. Glad you could make it . . .

Helen . . . It wasn't *that* far.

Tom No, I'm . . . I meant, switch days or whatever.

Helen I know. It's a joke. (*Beat.*) Tom, are you sure?

Tom Of course. Why?

Helen I'm . . . nothing. Let's eat.

Tom No, Helen. What?

Helen Same ol' stuff. Doesn't matter.

Tom Of course it does. Of course . . . Tell me.

Helen Look where we're at. I mean, Tom, it's . . . forget it.

She holds up a hot dog.

Ketchup?

Tom This isn't . . . Helen, I just wanted to get us near the sea wall here, so we'd have a little protection from the wind. That's all.

Helen Tom . . .

Tom I'm serious!

Helen But we haven't . . . we hardly talked to . . .

Tom I introduced you to people . . .

Helen In the parking lot! As you and I were unloading stuff out of the car. That's not an *introduction*.

Tom Shit. I knew this would happen!

Helen You knew it would happen because you know who you are, Tom. I don't think you're ready for this.

Tom Come on, I don't wanna fight . . . just eat something, alright?

Helen It's not fighting, Tom. When you and I talk, that's not *fighting*. It's *talking*. That's what people do.

Tom Whatever.

Helen *Tom* . . . what's going on?

Tom Nothing.

Long silence between them. The sound of the ocean.

Helen I told you . . . I've always said that you needed to be honest. More than anything else.

Tom I know. I *know* that . . .

Helen But you're not . . . this isn't . . .

Tom Helen, come on, stop now! Shit . . . this is my company picnic, OK? We're supposed to be having some fun.

Helen 'Fun'. OK . . . (*She slowly stands.*) Let's go join in the big game.

Helen jumps up and down a few times, miming a few shots as Tom watches. He looks over to where his friends are.

Come on, Tom! It's fun!

Tom Stop it! Stop! (*Grabs her.*) Helen, please stop that.

Helen Fine. Then let's *chat*, OK? (*She sits again.*) Because it's pretty damn hard to sit out here with a fake smile plastered on my face . . .

Tom Alright.

They sit in silence for a moment, then Helen reaches over and grabs a piece of chicken. Starts to eat. Tom sits and watches her – finally he has to say something.

Come on, slow down a little bit, honey. Jesus.

Helen Sorry. (*Beat.*) I can't help it. I eat when I get stressed out . . .

Tom It's fine. Me, too. Sorta.

Helen nods at this. Doesn't believe him. She waits.

Helen Tom . . . you're aware of how I feel about you. You already know that.

Tom Yes.

Helen But I get the feeling . . . I mean, it is now pretty obvious, that we're starting to have problems here . . . Issues, or whatever. And we need to get over them or . . . well, you know. Things that I don't wanna think about.

Tom I guess.

Helen waits for Tom to say more, but he keeps staring off toward the others. He is about to say something. Stops.

Helen Please, you need to stay in this. Focused on it, so don't drift off or anything. (*Beat.*) . . . I love you so much, I really do. Tom. Feel a connection with you that I haven't allowed myself to dream of, let alone be a part of, in so long. Maybe ever. But I can't be with you if you're feeling something other than that same thing that I am . . . completely and utterly open to that other person. I don't know what I should say here. I'm worried sick. Look at me, when did you ever see me not finish eating something that was placed in front of me? Huh?

She tries to grin.

I know you hate those jokes, sorry, but I'm . . . Tom, tell me about it. I know you're thinking something so we might as well just . . . One more thing. Just this. And I've never offered this to anyone, not any other person in the world. Ever. My family, or a . . . no one. (*Beat.*) I would change for you. I would. I don't mean SlimFast or that one diet that the guy on TV did . . . with the sandwiches from *Subway*. That guy . . .

Tom Helen . . . that . . . that's not . . .

Helen . . . I'll do something radical to myself if you want me to. Like be stapled or have some surgery or whatever it takes – one of those *rings* – because I do not want this to end. I'm willing to do that, because of what you mean to me. The kind of, just, *ecstasy* that you've brought me. So . . . I just wanted you to know that.

Tom sits there, taking it all in. Looking off. She nudges him with an elbow.

This would be an excellent time to say something sweet to me. If you at all care about my feelings.

Tom I know. I'm . . . (*Beat.*) Helen, that was such a nice thing to offer.

Helen . . . Oh–my–God . . .

Tom What?

Helen I just . . . the way you worded that right then. In the 'past' tense. It scares me.

Tom No, I just . . . it *is*. Really. And I appreciate it so much.

Helen . . . But what? (*Beat.*) Gosh, I wish those thousand ships would show up right about now . . .

Tom Yeah . . . (*Long beat.*) Helen, look, I've been thinking . . .

Helen . . . OK.

Tom I think you are an amazing woman, I honestly do. And I really love what we have here. Our moments together . . . but I think that maybe, you know, some time would be good here, or if you were to, I'm not sure . . . maybe take that job. It might tell us if we're . . . I dunno.

Helen Oh . . . (*Beat.*) Wow, that's a bit of a . . . you know . . . I mean, it's . . .

She tries to interrupt again but Tom stops her. Waits.

Tom Listen . . . if we were in some other time or a land that nobody else was around on . . . like that island from the movie, the Sinatra film – *None But the Brave* – then everything might be OK, I wouldn't be so fucking paranoid about what the people around me were saying. Or even thinking. Then it could just be you and me and that'd be so great. Perfect. But . . . I guess I do care what my peers feel about me. Or how they view my choices and, yes, maybe that makes me not very deep or petty or some other word, hell, I dunno! It's my *Achilles* flaw or something. I'm . . .

Tom stops for a moment, regrouping. Helen tries to speak.

Helen . . . Tom, don't do this, OK? Please don't. We can, I dunno . . . we . . .

Tom *No*, I need to . . . if I stop now I'm not gonna be able to . . . finish, so I'm . . . (*Beat.*) Helen . . . things are so tricky, life is. I know now I'm not really deserving of you, of all you have to offer me. I can see that now. I want to be better, to do good and better things and to make a proper sort of decision here, but I . . . I can't. I cannot do it. I mean, I could barely drive here today because of . . . my hands were shaking the whole time. They were. Jumping up and down on the wheel there. And these are all people that I know! That I . . . I'm just not gonna be able to do this, on, like, a daily basis. (*Starts to cry.*) God . . . look at me! It's . . . I'm sorry about this and I wish that I was saying what you wanna hear. I do. That would make me really happy, to please another person right now. I mean, a person that I'm feeling this . . . love for. Yeah, *love*. But sometimes it just isn't enough. You know? All this love inside and it's not nearly enough to get around the shit that people *heave* at you . . . I feel like I'm drowning in it – *shit* – and I don't think I can . . . I don't wanna fight it any more. I am just not strong enough for that, so I'm gonna lay on my back for a while and float. See if I can keep my head above the surface. (*Beat.*) I guess that's what I needed to say to you. That I'm not brave. I'm not. I know you want me to be . . . always believed that I *can* be, but I'm a weak and fearful person, Helen, and I'm not gonna get any better. Not any time soon, at least . . .

Helen touches Tom on the shoulder. Tom is still tearful.

Helen . . . But that's . . . it's something we could work on, right . . . Can't we, Tom? Right?

Tom . . . No. I don't think I can.

Helen slowly pulls her hand away. Tom continues to cry. big, rolling tears, with his face turned from hers.
After a moment, Helen collects herself and puts her hand back on Tom's body. Touching him.

Helen I don't accept that. I don't. I'm . . . I think . . . I dunno what, but I just don't. We take 'no' for an answer too easily and we shouldn't. Not when it's like this, not when it's worth it to fight back. So that's what I'm gonna do here. I'm gonna fight back . . . I'm gonna fight for you. For *us*. (*Beat.*) I'm not moving, Tom. You can get up and go see your pals over there or not but I'm staying here. With you, if you want. And it's not just because I don't have a ride home, OK? So . . . that's . . .

Despite himself, Tom smiles. Wipes away tears. Helen smiles, too.

I'm here and I'm not leaving. No. I'm staying right over here, next to you. Where I should be. *This* is how it should be – us together. I've felt that since the day I met you – since I watched you try to talk with me while you were eating that stupid chicken salad! I felt it in *here*, in my heart, that we should be together. You and me. And all you have to do is try, Tom. That's all. (*Beat.*) 'Try.' It doesn't mean we'll make it or that we'll always be a couple or we'll solve all the world's problems and our lives are gonna be sunny and wonderful for all our days through, for ever and ever more . . . but, you know, it's . . . Hey, we can at least *try*. Right? (*Beat.*) You're worth at least that much to me, Tom, and I hope I am to you . . . So . . . yeah. Let's do that. Okay? We can do that . . . Can't we? (*Beat.*) Course we can. Anybody can do that much. Just give something a try. (*Beat.*) So . . . let's . . . Just try. Come on . . . try it. *Try*, Tom. Just try it . . . (*Beat.*) Try.

Helen smiles over at him through her own tears. Hopeful. Undefeated.

You can do it, Tom. (*Beat.*) I know you can . . .

Tom finally looks over at her and smiles as well. It's faint, but it's there.

After a moment, he looks back out at the water. Seconds later, Helen does the same thing.

They sit together without speaking, quietly staring out to sea.

Silence. Darkness.

IN A DARK DARK HOUSE

In a Dark Dark House in its original version was first performed at the Lucille Lortel Theatre, New York, on 16 May 2007 in an MCC Theatre production with the following cast:

Terry Frederick Weller
Drew Ron Livingston
Jennifer Louisa Krause

Director Carolyn Cantory
Design Beowulf Boritt
Costumes Jenny Mannis
Lighting Ben Stanton
Sound Robert Kaplowitzz

In a Dark Dark House in the revised version printed here was first performed in London at the Almeida Theatre on 20 November 2008. The cast was as follows:

Terry David Morrissey
Drew Steven Mackintosh
Jennifer Kira Sternbach

Director Michael Attenborough
Design Lez Brotherston
Lighting Howard Harrison
Sound Howard Wood

Characters

Terry

Drew

Jennifer

Author's Note

The / in certain lines denotes
an attempt at interruption or overlap
by a given character

One

Silence. Darkness.

A manicured stretch of lawn surrounded by trees. Several areas to sit (benches, chairs, etc.) on two levels, with stone steps leading down from one to the other. It feels well hidden from the rest of the world. It is, in fact.

A man – Drew – staring out at the coming morning. Butterfly bandage over one eye. Sound of wild life. Maybe just a hint of traffic in the distance.

Drew goes over and checks a high hedge, trying to look through it. He wanders down a set of steps and studies a different wall (unseen). Stands on tiptoes.

Another man – Terry – appears out of the forest. He stands and watches this for a moment. Silent. Finally:

Terry . . . Go for it. Make it over and you're outta here. /

Startled, Drew turns around and then smiles – he takes one step forward. Terry keeps his distance for the moment.

Or you can fall back on your ass and I'll say I found you that way. Broken collarbone or however you wanna play it. / (*Beat.*) Should buy you an extra few weeks . . .

Drew Right . . . / You're funny. / Exactly! Hey, man . . . what's up?

Terry Not much . . .

Drew smiles at this and waves Terry over – another step from Drew but he doesn't commit just yet. Terry doesn't move.

Drew No, come on, dude, seriously . . . what?

Terry Nothing. Really. (*Beat.*) And don't say that, call me *dude*. Grown-ups don't use words like that – not if we can help it, anyway . . .

Drew Whatever.

Terry That one, either. (*Beat.*) Time to grow up, *dude* . . .

Drew See?! (*Smiles.*) You said it.

Terry Yeah, but who says I'm a grown-up?

Drew True . . .

Terry . . . I stopped doing that shit years ago. Growing up sucks.

The two men smile at this – Drew seems content to grin for a bit, but Terry stops pretty quickly. Listening.

The road's close . . . the highway or whatever that is. Freeway. / Place is right off the exit, almost . . .

Drew Yeah. / I noticed that – I mean, not today but, you know, like, at some point. Sitting in one of the, ahh, *six hundred* groups a day they make us go to here! / I heard traffic . . .

Terry Huh. / . . . probably five hundred yards 's all.

Drew Which is really stupid, right? *I'm* not gonna do anything – I was just looking around – but a bunch of the people they've got in here? Man . . . if they knew *civilisation* was just over there – it could really get messed up in this joint . . .

Terry S'pose so. Crazies all running up and down the road, dodging cars –

Drew Exactly! (*Laughs.*) / That'd be cool.

Terry Uh-huh. / Pretty funny . . .

Drew Although nobody around here likes it if you use that word, 'crazies'. Just so you know.

Terry Thanks for the tip.

Drew I'm just saying . . .

Drew points. Terry nods at this but doesn't say anything.

Terry Great. (*Beat.*) . . . so.

Drew Yep. So, so, so. (*Beat.*) So, you gonna stay for lunch or what? I mean, they'll let you in if you want some; chow's pretty decent.

Terry Sounds good. (*Thinks.*) I need to be back at six, but otherwise, fine.

Drew Too bad, gonna miss movie night . . . It's *On the Waterfront* or some shit. *Black and white.* (*Beat.*) Work?

Terry Uh-uh. 'S Friday. I'm off Fridays and Tuesdays . . . unless I get hooked up for some overtime, but usually no. / Fridays're mine.

Drew Huh. / Then what, some *lady* . . . ?

Terry Nah. Got a Little League game at six, I'm doing some ump-ing this year with the local kids – but I'd be happy to have a bite with you.

Drew Cool. (*Beat.*) I think it's stuffed peppers or something today . . . plus they've always got their sandwich bar. *Loads* of cold cuts and crap. / It's tasty . . .

Terry That sounds fine. / Good.

Drew Nice! (*Beat.*) Just like old times.

Terry Not really. Mom's cooking was the worst. / Christ help us if she did anything like a stuffed pepper!

Drew True! / That's totally true . . . thank God for Birds Eye, right?

They smile at this – apparently Mom wasn't much of a chef.

Terry Yeah . . . (*Beat.*) So, I'm not sure I can find the right . . . whatever-you-call-it . . . *segue* for this, so I'm gonna just jump right in – What's going on? / Huh?

Drew Nada. / Nothing.

Terry Nothing's gonna come of '*nothing*', Drew, so try again. (*Beat.*) You're in the hospital, little brother, OK? The *psych* hospital, so don't do the whole 'it's cool' thing . . .

Drew I'm serious, I'm just . . . you know. (*Beat.*) Anyway, this isn't the real hospital. It's only the *addictions* unit – for us *over*zealous wine drinkers . . .

Terry I'm not your wife, OK, so I don't need all the bullshit excuses . . .

Drew Terry, I'm not . . .

Terry I got called to come down here and do some family therapy, Drew, so don't tell me I drove a bunch of hours to have you play games with me. I got a *game* tonight – I need the *truth* from you . . . (*Waits.*) I don't give two shits what you do with these folks up here – that is your business and if the insurance pays for this, then all the better – but do not mess around with me because I'll come over there and kick your fucking ass, I swear to God.

A silence grows after this – the dynamic between these two is now pretty obvious.

Drew Great to see you, too, man . . .

Terry You're a dick.

Drew Yeah, it's my *specialty* . . . Just ask Judy. She keeps a running list of my failings in her purse . . .

Terry She should. / And I don't have time for your dumbshit act, either, Drew.

Drew *Thanks*, dude. / I know that, bro.

Terry I really do not.

Drew Alright, cool. I get that, and it is totally respected. / *Totally.*

Terry Then fine. / Drew! God . . . you sound like an episode of one a' those, you know . . . some bad TV show.

Drew What do you mean?

Terry You *know*, those, like, California-type television programmes. With the surfer kids and that sort a' deal. / 9-0-2-whatever-the-fuck it is . . .

Drew No, I don't. / Uh-uh . . .

Terry Bullshit! Dude, bro, totally . . . All your crap. I hate it. (*Beat.*) Did you used to do that in court?

Drew *Sometimes* . . . Forget it, man. Sorry.

Terry Don't be sorry, just stop. / Stop doing it when I'm around you . . .

Drew Fine. / OK.

Terry You're not a kid, alright? You are not some teenager who can run all over doing that because it sounds stupid. You sound childish, Drew. You just appear goofy and it's a little embarrassing . . . (*Beat.*) You are a grown man.

Drew Thirty's the new twenty . . .

Terry Yeah, well, you're thirty-five.

Drew So? That only makes me *twenty*-five then. Still young . . .

Terry . . . Right.

Drew Can't help it – I've got a lot of young people working for me. They rub off on you.

Terry Yeah, and how does Judy feel about that? Having a husband who sounds like that Tori Spelling girl . . .

Drew We're . . . I try and keep it to a low *roar* around her – this little mid-life thing I'm dealing with . . .

Terry So that's what this is? / *This*.

Drew Hmm? / What . . . ?

Terry Why I'm *here*.

Drew No, it's . . . (*Beat.*) What'd they say to you? I mean, do you have any idea . . . what'd they say?

Terry Nothing. That you were here and in for a while, that's all. 'S court-appointed or something . . . right? It doesn't really matter – you've done so much shit it all just *blends* . . .

Drew . . . I'm sure.

Terry They said you mentioned some stuff in session that . . . stuff that also would be of interest to me.

Drew Ahhh. Got it.

Terry Yeah, and so I drove down. I drove here today so that we could . . . you know. Talk about it.

Drew . . . They didn't really say 'stuff', did they? No offence, but that's not very professional if they did.

Terry Drew . . . don't bust my balls, OK? It was something like that . . . 'issues' or 'problems' or some damn thing. I don't remember now. It sounded urgent so I hopped in my Skylark and dragged my ass down here for *four* hours. / To be with you . . .

Drew Thanks, man. / I appreciate that.

Terry Yeah. You know . . . yeah.

Drew Not that I want you to see me in this place, but hey, that's part of my recovery, to get past the whole *vanity* thing. Be in touch with the 'real' me . . .

Terry Sounds good.

Drew Don't lie – that sounds gay even to me and I have a far greater threshold for that stuff than you do . . .

Terry Well, that's true!

For the first time in a while the two brothers laugh at something together. Drew suddenly pounces on Terry.
Bit of horseplay erupts – pushing and shoving. Wrestling.

. . . Faggot! / Get off me! / Well, you always did know, right?

Drew Come on! / Ohh, dude! / What's that?

Terry When something's queer or not . . . you've got this, like . . . / Yes!

Drew *Gay-dar?* / Oh yeah, I'm the king of that kind of stuff. The gay-osity of things!

Terry I figured.

Drew I'm *super*-gay when it comes to all that crap! / Curtains and *cologne* and shit . . . I'm a home furnishings fag.

Terry Exactly! / Haha! When you gonna do the ol' 'out of the closet' deal? I still got all that part to look forward to, don't I?

Drew Fuck yeah! / We'll have ourselves a big party and everything . . . fly Mom out for it, even.

Terry I knew it! / . . . Sounds great . . .

Drew She can make some *stuffed peppers* for us . . . (*Falls to ground.*) Ahhh!

Terry . . . and you can help her – being the big queen that you are now. / (*Pins Drew down.*) Slip on your Bloomingdale's apron and just go to town!

Drew Course! / You got it . . . Oww! Oww! Stitches, bro. *Stitches* . . .

The two men slowly stop, letting the moment pass – trying to keep it light. Drew gingerly touches his Band-Aid.

Terry . . . Here. (*Helps Drew up.*) Anyways.

Drew Yeah. Anyway. (*Beat.*) Nothing like a couple fag jokes to help break the ice, right? / (*Smiles.*) Yep.

Terry Good times. / So . . . (*Beat.*) What's up?

Drew Nothing.

Terry Uh-uh, try again. *Now*.

Drew I'm . . . Dude, you are a tad *intense*, anybody ever say that to you?

Terry Don't call me 'dude'. Really . . .

Drew Whatever.

Terry I mean it. (*Beat.*) I'm waiting to hear, Drew, so come on . . .

Drew It's not a big deal! I was in for a seventy-two-hour observation and they . . . you know, chose to extend – at *gunpoint*. (*Grins.*) . . . So I'm embracing the thing and I'll be here as long as it takes this time. That's a *promise*.

Terry Fine. / That's great, Drew.

Drew I'm gonna kick the pills and *every*thing. / Yep. Simple as that.

Terry Nothing is simple. Simple's not even simple any more . . .

Drew 'S that right?

Terry Yep.

Drew Sorry, didn't get the *memo* . . .

Terry Yeah, well, you best keep up, *bro*. World is changing on us, each and every second, so it pays to keep a close eye on things . . .

Drew I hear ya.

Terry Uh-huh . . . (*Beat.*) So?

Drew *What?*

Drew stares at Terry for a minute, a grin dropping off his face in waves. Terry doesn't say a word.

You're right, man . . . you are shit at transitions.

Terry Yep. (*Beat.*) So I'm gonna ask you again, and then after that, that's when I'm gonna get pissed and start in on the angry part of this.

Drew Terry . . .

Terry *Drew* – why the *fuck* am I here right now? Tell me.

Drew . . . Come on, dude.

Terry You're pushing it. You are, like, *really* pushing me here.

Drew It's embarrassing.

Terry I'm sure it is . . . I mean, wait'll this gets around your office! I don't care if it's a *private* wing or not – people are gonna talk.

Drew I don't mind about that. / Who do I know that their opinions are gonna matter to me? Huh?

Terry Oh, sure . . . / Somebody . . .

Drew *Who?!* (*Grins.*) I don't have a boss, I'm *fucking* rich . . . and my wife and kids've already heard. (*Beat.*) Only person I was nervous about telling was you.

Terry . . . And here I am.

Drew Exactly.

Terry And why is that?

Drew What?

Terry *Why* am I here, Drew? At this place with you, out in the *woods*, right now?

Drew Because, man . . . *because* I'm . . .

Terry Good, that's *good*. Get it out.

Drew Don't patronise me, big brother.

Terry Then just fucking say it, OK? This is getting a little silly . . .

Drew OK, fine. *OK*. I need you, alright? That's why . . .

Terry What's that mean?

Drew I'm . . . What does it *usually* mean? / I'm reaching out here . . .

Terry I dunno. / Fuck you are.

Drew That hurts, dude . . .

Terry Yeah, well, then put a bandage on it because it's already starting to stink . . . (*Beat.*) You don't *need* anybody, not one person, and you have proved that a thousand times over, *baby* brother . . .

Drew Wow.

Terry Uh-huh, wow's right. I get about *two* calls a year from you – and since it's not Christmas or the week *after* my fucking birthday – why don't you go ahead, enlighten me?

Drew . . . Fine. (*Beat.*) I need you to *do* something for me. Is that what you were looking to hear? That better?

Terry 'Better' is pretty relative – but at least it's honest. You need me to do you a favour, that sounds more believable than this other . . . shit you've been pitching my way. / Right?

Drew . . . S'pose so. (*Shrugs.*) / Yep.

Terry So, tell me, I'll see what I can do . . . if it gets me back for the first inning, you can probably count on it happening.

Drew sits down on the steps and fiddles with his ID bracelet for a bit. Terry waits, silent.

Drew . . . I just need you to tell 'em the truth about something, back me up on some stuff. / That's it.

Terry 'Truth'. / Well, that shouldn't be too hard . . . for me.

Drew What's that mean?

Terry Well, the 'truth' is not exactly your specialty . . . is it? / But if you've got the whatever-you-call-it – wool – pulled over their eyes then that wouldn't surprise me . . . par for the fucking course.

Drew Dude . . . / Ya know what, man, forget it.

Terry Fine.

Drew Seriously.

Terry Happy to. Take care, pal . . . Enjoy the fucking cold cuts.

Terry starts off, but Drew moves out in front of him; not blocking him exactly, but in the way. Terry steps back.

Drew . . . Terry, come on.

Terry Don't suppose you wanna go to your *art therapy* with a broken nose, so I'd step outta my way.

Stalemate as the two men stare at each other – just after Terry moves, Drew speaks:

Drew . . . It's about Todd. Todd Astin.

Terry comes to a quick stop. Freezes. He slowly turns.

I told them about him. / Come on . . .

Terry What? / . . . I don't follow . . .

Drew Todd Astin.

Terry I *know* his name, you don't have to keep saying the name, OK? (*Beat.*) I wanna know *why* you just said it . . .

Drew It's about when we were kids.

Terry And?

Drew And nothing, except for all the, you know . . . his . . .

Terry *What?*

Drew I told 'em about the stuff that he . . . I had to, you know, had to get some shit off my chest.

Terry People don't *have* to do anything. Not at all – live, die, breathe, OK, but other than that, you don't *got* to do much of anything else . . .

Drew Yeah, well, if I wanna keep Judy and the kids in my life, then I do. I *had* to.

Terry Huh.

Drew She made an ultimatum on me, like, a week ago, said if I didn't get honest with her about my life – my *history* and all that – then she was gonna leave me. Take the kids and go . . . Judy doesn't say shit like that without meaning it. *Un*like me. (*Beat.*) She's at the end with all this; surprised she lasted as long as she did.

Terry Me, too. You got a perfect family there and you piss 'em away . . .

Drew Yeah, well it's over now, dude – this here is the last chance I got, so that's why I need your help on it. I'm coming clean . . . about all my past and everything, that's what I'm saying.

Terry nods at this, considering what to say next. Waits.

What?

Terry I'm a little lost here, Drew . . . he never did anything with you. Right? 'S what you said.

Drew No, he . . . I mean, yeah. We . . .

Terry You told me that, *years* ago. / You looked me right in the face and you said that . . .

Drew I know . . . / I know I did, but . . .

Terry Then I don't get this . . .

Drew That's what I'm trying to tell you here, Terry . . .

Terry I warned you about that guy, like, a *billion* times, I told you that you needed to stay away from him and you said you would, you said that to me – said it over and over and *over*. Right? I told you to . . .

Drew I know, which I never understood.

Terry I TOLD YOU. And you said you did. (*Beat.*) Now, was that a lie or not?

Drew . . . It was, yeah.

Terry I see . . .

Drew I'm sorry, but yes.

Terry So . . . after *all* I did to tell you that, getting sent away and, and – basically tossed out in the fucking *trash* by our dad – you still went off with him? / Hmm?!

Drew No, I . . . / No . . .

Terry Bullshit! Bull-fucking-shit!! You said you're gonna get honest, then fucking do it! You and Todd spent time together, even after I *begged* ya not to . . . right? / RIGHT?!

Drew No. / NO! Not after, no – before. It was before you ever told me.

Terry . . . What? (*Beat.*) *Drew*, what?

Drew Sorry. It was already too late and so I just, you know, pretended. I acted like everything was still OK but by that point . . . No, it wasn't. I couldn't tell you, I'm sorry. I was too scared about it . . .

Terry It was *before*?

Drew Yeah, a lot before . . . (*Beat.*) All that stuff Todd did to me was before that. *Way* before . . .

Terry . . . You're kidding me . . .

Drew No. I mean, why else would I be in here right now? Talking about it?

Terry Ahhh, about a thousand reasons . . . look at your life, Drew.

Drew Dude, I'm trying to get myself on the straight and whatever, OK, so the truth is step one – I can see now that a lot of my behaviour can be linked to all this. Things that happened to me when I was a kid . . .

Terry Well, that's convenient . . .

Drew Fuck . . . that's a shitty thing to say!

Terry I'm not saying anything. I'm not saying it didn't happen – saying it's very *useful* for you to fall back on now . . . so . . .

Drew Hey, look, I don't need you so bad that I gotta sit here and take any ol' crap that rolls out your mouth in my direction . . . (*Beat.*) I'm not the greatest person, fine. I have lots to make up for in my life and with my family, well alright, I'll work on that, but I don't have to swallow a bunch of your shit, too. I really don't . . .

This seems actually to land for Terry – he nods at Drew and lets this soak in. Wanders off, considering. Silence.

Terry Listen, if that's the truth, that he and you . . . then I'm very sorry and . . . I'll do anything I can to help you here. All I can do. I just wish you would've said something to me . . . like, back in the day. When I could've done something about it. / Saved you.

Drew Well . . . / You can save me now.

Terry I know, but . . . I just . . .

Drew That's all that matters.

Terry True. Yeah . . .

Drew It's in the past. I'm just gonna put that behind me and move ahead. / That's what I want . . . I do.

Terry 'Kay. / 'S very forgiving of you.

Drew You have to, bro. Have to forgive to take the next step . . .

Terry You learn that here?

Drew Nah . . . people've been telling that to me for years! Therapists, a few doctors, but I was, you know, too out there to listen.

Terry I bet . . .

Drew Keeping it together for the kids, but just barely – little counselling here . . . some lady's undies on the floor of the Porsche . . . always just sneaking by. Wanting to get myself caught, really, but people letting it go, forgiving me, and all the time just handing me a free pass to do it again. A little smoother the next time, so it's harder to get busted . . . and then fucking up *again*. Bigger and better. Hoping that this'll be the one, this time somebody has *got* to stop me! But they don't, they never do. *Until* I ran a traffic light with some chick from work and we're both high – wrapped my Boxster around a fucking lamp post – and, well, ya know, I just watched it come down. My life . . .

Terry I really don't wanna know all this stuff, Drew. I don't.

Drew It's just *me*, bro. / This is where I'm at now . . .

Terry Fine, and I'm here to help you . . . / I just don't need all the blow-by-blow, OK? You can save it . . .

Drew Too messy for ya?

Terry Nah, just not interested.

Drew Ha! Well, at least you're honest . . .

Terry I always have been, Drew. *Al*ways. You probably never noticed because you've been such a lying fuck for most your life that you couldn't possibly recognise it.

Drew Ouch.

Terry Yeah, not so great being sober, is it?

Drew . . . Not when *you're* around . . .

Terry Hey, you asked.

Drew Guess so. That's true.

Terry Anyways . . .

Drew Yep. Anyway . . . you think you can do that for me, talk to those doctors I'm seeing? / Tell 'em about Todd?

Terry I can, sure. / I'll answer anything they ask me.

Drew Appreciate it. It'll help me out a lot, I think . . . both with them and Judy. She likes you.

Terry Funny how that works, huh? Married to you and she likes me . . .

Drew . . . Yeah.

Terry Wonder why that is?

Drew Probably 'cause you don't stay out late and fuck around on her, that sort of thing . . .

Terry Might be! (*Bitter laugh.*) Yeah.

Drew After a while, wives just seem to be able to tell when you're lying through your teeth . . .

Terry God bless 'em.

Drew Yep. (*Grins.*) Maybe Judy's just got a crush on you. / That could be it.

The two brothers smile at this one, maybe even a chuckle.

Terry Right! / Uh-huh. (*Beat.*) So you want me to tell 'em what? These people?

Drew Just that I'm not making the guy up or anything, that he existed . . .

Terry OK. That's easy.

Drew They're telling me that in lots of these cases it's a sibling or some family friend, a parent . . . a figure of some authority. That kinda deal is the usual case. (*Beat.*) Not some dude *drifting* 'cross the country.

Terry I see . . .

Drew They've even, you know – they asked if it could've been Dad, or, like, maybe . . . you. *Implied* it, anyway.

Terry Sounds like doctors – heads wedged up their fucking asses . . .

Drew Yeah . . . but I told 'em 'No.' I said it wasn't anybody in our house . . . and it wasn't! / It was *Todd* . . .

Terry That's OK . . . / Drew, it's . . .

Drew I mean it, though. It was! (*Beat.*) But, you know, can't *prove* it or anything. It's just true, and so, you know, they're finding it . . . 'difficult to corroborate'. (*Beat.*) Mom came up already but she can't remember *yesterday*, let alone, you know . . .

Terry Yeah, well, she's been a fucking *ghost* for as long as I can ever remember – how's she doing by the way? / Right . . .

Drew Same . . . back's killing her. The eyes are going. All that shit . . . / (*Beat.*) Anyway, she's no help and Dad . . . he's . . . whatever . . .

Terry Dead, I hope. (*Beat.*) Anyway, I get it – I'll tell 'em anything I can remember about the guy. Dates and names and shit . . .

Drew Good.

Terry . . . and hopefully that'll help.

Drew It will. / Definitely.

Terry Fine. / I'm fine with that, then . . .

> *Terry relaxes for a moment now, sits down on one step.*

Drew You OK?

Terry Yeah, course. Just hearing that name again. / It's weird . . .

Drew I know. / Sorry.

Terry What are *you* sorry about? (*Waits.*) It's just strange, that's all. I haven't thought about him for . . . you know. A while.

Drew . . . Really? Huh.

Terry What's that mean?

Drew I'm just saying . . . you guys were . . .

Terry looks over at his brother, holds his gaze. Finally he turns and looks away.

Terry I mean, yeah, he's *crossed* my mind occasionally . . . why wouldn't he? He was one of those people that – you know what he was like – you let 'em in, into your life when you're a kid . . . / You remember what a huge *event* it was when he first came to town . . .

Drew Yep. / Sure. Even *Dad* liked 'em.

Terry Yeah! He knew how to do everything and he was always just . . . cool. You know? Could play baseball and *golf* and helped us out with our chores, even. Taught us *both* how to dive the right way . . . (*Beat.*) I'll tell you what . . . I was only fourteen or something, but I thought he had a deal going with Mom.

Drew *Really?* / Wow, I never . . .

Terry Come *on* . . . the way she'd fix snacks for him and dressing up and stuff? / I noticed all that crap but it was nothing I could put words to; just spotted the behaviour and it made me . . . I got all angry about it, but not 'cause I worried about *Dad* – I didn't ever care about that piece a' shit – and he was oblivious, anyway. (*Beat.*) No, see, I just wanted Todd to be *my* friend . . .

Drew He was. You guys were . . . you spent, like, the *whole* summer with him! / Practically, anyway.

Terry Uh-huh. / Except for camp – when the folks made me go away to a fucking scout *jamboree*.

Drew Yeah, except for that.

Terry But by then I was, you know – I did a complete one-eighty on the guy. So . . .

Drew nods at this while Terry catches himself, not sure how to proceed. He takes a beat.

At that point – the last week or two before I left – he was being all different towards me. I had this bad feeling . . . so I tried to tell you, to *warn* you to be careful. And now you're telling me that he was . . . / You know . . .

Drew . . . Yeah . . . / Yes.

Terry . . . that it was already too late.

Drew I'm sorry . . . I know he was a big influence on you, so . . .

Terry Fuck it. If that's true then he deserves whatever shit gets told about 'em. (*Beat.*) . . . I can tell these people that much if it's gonna help you.

Drew It would. It'd help a bunch . . .

Terry And what're they saying about all this? Huh? About you and him?

Drew Well, you know . . .

Terry No, I don't. I do not. That's why I'm asking . . .

Drew It's what I'm *saying* . . . I'm *saying* it right now – they blame most all of my behaviour in the last year or so on it. / These memories that're coming back up for me – the trauma. That it sorta . . . I dunno, froze me, I guess, kept me in this perpetual age . . . like a *teenager* . . . all acting out and shit, because of it . . . that what he did to me – all the sexual stuff he tried – had a real effect on my development and is now sort of just pouring out . . .

Terry Huh. / I can see that – No, that'd make sense.

Drew Yeah, and so . . . you know, we're now getting to the bottom of all this and I think it's gonna make a real difference with the judge, on the drunk driving charges and probably some of the other stuff, too – even the *coke* I was carrying! / Yeah . . .

Terry That's great, then. / Good.

Drew But that's not why I'm doing it – I mean, I really do want to get to the bottom of this . . . / To put it behind me, what happened. (*Beat.*) I *really* do, man. I wanna get past all this shit that I've been living with. And doing.

Terry Sure. / No, I mean, yeah . . . I can believe that.

Drew Good. I'm glad.

Terry nods and wanders off, thinking for a moment. Drew lets him have some space but doesn't take his eyes off of him.

You OK there, bro? I mean . . .

Terry Hmm? Yeah. No, I was just . . .

Drew We can head back if you're . . .

Terry No, I'm just . . . the whole fucking Todd deal is (*Beat.*) I mean, no offence, but if *any* other word had come outta your mouth I probably would've been gone. You know? / I'm serious. (*Makes a whoosh.*) History!

Drew Totally understand. / No, I get it.

Terry Sorry, but you have not turned out to be the most trustworthy fellow I know. At *all*. (*Beat.*) But what ya said there, that story of yours . . . even though it makes me wanna, I dunno, shoot somebody in the goddam *face* . . . I believe you.

Drew Thanks, bro. (*Beat.*) Sorry. *Terry.*

Terry Yeah. (*Beat.*) And I suppose ya know why, don't ya? Hmm?

Drew What?

Terry I'm saying you know 'why' I'd feel that way, right? Obviously.

Drew . . . No . . .

Terry Bullshit, no. I wouldn't be here if you didn't have some idea. You are fucking *transparent* as hell, little brother . . .

Drew Terry . . .

Terry I've called you a lotta shit in your life but I never once said you weren't smart. Like a fucking *fox*, buddy, I don't think we have to argue that fact. (*Beat.*) Never would've asked me to this place if you didn't have some notion 'bout my history . . .

Drew thinks about this – it now looks like the all-or-nothing moment. Terry doesn't even blink.

Drew . . . I guess.

Terry You 'guess'. Huh.

Drew I mean, yeah, I suppose I must've had some . . . always figured that you had your reasons for . . . you know. The things you said to me. Back then . . .

Terry Right.

Drew But, Terry, honestly – I'm not sure that I put two and two together or anything, just had a *sense* that . . .

Terry Come *on*! You're a fucking *lawyer*! Used to be. (*Beat.*) Drew, I'm trying to tell you something – make this a little easier for you to live with. Some shit I've never told anybody else. / I mean *no*body.

Drew What? / Bro, then honestly . . . *what*?

Terry I mean, Jesus Christ – did all that schooling, passed the *Bar thingy*, you are one smart guy – you really think I just got up one morning and said to myself, 'Hey, this Todd fellow might not be so great after all?' Huh?! 'S that what you think?!

Drew I, I, I . . .

Terry I spent the *entire* summer with the guy, Drew. *Every* waking minute . . . You think he tried anything with you that didn't happen to me? I mean, grab me a piece a fucking stationery off your *walnut-topped* desk there and I'll spell it out for ya . . . I mean, goddam . . .

Drew turns and looks at his brother – Terry plunges on.

Yeah, now ya got it . . . see, that's not so hard, is it?! Pretty damn obvious, really, if somebody had taken ten *seconds* to give a shit about me. / Back whenever . . .

Drew Jesus Christ. / I'm sorry . . . / I just . . . fuck, that's so . . .

Terry It's OK. / Don't worry about it.

Drew . . . Terry . . . please let me . . .

Terry I mean, why start now, huh? Waste a' fucking time. (*Beat.*) So . . .

Terry looks over at his brother, his face a blank slate. Drew tries to hold eye contact but looks away. Silence.

What do I gotta do? (*Beat.*) *Drew.*

Drew Huh?

Terry These people. What do I gotta say?

Drew Just go over some details, fill in a few of the blanks that I've left open – you're, like, a couple years older and you can probably remember him a bit better. / Physically, I'm saying.

Terry Uh-huh . . . / I can give 'em a pretty fair rundown on the guy, if that's what they're searching for. Looks and all that. / Guy used to call me 'buddy'. Remember that shit? Would always call me his 'buddy boy'.

Drew That'd be a big help. / Sure, I do.

Terry Yeah, well, I can fill 'em in with a few tidbits like that.

Drew Cool. Thanks, bro.

Terry OK. *Bro.* (*Beat.*) I'll, uhh . . . yep.

Drew moves over and tries to say something but stops. Instead he gives his brother a hug. Unexpected – it's definitely a one-sided affair.

Drew That's so great, dude, honestly! / Very nice of you . . . Thanks.

Terry No problem. / Least I can do . . .

Drew Awesome.

Terry Yep. (*Beat.*) So, should we – where are these guys at? Back at the . . . ?

Drew Yeah, the administration building down by the gates there – it's that *Tudory*-looking deal.

Terry Alright. / Fine.

Drew Good. / You wanna eat first?

Terry Umm . . .

Drew We can just grab a sandwich . . .

Terry I guess. Don't you wanna get this over with?

Drew It's . . . I'm in here now, so it's OK if we wait a little. No rush.

Terry I've got that game, though . . .

Drew True, but that's not till – (*Looks at watch.*) – like, six, you said.

Terry Right. OK, great.

Drew Sweet – I wanna show you off a bit! My bro, the working man.

Terry What's that mean?

Drew Nothing . . . bunch of assholes up in here, you know? I want 'em to get a look at a *real* man . . . a guy who could've been . . . you know . . .

Terry What? (*Waits.*) Been what? Go ahead.

Drew Nothing. I just mean . . . a dude who listens to his own drummer and that shit. You know what I'm saying . . .

Terry Huh. (*Beat.*) You got show-and-tell today? That what's going on here?

Drew Come on, Terry, I'm just saying . . . I'm proud of you, isn't that OK? / (*Beat.*) These people are all fucked up for one reason or another . . . it does 'em good to see somebody who is well adjusted. Holding down the same job most his life, served his country, doing *regular* shit – you'd be, like, an *inspiration* for a lot of guys. / Some ladies, too.

Terry Sure. / OK, Drew, enough. (*Beat.*) Let's take it a little easy with the family reunion crap . . .

Drew What're you talking about?

Terry I'm saying I'm gonna do this, and that's fine, but let's not pretend we're all 'buddies' and shit . . .

Drew What'd I say?

Terry Nothing, no, you just – fuck, Drew, you don't *know* me. Moving toward forty years old and you don't have a fucking *clue* who I am. Alright?

Drew I just wanted to introduce you . . .

Terry Which is OK, nice . . . just don't ask me to act a certain way, smile my ass off to people that're . . . fuck. (*Beat.*) I'm not at all excited with the idea of sitting with a doctor and talking about my stuff, and I got a shitload, believe me. Stuff that just about strangles me, give it half a chance, so . . . that's . . .

Drew What? Tell me, Terry . . . please?

Terry *Drew*, don't do that little boy bit a' yours or I'm gonna smack you so fucking hard . . . goddam it!! Listen to me, what I'm saying here. OK? (*Beat.*) I've spent most of my adult life hiding, hiding in plain sight by being quiet and doing my work and never raising my hand. For the most part I live like some fucking *shadow*. I pay taxes and take the night shift and drift through shopping malls and movie theatres with my head down and like I've got somewhere to be.
   I was a good kid when I was young, most folks would tell ya that, but our old man beat all of that goodness out of me and now I am just OK and OK's pretty dangerous when it gets pushed even slightly in the wrong direction.

Drew . . . That's not true, Terry. You're a . . . I mean, you're a good guy.

Terry Fuck you. Don't call me that. YOU DO NOT KNOW. What's happened to me and I mean all of it – Dad and Todd and my years over in – they changed me. Got all this . . . *turmoil* inside and I never know if I'm gonna just explode and rape somebody or grab a guy by the throat or maybe beat the fucking life out of a person for no good goddam reason. *That's* me, Drew, who *I* am, and that's why I live like I do. (*Beat.*) You know I'm capable of it, right? I said, *right*, Drew?

Drew stares at his brother for a moment before nodding.

Drew . . . Yeah. I do. / Yes.

Terry Alright, then. / (*Beat.*) Wanna know why I'm working the baseball deal this season? Huh? To try and prove to myself that I'd never do that to some *kid*, what happened to us. Really. That is why . . . it's not for my love a' the game, believe me!

Drew OK, that's . . . I didn't mean that we had to . . . just shake a few hands is all.

Terry Fine, no, that's OK, but I'm gonna need ya to ease back on the 'Isn't my big brother cool?' shit right now. / Yeah? We're good?

Drew Fine. / I wasn't trying to be . . .

Terry No, I know.

Drew Seriously. / You've just . . . you've been *that* guy in my life, ya know? A bunch more so than Dad ever was, and . . . that's . . .

Terry OK, Drew, fine. I'm just telling you. / Sure, no, I get that. I do.

Drew Seriously! You have always been a real flagpost for me, even when I was acting like an asshole, didn't call you for months – still admired you. Honest. (*Beat.*) I don't always know how to say that sorta shit . . . feelings that families or, like, a relative'd have but I do get it.

Terry Thanks. / That's . . . thank you.

Drew Yep. / (*Smiles.*) So, come on, turkey sandwich on me, then we'll go find my shrink and fill 'em in on Todd Astin . . .

Terry OK. Sounds good.

Drew throws an arm around his brother and smiles.

Drew . . . Shame we can't find the fucker.

Terry Yeah, why's that?

Drew . . . Oh, nothing . . .

Terry What?

Drew Just . . . (*Shrugs.*) Whatever.

Terry No. *Why?*

Drew Because I'd . . . you know . . . I'd wanna beat the shit outta him, I guess. If I could get my hands on him again . . .

Terry Ahhhh, you never punched a guy in your life. Not that I've heard of, anyway . . .

Drew OK, well . . . fine, then I'd have you step in for me. / You do it.

Terry Ha! / Just like the ol' days, huh? I fought every battle you ever had as a kid.

Drew . . . I don't know about that . . .

Terry Any bully, fucking beatings from the ol' man . . . *all* of it. / I ran interference for you *every* day of our lives, growing up . . .

Drew Yep. I know. / Second you stopped, my whole life went to pot . . .

Terry Literally! (*Laughs.*) / Anyways . . .

Drew Exactly! / Anyway, *you* could kick his ass . . . that'd be so sweet!

Terry Thought you wanted to *let it go* . . .

Drew Yeah, well . . . nothing wrong with a little ass kicking. For old time's sake. (*Beat.*) Fuck 'em up a little, like you did over there in Kuwait to people. / Come on, man – chestful of fucking *medals*?

Terry *Uh-huh*. / Yep . . . for being a punk and pissed off. I was a fucking dick when I was in the service, trust me.

Drew *Any*way . . . it wouldn't bug you so much if it was Todd Astin, right?

Terry . . . I dunno . . .

Drew Come on, bro, be honest! After what we've both gone through?

Terry S'pose not, no. (*Grins.*) Wouldn't hate that myself.

Drew Hell yes. I'd murder the dude, you gave me half a chance . . .

Terry Yeah?

Drew I mean . . . if I could get away with it, sure. (*Laughs.*) Then yeah . . .

Terry Huh.

Drew Drop his ass in a dumpster and I'd still be able to sleep like a baby at night . . .

Terry I doubt that.

Drew 'S true!

Terry That's a lot of big talk, Drew . . . but I think you'd puss out in the end. / You're more of a 'puss-out' type . . .

Drew Dunno. / You might be surprised . . . I might just do something that'd bewilder the shit outta you . . .

Terry Maybe. Figure you might *sue* 'em – if you were still a lawyer, that is . . .

Drew You might be *very* surprised what I'd do to that guy, Terry. (*Beat.*) Took away a part of me that's not ever coming back, so . . . no, I don't think I'd weep if that son-of-a-bitch ended up the bottom of a *lake* somewhere.

Drew shakes this off and gives his brother another hug. He motions toward a distant building, starts off.

Come on, let's get you fed . . .

Terry Alright.

Drew Maybe we can start a food fight or something . . . / Have a little fun . . .

Terry Sure. / OK. (*Beat.*) Hey, Drew?

Drew Yeah? / It was . . . what do you mean?

Terry Where did all this happen . . . times he came to you? / I just wanna . . .

Drew Why?

Terry I just . . . in case they ask me, I should know some details. Right? / I mean, if I'm . . .

Drew . . . I guess. / No, that makes sense. Sure. (*Beat.*) . . . 'S the tree house. You know . . . that one tree fort we built, like, down past the creek? (*Beat.*) He'd meet me up in that . . . in the dark's where we'd do it – usually when you were off on your paper route. He'd get me to . . . he'd get all up close to me and then he'd, he would ask me to take his, make me hold on to his . . . you know, *thing* and then I'd have to, I . . . would do all these – with my mouth I had to, to . . . you know. He would put his . . .

his dick in my – (*Cries.*) He would make me suck on his cock, Terry . . . that's what he did. He forced me to! Forced me as I'd lay there staring up at the trees. And he . . . he'd . . . (*Waits.*) 'S that enough? I mean . . .

Terry Course.

Drew I'll go on if you want me to, but it's . . . you know . . .

Terry No, Drew, that's OK . . . I just . . . / 'S fine.

Drew 'Kay. / (*Wipes his eyes.*) I'm glad.

Terry Let's get a sandwich and then I'll go tell 'em about it. (*Beat.*) I just need a second to myself to . . . you know, take all this shit in. That alright?

Terry waits for his brother to agree. Drew nods at this.

Drew Yeah. (*Smiles.*) I'm gonna run ahead and get in line. The best items're usually snapped up pretty fast . . . all the desserts and stuff.

Terry Great. / Right behind you . . .

Drew Cool! / Thanks a lot, bro.

Terry You bet.

Drew I mean it, though. *Honestly.*

Terry I know ya do.

Drew *Thank* you . . .

Terry . . . Sure.

Drew runs off down the path and disappears. Terry stays for a moment, standing perfectly still – after a moment his phone rings.
  Without warning Terry brings out his phone and rips the cover right off the thing. He drops the pieces

to the ground and pulverises the rest of it with one shoe. Completely shattered now.

Terry looks down without emotion and picks up the pieces. Plops them into his pocket. Remains where he is. Silent.

Sound of traffic and the woods.

Two

The grounds have now been converted into a kind of play area – not for children but families. It's a double green for a putt-putt course, with two tubes that run from one level to the next. A hole with a mini-flag down below.

A teenager – Jennifer – in shorts and a tank top, ass pointed out as she works her arm up into one tube. Searching.

After a moment, Terry appears. Dressed casually and with a putter in one hand. Jennifer notices him watching her – she gets to her feet. Wipes her hands off on her shorts.

Jennifer . . . Go for it.

Terry What's that?

Jennifer You can go ahead and play through. / Don't worry about me . . .

Terry Nah, that's OK. / No, finish, it's alright. I can . . . I'm waiting for my car to get done anyway. I'm getting it 'detailed' over there at the . . . 'Glimmer-King', is it?

Jennifer Yep. They do a good job . . . (*Beat.*) But I'm just, you know, doing the Ajax thing right now, so . . .

Terry nods. Watching her. Staring almost, but he catches himself at the last moment and looks away.

I'm cleaning out the tubes on 13 and 14 – they clog up after it rains.

Terry Got'cha. (*Beat.*) I think you're talking about *Drano*, by the way . . . not the other one. Common mistake, really, but only one of 'em'll get rid of your problem. / Blockage.

Jennifer Yeah? / What do you mean?

Terry Ajax is just, like, a cleaner . . . for making sinks sparkle and shit like that. Drano's the one people use for their clogs. There's other stuff, of course, but Drano's the one you're always hearing about. / On TV.

Jennifer Oh. / I see.

Terry Yep.

Jennifer . . . What're you, some professional *spokesmodel* or whatever?

Terry Ha! (*Smiles.*) 'S that what I look like?

Jennifer Kinda. You sorta have that feel . . . all handsome or something.

Terry *Thanks.*

Terry shuffles his feet at this, embarrassed by all the attention. Laughs to himself.

Jennifer Yeah. (*Beat.*) So, do you do that? Correct people on their cleaning supplies for a living . . . ?

Terry Nah, I just know about that one . . . that and, umm, Liquid-Plumr.

Jennifer I see.

Terry I get crap jammed in my pipes all the time out where I live . . . I'm a little off the beaten track, house of mine. / It's on a well and septic.

Jennifer Hmm. / What's that mean?

Terry Means *trouble*, most times! I'm not on city utilities.

Jennifer Ohh, I get what you're saying . . . yeah, we aren't, too. At my house.

Terry nods without having a response. Jennifer smiles.

Terry Sooo . . . this is your *job* . . .

Jennifer Yep! Pretty fancy, huh?

Terry Yeah, nice . . .

Jennifer I was thinking *Harvard* and then I got this gig and said, 'Hey, fuck that shit.'

Terry Good one.

Terry watches her as she smiles and takes her bucket over to the high weeds nearby – tosses out the dirty water.

Jennifer . . . The world doesn't really need any more lawyers . . . it needs a few extra menial labourers. So I'm just doing my part!

Terry I hear ya. (*Smiles.*) . . . and you're right, by the way. I mean, for my money.

Jennifer What's that?

Terry About the lawyers.

Jennifer Yeah? So, you spend a lot of time on the wrong side of the law?

Terry Oh, you know . . . I took Lou Reed's advice and did a little walk out there but nothing too bad . . .

Jennifer Who's he?

Terry Nobody. / (*Grins.*) Some singer. Too long ago for you to worry about . . .

Jennifer Huh. / My dad does shit like that – quotes people and then won't tell me who it is. / That pisses me off.

Terry Sorry . . . / You heard of the Velvet Underground?

(*Waits.*) He's one of the guys in that. And then had a solo thing, too . . . doesn't really matter. I was just trying to be a little funny.

Jennifer Then you should throw a punchline in there every so often . . .

Terry Ha! (*Laughs.*) Anyway, point is, I've got a kid brother who's a hot-shot lawyer; he's a prick, mostly, so I just lump it all together . . . excuse my French.

Jennifer . . . I don't think that's actually *French*.

Terry Ha! (*Chuckles.*) And, actually, he's not even a lawyer any more. Made a bundle when he bought up a company out from under a client of his . . . Apparently that was *unethical* or something, so they asked him if he would kindly fuck off. I mean, in so many words. / Disbarred 'em.

Jennifer Ahh. / Well, thanks for the info . . .

Terry Sorry! Shit, forgive me – sometimes I just babble on about nothing if I'm around people I don't know . . . I mean, I'm not no Cary Grant.

Jennifer looks at Terry like he just spoke Chinese.

Don't worry about it . . . (*Beat.*) You go ahead and do what you gotta do.

Jennifer Nah, that's cool. (*Pointing at the pipe.*) 'S either you or dead mice, so . . . you win out by a slim margin.

Terry *Thanks.*

Terry smiles at her then looks off into the distance. Jennifer watches him.

Jennifer Well, you might as well go for it while you wait. Finish the hole . . .

Terry No rush. / 'S OK, I'm not really playing. I'm kinda looking for the owner.

Jennifer Yeah, but I'm in the way, so . . . / Oh. Well, I'm the manager.

Terry Pretty young for a manager. Good for you.

Jennifer Well, I grew up around it, so . . . it comes natural, I guess.

Terry This your place?

Jennifer Funny . . . (*Beat.*) Fifteen-year-olds don't have *places* – we just exist.

Terry That's true . . .

Jennifer Actually, it's my dad's business. This here. / Yep. / Uh-huh. I mean, among others . . .

Terry *Really?* / Your *dad*, huh? / Wow, he sounds like a very successful . . . something. Entrepreneur-type. Guy.

Jennifer Nah, just means he can't make shit happen, so he desperately tries a bunch of crap . . .

Terry Ouch!

Jennifer Hey, truth hurts.

Terry Sometimes it does. (*Beat.*) So it's him I'm looking for I guess. / Yep.

Jennifer OK. / He's not here on the weekends. He works at Big T's Gas-n-Go, 'cause his people're always calling in sick on Saturday and since I can't sell any beer or whatever. / Not old enough . . . so I run this place for him. (*Beat.*) Big T's is only about five, ten minutes up that way . . .

Terry I see . . . / Huh. And you're the name up on the sign there?

Jennifer Yep, that's me. (*Holds out a hand.*) Manager of Buddy's Putt-n-Play. My real name's Jennifer, but my dad calls me 'Buddy' sometimes.

Terry . . . Isn't that something? (*Smiles.*) Nice to meet you. It's . . . well, it just is.

Jennifer Cool. You too.

Terry So, your dad must be proud, huh? Of you, I mean.

Jennifer Yep. I'm a chip off the ol' block.

Terry Well, he's lucky to have such a . . . you know . . .

Jennifer No, what?

Terry Just a . . . I mean . . . (*Haltingly.*) Such a pretty *chip*.

Jennifer Aww, shucks, mister . . .

Terry I'm just saying!

Jennifer No, thanks, that's sweet of you. *Kind*, or whatever.

Terry Believe me, I'm not being kind . . . you're a bit of a knockout there.

Jennifer I can yell if I need to . . . I mean, if you're gonna get all *creepy* on me here.

Terry Well, you better start screaming then . . . (*Smiles.*) Just kidding ya.

Jennifer Ha! I *know*. (*Laughs.*) Ya can't fool me – you're a nice guy.

Terry Pretty much. / Then good.

Jennifer 'Pretty much' is close enough for me. I'll take it. / (*She indicates.*) Well . . . your car's probably done.

Terry Oh yeah, alright. (*Nods.*) Good . . .

Terry stands there, not committing to anything just yet. Jennifer decides to break the silence.

Jennifer . . . Wanna see something?

Jennifer walks over to a bottle of soda she's got hidden in the grass. She bends over and down to the bottle; she puts her mouth over the opening and stands – turns it up and drinks.
  Tilts her head back down; drops the bottle into her hand.
  Terry turns a quick circle to see if anyone is watching.

See? No hands . . .

Terry . . . Very clever stuff there, young lady. / Yep. That's . . . huh. Geez.

Jennifer Thank you. / I do gymnastics during school. It's a trick I learned . . .

Terry Not so sure your *dad'd* approve of that trick – showing it off to just anybody – but hey . . .

Jennifer I won't tell if you don't.

Terry OK, well, fair enough.

Jennifer He's a hypocrite, anyway.

Terry Yeah, why's that?

Jennifer He does the whole 'don't speak to strangers' routine, like, each day of the week, but he's always up in the face of the kids here. Talking with 'em, I'm saying . . .

Terry Yeah?

Jennifer *Always* . . . every guy who wanders in, he's gotta be asking 'em all kinds of shit – it really is nauseating.

Terry He's probably not seeing it the same way, though.

Jennifer What?

Terry Talking with people . . . He knows who he is, so no worries, but with you it's probably more about your, you know, *safety* or whatnot. He's just doing it because he loves you . . .

Jennifer Yeah, yeah . . .

Terry Your mom too, I'm sure.

Jennifer Well, when you find her, you can ask her for us . . . (*Shrugs.*) It's really just me and my dad now.

Terry Got it. Sorry.

Jennifer No big deal.

Terry Still.

Jennifer Just the way it is.

Terry Well, dads love their daughters . . . it's a known fact – anywhere on the planet it's true.

Jennifer S'pose so. / Maybe . . .

Terry I *know* so. / He does, right?

Jennifer Yes, OK, I'm his little princess and all that crap – it's true! His shining star or whatever . . .

Jennifer laughs at this and hides her face. Terry smiles and tentatively pats her on the back.

Terry See? / Told ya so.

Jennifer Fine! / God, it's so . . .

Terry That's cute.

Jennifer . . . It's *so* gross, all that gooey junk they say – parents, I mean – when you get older. Just so damn embarrassing . . .

Terry Hey, it's a hell of a lot better'n being told you're a stupid asshole or something, believe me . . .

Jennifer Nice. You get that often?

Terry Just from *birth* on.

Jennifer Wow.

Terry Yep. After a while, it sticks . . .

Jennifer Sorry.

Terry Ahh, not your fault – unless you're thinking it to yourself right now.

Jennifer No way. / I think you're pretty OK.

Terry Good. / Ouch . . .

Jennifer 'OK' is totally great – geez, you don't know much about teenagers, huh?

Terry Not really . . .

Jennifer You got kids? / *None?*

Terry Uh-uh. / No. Not that I know of . . .

Jennifer You want one?

Terry Only if she's a princess . . .

Jennifer Ha ha! (*Grins.*) Seriously, though.

Terry Umm, I dunno. We'll see . . . I still got a few good years in me yet.

Jennifer Maybe . . . (*Laughs.*) Got a girlfriend or anything?

Terry Nope. Not a one. / My God, you're a nosy little thing! That's . . .

Jennifer Ex-wife, then? / Just wondering . . .

Terry And why 'ex'? How do you know I don't have a wife waiting at home?

Jennifer . . . You wouldn't be yakking away on the thirteenth tee of this shithole if you had somewhere better to be . . . How's that for being Nancy Drew?

Terry Not too bad! (*Smiles.*) Nah, I'm a single man. And you . . . what do *you* got? Some cute guy, I'll bet . . .

Jennifer Yeah, I know a few, sure. Boys, I mean . . . that I've dated or who, you know, wanna try stuff with me – but no, I'm not hooked up with anybody at the moment, if that's what you're asking . . .

Terry Great. (*Mumbles.*) What was your name again – 'Buddy'?

Jennifer No! I don't know why he named the place that. It's so gay! *Buddy's* just sounds so, so retarded . . .

Terry I don't mind it . . .

Jennifer Yeah, well, then you're probably a little bit retarded or something.

Terry I like to think of it as *special*.

Jennifer I bet . . . *very* special.

Terry That's me . . .

Jennifer Anyways, I'm Jennifer. I've told you that already . . .

Terry Oh, that's right. Jennifer. I do remember that now . . . sure.

Jennifer Good. (*Offers up her soda.*) Here . . . Have some.

Terry No, that's OK . . .

Jennifer Go ahead, I don't have a disease or anything . . . promise.

Terry Umm . . . No, I don't need your . . .

Jennifer It's hot out. Go on.

Terry I can buy one, that's no problem.

Jennifer The machine is way back there . . . by the clubhouse.

Terry 'Clubhouse'. That's a good one.

Jennifer Whatever! (*Grins.*) You know what I mean . . . the *snack shoppe*. Go ahead. Have a swig. / 'S 7-Up, so it won't kill ya.

Terry Alright. / Thanks for the warning.

Terry carefully reaches for the twenty-ounce. Takes a swig.

Jennifer Geez, I didn't mean finish it . . .

Terry Oops! (*Spits some up.*) Shit . . .

Jennifer Ooh, that's pretty . . .

Terry God, I'm sorry . . . how suave was that?!

Jennifer Kinda right up there.

Terry Damn, that's embarrassing . . .

Jennifer Don't worry, I do a bunch of shit like that – I'm practically *famous* for doing goofy crap. / . . . I'm not just gorgeous; I'm a spaz, too.

Terry Good to know! / I'm glad . . . and you are, actually. You really are.

Jennifer What's that?

Terry Gorgeous. I mean, for some fifteen-year-old cleaner-upper person . . .

Jennifer *Thanks.* (*Laughs.*) You're a riot . . . that must be another one of your jokes. The 'un-funny' kind.

Terry Hey, I'm just warming up. (*Taking another guzzle.*) Umm, what is that? Strawberry or . . . ?

Jennifer Yep. (*Grins.*) Lip gloss. (*Beat.*) I . . . might want another sip outta there at some point . . . so don't take it home with you.

Terry Oh, hey, here . . . have it.

The two of them stand looking at each other for a moment without saying anything. Traffic sounds in the distance.

Jennifer So . . . what kinda car you got?

Terry 'S an old Buick that I fixed up . . .

Jennifer Cool. I like cars.

Terry That's nice.

Jennifer Is it?

Terry Yeah, it's nice to like things . . .

Jennifer I like all kinds of stuff. (*Beat.*) Fact is, I'm gonna do that when I get older . . . buy up old stuff and maybe even sell it again.

Terry Like, what, a junk dealer?

Jennifer Something like that. You see that show on television where guys go around and judge other people's things? / Tell them how much it might be worth?

Terry Yeah, I think so . . . / Uh-huh.

Jennifer They call it a 'roadshow'. That's the name of it on PBS, an *Antique Roadshow*. 'Cause they travel from town to town, I guess . . .

Terry You're *fifteen* . . . How come you're not watching *The OC* or whatever they call it?

Jennifer I do, I watch all kinds of stuff. Look around, mister . . . / (*Pointing.*) Not, like, *tons* to do in town . . .

Terry Right. / I hear ya.

Jennifer So, yeah, the tube gets a workout at our place . . . And by the way? I'm not, like, a genius or anything . . . but why is it *'The'* OC, anyway? It's Orange County, where they come from in California – they say it right there on the show. *Orange County.* I mean, you wouldn't say 'the' Orange County, right? Anyways, it's stupid . . . that's not how come I watch my other shows, but still. *'The'* OC. Dumb. (*Beat.*) 'S probably why it got cancelled . . .

Terry Could be. (*Smiles.*) And so that's your goal in life? To check out other folks' crap and then . . . what?

Jennifer Just that. Look at it, decide how good it is – tell 'em what they can sell it for or what it's worth . . . (*Grins.*) That'd be pretty neat.

Terry I guess.

Jennifer And maybe I can even cheat 'em at it sometimes – you know, like, tell 'em a false price and then buy it from them. Get an old painting or a chest of drawers dirt cheap . . . without 'em even knowing it – that I practically stole right out from under their noses!

Terry Nice goal. (*Laughs.*) Jesus . . .

Jennifer Hey, it's a living. / Kind of like what your brother did . . . right?

Terry True. / Right! Good memory, kiddo.

Jennifer Thanks. (*Beat.*) And what do you do, anyway?

Terry Umm – I'm sort of a security guard.

Jennifer Like a *cop*? Eeeww . . .

Terry Well, not really. I'm *un*armed . . . can't be a full-on cop 'cause I got a little bit of a *record* . . . / Apparently I was a bad boy when I was younger.

Jennifer Oh. / Hmm. Interesting . . .

Terry Yeah . . . I work nights mostly now, and I guard shit for folks. (*Beat.*) From little thieves like *you*.

Jennifer Ha ha! (*Laughs.*) You mean, like, at their houses?

Terry No, not always . . . Usually I work at a store or some warehouse, few construction sites . . . that sort of deal. / Evenings.

Jennifer Oh. / That's interesting . . .

Terry No it's not. It's a job, which is OK, and I have days off, which is the good part. I'm not the *deepest* sleeper, so it gives me more time to, you know – do stuff like this. / Drive around. Read. (*Grins.*) *Golf*, of course . . .

Jennifer Nice. / Sweet!

Terry Why is that 'sweet'?

Jennifer Well, otherwise we'd've never met.

Terry That's true. / I do . . .

Jennifer See? / Shit always works out for a reason – that's what I think.

Terry 'S a good philosophy there, lady.

Jennifer Yep. I think it's fate . . . you and I met for a reason.

Terry That'd be nice if it's the case.

Jennifer I think it is . . . / Oh, wait, except you're looking for my dad, right?

Terry Then great. / Yeah. Kinda.

Jennifer And why's that? Not that I'm all, like, nosy or whatever, but . . .

Terry Just 'cause. / Wanted to say hi. Thought I'd drop in, surprise him.

Jennifer Yeah, but why? / Oh. So, you know each other? I mean, like . . . / Cool. (*Beat.*) I can call 'em for you if you want. Or . . .

Terry Umm-hmm. From a while ago . . . / No, that's OK. I'll get over there soon enough . . . (*Beat.*) You know what? You've got his eyes . . .

Jennifer Oh. (*Quietly.*) You like my eyes?

Jennifer grins at him; Terry blushes and turns away from her. To divert this thought, he studies the golf course.

Terry So . . . how good are you at this?

Jennifer At putt-putt?

Terry You could probably kick my ass, right?

Jennifer Prob'ly.

Terry Don't be so sure, now . . . I learned it from a pro.

Jennifer No way.

Terry True, no, he wasn't a *pro* golfer or anything, but he was good at this. At all sports, really, but this one the most . . . putt-putt. It was years ago, but still . . .

Jennifer Yeah? / Huh.

Terry Yep. / We did it all the time when I was about your age. Him and me.

Jennifer So lemme see you, then.

Terry What do you mean?

Jennifer Do it. This hole . . .

Terry *Now?*

Jennifer Sure. Show me what you got . . .

Terry You're kidding, right?

Jennifer Nah, come on! If he was such the superstar, this guy you learned from . . .

Terry He was pretty damn good.

Jennifer OK, then.

Terry studies her for a moment – a light seems to click on in his head. He slowly smiles at her. A bit unnerving.

Terry Fine. (*Beat.*) What's the bet?

Jennifer What bet?

Terry Hey, we gotta play for *some*thing, if I'm gonna humiliate myself . . . some little treat, the end of the rainbow. / (*Beat.*) You're gonna make it worth my while, aren't ya?

Jennifer Oh, I get it. / I see . . .

Terry Yep. (*He smiles.*) So?

Jennifer Umm – whatever you say. Up to you.

Terry Fine – I get a hole-in-one . . . I can have anything I want. How's that?

Jennifer . . . Like?

Terry Now . . . come on. Don't make me spell it out. *Any*-thing. / As in, what-ever-I-choose.

Jennifer Oh. / *Ohhh* – so that's how it works, is it? Ha! You're bad!

Terry I knew you weren't ready for this.

Jennifer Hey, I've *done* plenty, so don't do that 'you're just a kid' thing . . . (*Beat.*) I mean, not, like, *every*thing, but lots. (*Grins.*) Some.

Terry OK, then there it is. A challenge. I'm throwing down the gauntlet or whatever, like they used to . . . back in olden times. (*Mimes dropping a glove.*) There.

Jennifer Ha! (*Grins.*) And if you don't? Make it in one, I mean . . . then what?

Terry I'm screwed.

Jennifer . . . Sounds like the opposite to me.

Jennifer laughs at this – long and loud. Terry joins in.

Terry Exactly! That's a good one . . .

Jennifer See what happens when you add a punchline in there?

Terry Yeah, it really works, huh?

Jennifer Sure does. (*Grins.*) So, if you're not able to get it in the hole – let's see . . . alright, here we go. / You miss, then I get a shot at it. I win, I pick. Fewest shots to get it in's the winner . . .

Terry What? / That's the game?

Jennifer That is the game. Sound good?

Terry . . . Not if I was smart it doesn't. (*Grins.*) Sounds like the cops are waiting off in the bushes there to jump my ass . . .

Jennifer Ha! (*Laughs.*) That'd be so cool!

Terry Yeah, *great* . . .

Jennifer You know what I mean. It'd be so funny if that were true – but it's not. It's just little ol' me.

Terry That's OK . . . Anyway, they'd never find where I hid the body. (*Grins.*) Would they now, Buddy?

Jennifer stops short and looks at Terry. Not happy with that one.

Jennifer Eeewww . . . don't say that. 'Buddy.' / I don't like it . . .

Terry Sorry, I thought that was your . . . / Isn't that what you said was . . . ?

Jennifer Yeah, but it's what my dad says to me. He calls me that. That's gross if you do it, too . . .

Terry Oh, I see. Sorry.

Jennifer Right? / It's . . .

Terry Sure. / No, I understand now . . .

Jennifer 'Jennifer' is fine. Or 'J'. A few of my friends call me that. 'J'.

Terry Good, then that's the one for me. Hey, J.

Jennifer Hey there, mister. Whose name I don't know, by the way . . .

Terry That's 'cause you never asked . . . Go ahead. Guess.

Jennifer Umm . . . Lance?

Terry *No*!! 'Lance' sounds like . . . God, like one of those male strippers or some shit. / 'Lance'!

Jennifer Yeah, exactly! / Must be that smile of yours . . .

Terry You sure it wasn't this? (*Does a few very self-conscious moves.*) How 'bout *this*? Oooh, baby, *ooooh* . . .

Jennifer bursts out laughing again – she thinks Terry is the funniest thing around. He may well be, in fact.

Jennifer Oh-my-God. That's so sick! / Stop! / I'm gonna puke, stop it! Eeewww!

Terry What? / I'm amazing, right? / You're loving it, aren't ya? Huh?!

Jennifer You wish! Don't *ever* do that again or I can't be seen near you . . .

Terry Then I will stop immediately.

Terry is true to his word; he stops after one last little ass shake, just for effect – the effect is Jennifer having another nice chuckle. Terry smiles, too.

Jennifer Man, that was *really* ugly. / Awful!

Terry Thanks. / Thank you, J . . .

A moment between them – Terry breaks it by pointing back up the steps to the upper level and towards a small mat.

I tee off from here?

Jennifer Yep. Unless you wanna go from the kids' spot. / Just to be safe . . .

Terry No thanks. / I'll roll the dice on this one . . .

Jennifer Then go for it, *Lance*.

Terry does a quick hip shake – Jennifer laughs again.

STOP!

Terry 'S your own fault.

Terry lines up his ball with a hole on the top level. He shoots it through the windmill and he waits. The ball is slow to arrive; it comes to a halt far from the hole.
A burst of real anger from Terry – he quickly controls it.

FUCK!! / Goddammit!! / Yeah, sorry, it's . . . family trait.

Jennifer I'd probably go with *motherfucker* on that one. / Too bad for you . . . *some*body's got a little temper there. / Nothing I haven't heard, but you should work on that. Give yourself a *heart attack* that way.

Terry nods. He walks back down and shoots the ball into the hole. Stands up and grimaces over at Jennifer.

Terry Two.

Jennifer walks over and puts out her hand for the putter. Terry gives it to her, but keeps a hold of it.
Jennifer looks up at him innocently. Neither person moves for a moment, then she pulls him to her. A kiss. Slow and simple – over before either one can think better of it.

. . . Hey.

Jennifer Sorry.

Terry I didn't say it was a problem. All I said was 'Hey.'

Jennifer Good 'hey' or the bad type?

Terry Which do you think?

Jennifer I'm holding out for the first one.

Terry . . . I'll get back to ya on that. (*Beat.*) You're pretty young to be throwing kisses around like that.

Jennifer Says you.

Terry Hmm. (*Puts hands on her shoulders.*) Maybe I should just keep you right here till I decide what to do with ya . . .

After a second, Terry kisses the top of her head and then slowly removes his hands. Jennifer takes the putter and saunters over to the stairs. As she walks slowly up and over to the tee, she trips on the lip of the last step.

Jennifer See?! *Told* ya . . .

Terry smiles and waves her off – Jennifer chuckles, then bends over and drops the ball. She stands and hits it.

They both wait and watch – the ball drops quickly through the first tube and towards the hole. Rolls past and stops.

. . . Shit! / That wasn't supposed to happen.

Terry *Hell*, yeah! / Ohh, baby!

Jennifer So funny. (*Moves down the steps and into place.*) God . . .

She takes another shot and misses. Throws down the putter in disgust. Terry does another little 'dance' then stops.

Fuck. Awwwww, that's so fucked! / I mean, God! / Shit . . .

Terry Oh yeah! / Yes! / Whew-heeww!!

Jennifer . . . Silly.

Terry Yes, I am. I'm very silly. (*Starts to dance.*) But you still lost . . .

Jennifer Yeah, yeah, yeah. And you *promised* about the dance . . .

Terry True. / Sorry . . .

Jennifer You did! / Whatever. So?

Terry What?

Jennifer *So* what's the damage? / Come on . . .

Terry Oh. *That.* / (*Beat.*) Why don't we . . . you know. Let's get outta here.

Jennifer Yeah, but to where?

Terry I dunno. Let's go for a ride.

Jennifer Just you and me?

Terry *Us* – let's drive around a bit. Talk about stuff.

(*Nervously.*) Don't worry, we can figure something out . . . It'd be fun, right? Little drive around town and we'll just . . . you know . . . see what happens. (*Beat.*) Come on.

Jennifer . . . I dunno. (*Beat.*) I'm not s'posed to speak to strangers, remember? / And you could be a bad man . . .

Terry 'S a bit late for that. / . . . Could be.

Terry provides the best smile he can muster – Jennifer swallows it down whole. Shrugs.

Jennifer *Fine.* Better'n hanging around this place. People here suck.

Terry Yeah? Even your friends?

Jennifer Uh-huh. Even them. Most times, anyway. (*Beat.*) So, you gonna go get your car or what?

Terry Yep . . . I'll park in that side lot.

Jennifer OK, see you in a few minutes. I gotta go lock up now . . .

Jennifer pulls an elaborate key chain out of her pocket – glass ball or something. Twirls her keys and looks at him.

Terry That's fancy. What is it? / No?

Jennifer Nothing. / My dad gave it to me . . .

Terry Huh. (*Beat.*) And what's your *daddy* gonna say to you taking off early?

Jennifer Why, you wanna drive by and ask?

Terry Uh-uh – don't think I do, J. / Nope.

Jennifer No? You sure? I can swing ya right past there. / Good. Me either.

Terry Fine . . . I guess it'll be our little thing, then, right?

Jennifer Yeah. Just yours and mine. (*Gives him a peck on the cheek.*) A secret.

Terry Yep.

Jennifer You can keep a secret, can't ya?

Terry . . . Sure.

She moves off and down a trail back towards the clubhouse. Terry watches her – he stands completely still.
  Sound of traffic and the woods.

Three

The space has been converted once more – this time into a bi-level section of manicured lawn. Expensive plants and flowers spilling from various cultivating beds. Several tasteful benches placed carefully about. A statue or two.
    Terry stands by himself, looking out into the surrounding woods. He is dressed in a sports jacket and tie. He holds a small plate – it has the remnants of cake and ice cream on it.
    After a moment, Terry looks around and then goes to tuck his garbage inside a bush. Drew – dressed in an expensive suit – enters and watches. He's holding a fluted glass.

Drew . . . Go for it.

Terry whips around and steps away, a little embarrassed. Drew smiles and holds out his arms – Terry stays where he is. Drew walks over, gives his brother a half-assed hug.

Terry Hey there, Drew.

Drew Hi, dude . . . thanks for coming.

Terry Look, do we have to do this again? I've asked you before – do not call me that.

Drew Right, sorry . . . bro.

Terry Asshole.

Drew I'm just *joshing* you, man! I know, I know . . . I remember all about the lingo. / Off limits, I get it.

Terry OK, just so you do. / Yeah.

IN A DARK DARK HOUSE

Drew *Totally.*

Terry You are such a dumbfuck, man. It's really almost hard to fathom . . .

Drew I just do it to piss you off.

Terry Yeah, well, it works . . .

Drew Awesome! (*Smiles.*) Hey . . . how's your baseball team? 'S all good?

Terry I don't have a team, Drew, I'm the *ump*. I told ya. / Yeah, really . . .

Drew Really? / Oh. I thought . . . huh. (*He shrugs.*) Anyway.

Terry Yeah, anyways . . . nice to see you, I guess.

Drew You too. / Honestly it is . . . (*Beat.*) You look all . . . I dunno. Something. Rested or whatever. / Could be that tie ya got there! 'S a *beauty* . . .

Terry Yep. / Good. / Yeah, thanks! Pulled it outta my *sock* drawer . . . (*Beat.*) You happy to be outta that place?

Drew Course! I mean, of course I am . . .

Terry I bet.

Drew Great to be home and all that, off with my kids and everything . . . it's fantastic. Absolutely.

Terry Then I'm happy for ya . . . (*Pointing to the drink.*) . . . I mean, *cheers*.

Drew Ha ha! I'm only having the one . . . anyway, it's just some sparkling cider. (*Smiles.*) *Mostly.* / So . . . (*Beat.*) But thanks, Terry. It is very much appreciated.

Terry Oh. / No problem.

The brothers stand looking at each other – unsure how to proceed. Listening to the various sounds around them.

Drew You believe that? I pay a million-eight for this house and a fucking *farmer* next door sells off two of his fields to somebody else . . . now I've got this *sub*division going on right over there, some shitload of condos – fuck! Thanks to that money-grubbing piece a' shit.

Terry That sucks . . . sounds like something *you'd* do.

Drew Yep! (*Laughs.*) Offered the son-of-a-bitch twice what he was asking but he held out and probably made *ten* times that . . . got it *zoned* and now my land value is screwed on this place. Back in the day I would've blasted his ass with a lawsuit, but you know what? I'm just gonna breathe deep and let it go. / (*Beat.*) 'S the 'new' me.

Terry Pretty cool. / Impressive . . .

Drew Ahh, I couldn't win it or I'd probably still sue the cock-sucker . . .

Terry No doubt.

Drew I hate that shit! When somebody's actually in the 'right'.

Terry Yeah, that just eats at the heart a' you lawyer types.

Drew Hey, hey . . . I'm a businessman now. All *respectable* and whatnot . . .

Terry Yep. You and Don Corleone there.

Drew Exactly!

Drew laughs it up at this one. Terry goes over and pulls his plate back out of the bushes. Drew waves him off.

Hey, man, leave it . . . that's what the *Mexicans* are for. Seriously. / (*Beat.*) It's only worth paying 'em if they gotta scramble around and do the dirty work . . . otherwise I'd just use the neighbour kids.

Terry Nah, it's OK. / I got it.

Drew Dude, they'll probably *eat* it, I'm serious – they'll thank me later.

Terry No, I shouldn't've done it – it was rude. I know Judy does a bunch of stuff out here, so I'll just carry it back with me. Wasn't thinking. / (*Beat.*) Figure I'm gonna get going.

Drew Whatever. / . . . Already?

Terry Yeah . . . it's a bit of a drive and I don't wanna get tied up in Sunday traffic.

Drew Everybody's gonna be coming back in this way. You'll be fine.

Terry Still . . .

Drew I mean, whatever you want, but the kids'd love to see you a bit. They always ask about you . . .

Terry That's nice. (*Beat.*) Hope they like that stuff I brought 'em. Not much but it's, you know, some puzzles – *games* and shit. Children like that kinda thing, right?

Drew Sure. / Of course they do.

Terry Good. / Great.

The two men stand silently for a beat, nodding at each other. Sound of construction in the distance.

Drew . . . But they'd love to *see* ya, bro. That's what I'm saying. Spend some time with you . . .

Terry . . . Maybe next time . . .

Drew Yeah, but you're here right now . . .

Terry Drew, *next* time, OK? Just leave it there, would ya? (*Beat.*) You always gotta push things – let it go. It's what I've been working on and I'd suggest you do the same. Let. Go.

Drew Fine. / I'll tell 'em . . . fine.

Terry Alright then. / Good. See you . . .

Terry nods and starts off – Drew calls out before he can disappear.

Drew . . . What's the problem, man?

Terry What?

Drew I'm just saying, where's the five-alarm blaze all the sudden?

Terry I told you. I'm tired and I need to get back . . .

Drew You didn't say that before. About being tired . . .

Terry Yeah, well, I was *implying* it. / My 'drive back' and all that.

Drew Right, right . . . / Then go for it.

Terry Thanks.

Drew holds out his hand for the plate. Terry slowly walks back to him but doesn't give it up yet.

Drew I'll take it . . . that way you can go out the side yard. Sneak off if ya need to so badly . . .

Terry . . . I'm not sneaking off . . .

Drew Bullshit. That's OK, just say it.

Terry I'll walk right across the fucking *bandstand*, you want me to so bad. (*Beat.*) I need to go – not trying to make a big deal out of it . . .

Drew Fine. I mean, 'S just my 'welcome *home*' party, that's all, so . . .

Terry Man . . . *don't*, alright? Do not do that shit or I'll – (*Works to stop short.*) NO. Used to be I'd wanna smash you right in your . . . fucking face. Ya know? But I been letting it go – my anger – and this is how I handle things now. What you see happening here. Got a little bit of *control.* (*Lets out his breath.*) 'S OK. OK, I'm good.

Drew Wow. Impressive. / Very cool. / No, I mean, it's fine, I just . . .

Terry Yep. / Uh-huh. (*Breathes out.*) So . . . that's, you know. / Doesn't matter, anyway . . . (*Beat.*) You don't care if I'm here or not.

Drew Now, where'd you get *that*?

Terry Ahh, maybe because it was *Judy* who called me, to even lemme know this was happening – or 'cause I'm standing around for an hour and a *half* while you're yakking away to all these other people . . . Maybe some thing like that.

Drew Shit, bro, that's not . . . / *Dude* . . .

Terry STOP IT! / Stop fucking doing that! You make me sick with your silly little act, OK, so shut the fuck up, I swear to Christ! / I mean, *fuck* . . .

Terry tosses the dirty plate to the ground, angry and disgusted. He is seething now.
 Drew cringes and looks over his shoulder, towards the house.

Drew Terry . . . / It's alright, they can't hear us way out here.

Terry I don't give a shit who hears us, Drew! I don't know any of those *people* . . . *associates* a' yours.

Drew The kids, then. I don't want the kids to get worried . . . / (*Beat.*) 'Kay?

Terry God! . . . / (*Frustrated.*) Aaaahhh!

Terry takes a moment, gaining back his control. Few more breaths and a little muttering to himself. He paces.

Come on, come on now, come *on* . . . (*Deep breath.*) Do it. / Kinda. / Yep.

Drew 'S OK. Guess it's hard to stop it overnight, right? / Big personality change like that. / Sure. I get it.

Terry Sorry, that just made me . . .

Drew 'S no big deal. I'm just saying . . . Anyway. Look, If you need to take off, I understand . . .

Terry Fine. It's not you entirely – I'm no good at stuff like this. Meeting folks and all that . . . fucking hate that shit. As you know. Not anybody's fault, it's just . . .

Drew You were doing great in there.

Terry looks. Drew takes a step toward his brother but keeps a bit of distance too – the guy's not stupid.

I'm just saying . . . I saw a girl or two trying to come up to you. They were checking you out, bro! (*Beat.*) Seriously, a chick from my office, she came over to me specifically to ask who you were, so . . .

Terry What're you . . . watching me? Making sure I don't embarrass you now?

Drew Not at all, dude – sorry, man, it's a *habit*! – that was not at *all* the case. (*Smiles.*) I was happy to see you there, talking with Judy and, you know . . . this makes me happy.

Terry Yeah, well, congrats again on your getting through that programme . . . / *Really* seems to be working.

Drew Yeah. / Absolutely . . . I feel like a *hundred* bucks! / 'Cause two months of being there – 'S all I got left.

Terry Right? / I bet. (*Beat.*) Seemed like a really expensive place.

Drew The best. Best in this area, anyway.

Terry Well. So long as it helps . . .

Drew Uh-huh . . . (*Beat.*) Your testimony really did sway the judge, too, so I got you to thank for . . . anyway. Thanks. / I know it's not easy for ya, opening up like that. / *Both* times – up there *and* in court.

Drew quickly crosses and hugs his brother without any consent. Terry basically just waits it out.

Terry Welcome. / 'S not my *favourite*, no. / Hey, you do what you gotta do . . . right?

Terry shrugs again, passing this off without fanfare.

Drew I mean it, man – I've done a bunch of stupid shit in my day and, so, you know. Thanks. You saved me . . .

The two brothers stop again for a moment, listening to a sound of construction in the distance. Drew points to it.

Listen to that . . . on a fucking Sunday even!

Terry . . . Yeah, I can hear 'em.

Drew It's the *sabbath,* for Christ's sake! (*Beat.*) I mean, for *somebody.*

Terry Yep. No rest for the bad guys . . .

Drew It's 'the wicked', right? I'm pretty sure it's not just limited to men . . . at least I think so.

Terry . . . Most women'd disagree . . .

Drew Yeah, well . . . fuck 'em, they can't take a joke.

Terry grins at this. Drew walks down the steps and takes a look around. Points out a spot overhead to Terry.

Gonna put a tree fort up there for the kids. Keep saying it, anyway.

Terry That's good.

Terry nods at this, drifting for a moment. He looks up at the trees overhead – turns back after a bit. Thinking.

Drew Yeah, should be. *Lots* of memories, but yeah . . .

Terry Right. (*Beat.*) Don't do it if it's too hard.

Drew We'll see. Trying to make up for lost time and all that, you know?

Terry I hear ya . . . (*Changing topics.*) So. I went and saw 'em . . .

Drew Huh? / Who?

Terry You know. / Todd.

Drew You *what*? You . . . (*Looks about.*) You *saw* Todd Astin?

Terry I did, yeah.

Drew Where in the hell did you do that? I mean, how'd you even . . . ?

Terry Wasn't easy . . . (*Beat.*) Some person doesn't wanna be found, even today it's tricky – all the fucking *email* and computers in the world, if you don't want people to know who you are – you can still do it. Hide.

Drew But you found the guy?

Terry Oh yeah. (*Smiles.*) 'S the one nice thing about being in security . . . you meet up with a lot of cops and men like that. Investigator types.

Drew Wow, that's . . . I don't believe it.

Drew wanders away for a moment, listening to the sounds around them but keeping one eye on Terry.

Terry It's true. Looked that *dude* right in the eye – fuck, *see*? Now you got me doing it!

Drew Yeah. (*Grins.*) And so, Todd was . . . I mean, what'd he say?

Terry To me?

Drew Yes, to you! *Fuck* . . .

Terry Nothing.

Drew Seriously, come on! What?

Terry Honestly? (*Beat.*) . . . I'm standing there, looking him straight in the face – dead into his eyes – and I'm trying to decide what to say to the guy. It's been twenty years, right? And he's there in front of me. Takes a glance my way – he lost most all of his hair, you remember that, like, *golden* hair of his? – and he says to me, says: 'Paper or plastic?'

Drew *What?!* / You dick . . .

Terry I swear to God. / That's what I . . .

Drew You saw him at, what, the grocery store?!

Terry Worse. Some fucking Gas-n-Go – that he *owns*. / Yep, runs it, too – he's got himself all set up, five hundred miles south a' here.

Drew No! / Holy shit . . .

Terry Exactly. / 'S exactly right.

Drew That's . . . / Hard to believe.

Terry Yeah. Has a little diner, too, and one of those mini-golf courses . . . which his daughter runs.

Drew Shit! He *told* you all this?

Terry Oh no – stared right at me . . . didn't know me from Adam. (*Beat.*) Like I said: he took my money, he gave me directions, mentioned the weather and a place to eat – that restaurant of his – and that's it. 'S no big event. (*Waits.*) Only part I hated was that he didn't recognise me, you know? / Even after a bunch a' years . . . I figured he'd still know when a guy was me or not.

Drew That's . . . I mean, fuck. / Holy shit, Terry! I can't believe that you . . . I mean, that you *actually* went . . .

Terry Why? I thought you wanted me to.

Drew Well, yeah, but . . . I mean, I said a *lot* a' stuff to you up there, I still never figured that you'd run into the guy . . .

Terry I didn't. I went and found him. / I hunted 'em down . . .

Drew Right, but . . . / Still . . .

Terry Took me, like, *five* weeks but . . . we got 'em.

Drew We?

Terry You and me, little brother.

Drew What's that mean?

Terry I did it for both of us, Drew.

Drew Terry, that's . . . that . . .

Terry Don't worry, I didn't *kill* 'em . . . if that's what you're all nervous about.

Drew No, I'm not worried, I just . . .

Terry Bullshit. Course you are, but forget about it – it's done now. / I took care of it.

Drew I'm . . . what's that mean? Terry . . . what're . . . ? / I don't know what you mean by . . . (*Beat.*) Listen, I only wanna know you're alright, that's all – seeing somebody like that again can be a real emotional deal. *I* oughta know . . .

Terry That's true, you *oughta* . . . But you don't. You don't because it wasn't you that did it. / It was me.

Drew That's true. / I know . . .

Terry I'm the one who found the guy. It was *me* in that place, smiling over at him – and he didn't have a *speck* of a notion that I was anybody he ever met. (*Beat.*) *I* did that. ME.

Drew I'm sorry, bro. I mean, *Terry* . . . I'm really sorry if you feel like I put you up to that.

Terry Nah, it felt good. Like closing a book, really, some book that you'd already read a long time ago, and it needed put back on the shelf – it was a little like that. / (*Beat.*) You should probably do it, too . . . gives you a whole different, you know, on the thing. *Perspective*.

Drew I'm . . . / Terry, listen . . .

Terry I'm glad I saw him. I actually am.

Drew OK.

Terry Yep. (*Beat.*) Met his daughter, too. She was a really sweet girl . . . *and* a pretty nice kisser, too! / Yep.

Drew Huh? / Terry, what're you . . . ?

Terry You know what he calls 'er? Guess.

Drew What?

Terry I said 'guess'.

Drew I dunno . . .

Terry *Buddy*. That's his pet name for her. It's *Buddy*. / Even put it up on the sign of his golf place . . . '*Buddy's*'. Believe that shit?

Drew Wow . . . / That's . . . I mean, that's a little weird, huh?

Terry Uh-huh. It sure is – calls his own *daughter* Buddy.

Drew That's wild.

Terry Yeah, I thought so. Kinda took me by surprise, that one . . .

Drew I bet. (*Beat.*) So why did you . . . ?

Terry *But* a real nice girl, and funny, too! Got that from him, I guess.

Drew Right. He *was* funny, wasn't he?

Terry Sure was. He was always a comical guy . . . I mean, when he didn't have his *cock* down your throat . . . right?

Drew nods at this, even tries a chuckle, but it quickly fades away. Terry stares straight at him.

Drew . . . Yeah. Maybe we should head back over to the tent, bro.

Terry Nah, I gotta go. I told ya that . . .

Drew Sure, OK.

Drews starts off again, but Terry isn't going anywhere. He stops his brother with a sentence. Drew turns back.

Terry I could've done anything to her . . . whatever I wanted, I could've gone ahead and done it. (*Beat.*) I mean, once she kissed me, then yeah . . .

Drew What's that mean? / No, seriously. What?

Terry Nothing. / Not a thing – just that I had her, right there in my car for a couple hours. Alone, Drew. Alone and all mine.

Drew Why? How'd that happen?

Terry Doesn't matter. Fact is that's how it went down – Todd's daughter was in my car and she was ready to do basically anything I asked her to. At *fif*teen years old. Anything . . . Not just kiss.

Drew . . . Terry . . .

Terry And for a second there, man! Well, the mind wanders . . . (*Beat.*) I was in complete control and I mean, I was shaking – sitting next to her and shaking like a wet *dog* . . .

Drew involuntarily looks over his shoulder to check that they aren't being overheard – he obviously wants no part of this.

Parked in a little side street and my mind is screeching, 'Take her! Do to her what he did to you!' But I can't, cannot do it . . . so I let her go. Drove her home, a peck on the cheek and a promise to see her again. (*Beat.*) Know what she did? Huh, Drew? Gave me this . . . here, look at it . . .

Terry pulls the elaborate key chain out of his pocket; the glass ball on one end dances in the fading light.

A thing that means a great deal to her. Yeah. She gave it to me as a memento to remember her by as she ran off up the driveway to home . . . place she shares with her father. *Todd*. (*Beat.*) After that I got back on the main road and went over to that gas station to see him. Look at him right between the fucking eyes. / The rest of it you already heard. (*Beat.*) I stood there with my plastic bag in one hand, pretending to study the map he had hanging there – not sure if I was gonna pull him over the counter or scream at him or just start – I didn't know what to do! Right then. I finally just gave a nod and wandered outside to my car. (*Beat.*) Sat there in the parking lot for about an hour or so and *wept* like a five-year-old . . .

Drew Jesus . . . / Shit. God! That's just about unbelievable, Terry . . .

Terry Nah, that's one thing it's not. I have spent too much life realising that fact – craziest shit you hear these days, still possible that it might happen.

Drew Right, no, I just mean . . .

Terry People are capable of fucking *any*thing. *That's* what I've learned. (*Beat.*) Which is part of why I've done this shit – worked on trying to be a different person. *Better.* 'Cause you can, you really can do it, if you wanna be. If not . . . I mean, if you choose *not* to be good or to make some . . . well, fuck. Who knows how ya might end up. / Right?

Drew Uh-huh. / Suppose so.

Terry I *know* so. (*Beat.*) Couple ordinary guys like us and we've got – both of us – so much shit buried down . . . *crap* we couldn't ever even believe about the other person. Right? And I mean stuff that makes us a whole lot more alike than we'd ever care to admit . . . (*Beat.*) You know?

Drew Maybe.

Terry Drew – you're not an idiot, so you know the truth, right? / I mean . . .

Drew What? / What, Terry?

Terry *Dude* . . . Does that help? If I talk like one of your buddies? (*Beat.*) You *know* what I'm saying without me saying it, correct? About Todd and me, right? Our history . . . and not just that, *history*; I'm saying the 'real' story. Him and me.

Drew . . . I don't, man, no.

Terry Come *on* . . .

Drew Really, bro, I'm not kidding . . . what are you talking about?

Terry Fine. You wanna play these games, then fine.

Drew Dude, *seriously* . . .

Terry Fuck you with that shit, Drew. You and all your *chummy* bullshit . . . We are not friends, little brother, we never have been, so do not act like it now, 'cause I hear you say shit like that and, and, I want to *puke* my guts up – right up on your fucking *gardenias*!

Drew . . . I know you're trying and all, I do, but you still got some serious anger issues there, Terry.

Terry Yeah, you *think*?

Drew I am, like, a hundred-per-cent sure of it. (*Beat.*) Look, if I offended you in some way, then I'm . . .

Terry Nope. We just don't click as two people, that's all. Shame that we had to end up related, otherwise I could just walk the fuck outta here and be done with it . . .

Drew Why, man, what'd I do to you? Like *specifically*, I'm saying. Not just 'cause I have money, which I know pisses you off . . . / It does . . .

Terry . . . Oh, please . . . / *Nooo* . . .

Drew You *know* it does.

Terry I wouldn't take that shit if your kids crawled up to me and begged me to have it! / *Pleaded* with me to take it from 'em, I wouldn't . . .

Drew Yeah, right . . . / Sure . . .

Terry advances on his brother a bit – not threateningly but with enough force to make Drew begin to back up.

Terry I *mean* it. You've got a seriously demented sense of what I consider important.

Drew Whatever, man. / *Whatev*er you say.

Terry That's right! / (*Beat.*) . . . Trying to *share* something with you and I get this phoney 'I dunno' shit again – You wanna play that tune then it's OK by me . . . We'll go back to a call at Christmas and say we're even . . .

With that Terry starts off, but Drew hops over to him. He gets in the way, with his arms up.

Drew Wait, Terry . . . / Come on, hold up!

Terry *What?* / WHAT?

Drew I'm just . . . Come on, man, I don't wanna part on bad terms again. We have done that routine too many times, right? Haven't we? (*Beat.*) Sorry that I didn't call you, it has been crazy busy since I got back – work and everything – but I really did want you here, to see you again outside of that, umm, you know . . . that place. Not what you'd call my 'finest hour' or whatever . . . right?

Terry . . . Nope . . .

Drew And if Judy was the one to call you about the get-together then forgive me, *my* fault, but it was not some slight to you . . . It's an oversight and I'm standing up here in front of you saying – honestly – I didn't mean you any harm by me doing it. (*Grins.*) Scout's honour . . .

Terry . . . Alright then, let's let it go.

Drew Cool. I 'preciate it. (*Beat.*) You sure you don't wanna say goodbye to the kids?

Terry Nah, I should be . . . Ahhh, fuck . . .

Drew What? Terry, what's going on?

Terry Nothing. / Doesn't matter.

Drew No, come on now, seriously here . . . what did you wanna say to me about you guys? / Course it matters! Of *course* it does . . .

Terry . . . Nah, it's just . . . / No, that's not it, Drew . . . You didn't . . .

Drew I mean, I'm sorry that I didn't see it, you know? Before. What I'd be opening up here, for you . . . / It was wrong of me to do that. To use you in that way – don't mean 'use' so much as just – if I had any sort of awareness about you guys, even the faintest sort of – just forgive me, OK? I don't wanna believe that I'd make use of something so painful for you . . . even though you . . .

Terry I never said 'painful'. No, I . . .

Drew Yeah, I know, but come on . . . / No, I *hear* ya, Terry, but it's . . .

Terry Didn't say it. / I never once disliked it, that's the funny thing. I didn't . . . you see books they got out there now, *thousands* of books about this shit – and I've read all of 'em – most of 'em talk about how a child is not 'culpable' or something like that, why you're not to blame, but you know what? I loved it, I did . . . from the very first time that he placed a finger on me.

Yeah . . . it was this joy that I felt with him, which was a little bit maddening, you know? But perfect, too. That's why I was always watching him and Mom and warning you to stay away from the guy. Not 'cause I was all worried about you . . . or cared so *deeply* for your safety, 'cause I didn't. All I was trying to do was protect the one thing that I cared about, which was this guy . . . this man who came to me and showed me a kindness . . . this sorta *love*, I guess. When I was young. (*Beat.*) 'Love' I now see, thanks to you, that he was spreading around like the Pied Piper of . . . wherever the fuck that fella was from.

Terry stops now, the truth having spilled out of him. He looks at Drew, who is frozen in his tracks. Silent.

. . . You don't need to say anything.

Drew No, I . . . I . . . I'm just a little . . .

Terry I know I should hate the guy, I do know that . . . but I can't find it in me to, even after all this time . . . and I've tried. Standing there . . . I'm looking at his stupid fucking middle-aged face and I'm trying to despise him . . . but I can't do it. I just . . . (*Beat.*) I dunno.

Terry looks off for a moment, trying to find the right words. Drew doesn't speak. Just watches his brother.

All I *do* know is I'm scared a lot; how 'bout that? Doesn't sound like me, does it? Uh-uh, but I am . . . scared of . . . shit, *every*thing. Who I am now, what I want or might be capable of . . . all that. So I keep myself to myself, alone, and work hard at not going where I really don't belong. I'm afraid of, like, relationships, scared maybe I'm a *fag* because of what happened and not hating it . . . all kinds of things. (*Beat.*) . . . I keep trying to figure out in little ways if I'm normal or not and so far I'll tell you what: I just don't know.

Drew Terry . . . course you are! You're . . . fuck, I don't know how to say it, but you're . . . you know . . .

Terry nods at this – listening without really believing what his brother is saying.

Terry Growing up like we did . . . who the fuck has any idea what oughta be considered 'normal'? Right? (*Beat.*) The son-of-a-bitch used to delight in beating on us, you know he did; the look on Dad's face when he was hitting me . . . *Fuck* him! I don't think he ever got pleasure from Mom the way he did from using his belt on my backside. I doubt it. And you, too, once I was gone, I'm sure of it. (*Beat.*) So I don't care what I hear from any doctors or, or from some asshole who has a TV show most afternoons – this guy came to me and made me feel important. Todd gave me something that I had never felt before and cannot find from anything else out there . . . he made some kinda difference in me, and, you know, hey. So be it.

Drew Terry, I'm . . . Look, it's . . . if it matters at all, I'm . . . I get it . . . I *do*.

Drew tries to decide how to continue here. Terry keeps an eye on him as his brother searches for the right words.

Terry You 'get it'. 'S that it? (*Beat.*) You wanna know the *real* reason I ran away from camp that summer? Because before I went, Todd made a joke, one about you . . . how he was gonna have to move over to you now that I was leaving. He *promised* me that he was kidding, that he was just being silly, but you know how you are when you're a kid . . . He's practically an adult and the shit coming outta his mouth is *gospel*. (*Beat.*) So, I get out in the middle of this big ol' scout deal, trying to concentrate on *canoeing* and crap like that and I'm, like . . . 'fuck this'. (*Beat.*) Took me four days to make it home. Had to hitch some, plus the car that I finally took – four *days*. But, see, now you know the truth – I'd been warning you to stay away from him for *my* sake. Because he was *mine* . . .

Drew I'm . . . yeah. I see that now . . .

Terry *Irony* being, once I got back there, it was me who needed help. / Needed you to help *me* for once . . .

Drew I tried . . . / I *tried* to . . .

Terry By telling the old man that I was hiding out in the *garage*? Huh?!

Drew Terry, listen – I was, like, *twelve* years old. Just a little kid . . . / I only told 'em that you were, you know, that you'd come home . . .

Terry Right. / After I asked ya not to . . . *begged* you, in fact! I – *begged* – you.

Drew I had no idea he was gonna react like that! Freak out and, and . . . call the cops and everything. / I don't know! I was . . .

Terry How the *fuck* did you think he was gonna act?! / He used to smack me in the mouth if I dropped a *fork*!

Drew It all happened so fast! We . . . Mom *dragged* me outta there and into the house . . . / Yes, she made me go up to our . . . I, I had to go up to . . .

Terry No. That's . . . / *No*, Drew.

Drew What?

Terry Don't.

Drew *What*, Terry?

Terry Do not do that. Rewrite history.

Drew I'm not.

Terry Yes, you are . . . because that's the way we do in our fucking house. We lie about it or we don't say shit; we clam up and don't utter a fucking *syllable* about things . . . about the real truth. *Yes*.

Drew What're you . . . ?

Terry I'm – talking – about – you – and – Mom! OK? That's what. The fact that you two could stand there and let me be . . . like I was *some* . . . *asshole* that you never met before. Even as the cops are asking you . . . *directly* in your fucking faces you didn't say shit, either one a' you. (*Beat.*) You had the chance to *say* something – say that not a day of our lives went by without that motherfucker hitting me or, or that he was a piece a' shit. That it was self-defence or *any*thing!

Drew . . . Terry . . .

Terry WHAT? When I finally needed you . . .

Drew I did! Terry, that's not true . . . what did you expect?! . . . You know how Dad was when he got going like that! *I* wanted to try and . . .

Terry Fuck you, Drew, you lying prick! I mean *after*. (*Beat.*) I saw you out there on the lawn as the cops were taking me away . . . You just watched me go. (*Beat.*) You two never said a word. NOT ONE WORD in my defence. *Ever*.

Drew No, Terry . . . that's not the . . .

Terry That's the story, Drew – you sold me out to our fucking father and then when you had a chance to do the right thing . . . you hid behind Mom's skirt like a little *bitch* and let 'em drag me off!

Drew . . . No . . . no . . . NO . . .

Terry You piece a' shit – look at you. A glass of *bubbly* in your hand and you're feeling pretty good about yourself, huh?

Drew What does that mean?

Terry Means you're a self-medicating fuck who can sell himself on just about anything! *Always* have been!

Drew Jesus Christ, Terry . . .

Terry SHUT UP! (*Seething.*) I have been there for you, Drew, tried to help as you've thrown your life away and you have never even acknowledged that night . . . not *once*!

Silence as Terry stops for a moment. Drew regroups.

Drew Look, Dad did all that to you and I'm sorry, I truly am – if you feel like I was to blame. I'm, I really didn't mean for anything like that to happen to . . . how could I? Terry, please . . . I'm not a bad guy, you know that, I'm not . . . at least not when I was twelve! (*Tries a laugh.*) Bro, please now – I mean, if we're gonna get all . . . 'full disclosure' here – ya jacked a *car*, Terry! Nobody made ya do that, they didn't, and I'm sorry if that was . . . you know. I dunno . . . (*Beat.*) I never wanted him to *hurt* you . . . God . . . even when it helped keep Mom and me from getting smacked around, that doesn't mean I ever would've wished it on you! I mean, no . . .

Terry That was *nothing*, Drew. You know that.

Drew It wasn't *nothing*, Terry, he . . .

Terry He could smack me all day long and I wouldn't say a thing. I was used to it by then – ohh, and as far as that 'car' goes, hell, I could've been outta custody in a few *hours* if somebody would've vouched for me. *Instead* they threw me in juvie for *four* years! (*Beat.*) Never did a thing wrong up until that age – not a stolen candy bar, *nothing* – and I was tossed out of that family like some carton a' bad *milk* . . . It was pretty breathtaking, I gotta tell you. To have it happen to you *as* you're watching it and not a *thing* you can do about it to save yourself – not one damn thing.

Drew Yeah, but, you . . . / OK, fine, I'm just a little confused here . . .

Terry It's true! / No, I think maybe what you're feeling is guilt . . . which must be an odd fucking *sensation* for you.

Drew What?

Terry You heard me.

Drew That's . . . for *what*? I didn't do anything!

Terry Exactly. That's exactly right.

Drew Oh, come on! – You wanna talk about the 'truth', why don't we at least *mention* the fact that you . . . before the police came you . . . / You know . . .

Terry Go on . . . / Go on, man . . .

Drew . . . you almost beat 'em to death! / I'm not saying that he didn't . . . but let's be *honest*, Terry . . . you put Dad in the hospital for *two* months!

Terry I know. / I know that . . .

Drew OK, then. So . . .

Terry And I'm sorry. I really am. (*Beat.*) I'm sorry I didn't kill 'em.

Drew . . . Terry . . .

Terry I will regret that every day for the rest of my life . . . (*Thinking.*) Standing there, in the dark of the garage with him all up in my – the light spilling in from outside – and after whacking me a few times, he gets right here, I mean, real close and sorta . . . and he kind of smiles and that hot breath of his . . . he says, 'You are outta here, you little fucker,' and he looks at me funny, looks and then adds: 'Ohh, and your boyfriend there's a goner, too.' And – for the first time – it hit me. That was *it* . . . this son-of-a-bitch was gonna ship me off and I was never gonna see Todd again. (*Beat.*) So I grabbed him, grabbed him so fast that he couldn't even react and I started to – I just launched in on him and I . . . I . . . it wasn't even me any more! He'd dropped to the ground after . . . I dunno, like, a few punches to the head and I got down there on top of him because, I mean, I was not through with him yet. I wanted to, to *just* . . .

Drew . . . Don't, Terry . . .

Terry But it was so *good*, Drew! It was so, so good to see the skin peel back off his face as I was . . . as I hit him there. Goddam! I'm always gonna remember that. How that made me feel . . . how *great* it felt to almost kill my father.

Terry stops now – there's nowhere else to go. Drew is off to one side. Silent.

Drew I'm sorry, Terry . . . I mean, if that is how you've felt for . . . / If that is what you think of me now then I don't know what to . . . say to you . . .

Terry I'm not angry, I'm really not . . . / Just clearing the air here, little brother, that's all. (*Beat.*) Every *pamphlet* I've read says to do that same damn thing. So there ya go.

Drew starts to say something but catches himself; instead he lets the idea soak in. Overtake him.

Drew . . . Yeah.

They seem to have reached a détente for now. A separate peace.

Terry Let's call it a day and I'll head out.

Drew You're always welcome – my *casa* is your *casa* or however those people say that shit. / Whatever.

Terry Dunno. / Maybe ask 'em when they're eating the *cake* outta your bushes.

Drew Ha! (*Laughs.*) You're still a funny guy, you know that? / Even if you walk around with this *dark cloud* thing going on, you're still very comical . . .

Terry Yeah. / Yep, I am one funny fella.

Drew drifts over and gives his brother a hug. Terry waits for him to finish. Drew smiles and hits him on the arm.

Drew I should prob'ly scoot back, dude. / Yep.

Terry Right to the end with that shit, huh? / Figures.

Terry nods at this and Drew reacts silently – shaking his head. Drew starts to say something, stops. Tries again.

Drew Look, Terry, I've been . . . I . . .

Terry What is it?

Drew It's . . . fuck, bro, nothing, I'm . . .

Terry Go on. (*Beat.*) Drew, *what*? Please.

Drew I'm just . . . wondered when, you know . . . we might see you again.

Drew looks off again toward the house and the party. He makes an involuntary step, even. Terry watches and waits.

Terry Maybe Christmas.

Drew Sounds good . . .

Terry Get some time with the kids.

Drew That'd be cool . . .

Terry Kids aren't 'cool', Drew. They're all that matters in this fucking world . . .

Drew I know. (*Beat.*) . . . I'll tell 'em goodbye for you. / I will, right when I get back.

Terry You do that. / Fine. Take care.

Drew You too, bro.

Terry You're an asshole, you're aware of that, right?

Drew I am. You have made it very, very clear for me . . .

Terry Good. Then we're covered . . .

Drew nods and starts off – he stops for a moment and watches Terry, who is looking up into the trees. Searching.

Where you gonna put it?

Drew Huh?

Terry The tree house – which one a' these you plan on using?

Drew Oh, I dunno yet. / Haven't got that far with it – just an idea, really.

Drew goes and looks into the sky where Terry is pointing. A light seems to click on inside Terry – he turns to Drew.

Terry OK. / Sure. (*Points.*) This one's good right up – see that pocket on your maple over there? It's nice.

Drew Yeah, right – I see the spot.

Terry 'S perfect.

Drew Yep.

Drew stares upward at the trees. Terry studies him.

Terry Strong . . .

Drew Uh-huh. I think that could work . . .

Terry suddenly grabs Drew into his arms, pulling him in tightly from behind. Drew resists, then slowly gives in.

Terry Lemme just hold you a second . . . Come on . . . / Stop it, Drew . . .

Drew . . . No . . . / Don't, Terry, you're . . . / Terry, please, I don't wanna.

Terry It's OK, Drew – Drew, stop . . . / Just relax for a second – Drew, STOP – IT! (*Beat.*) I know, OK? I *know* . . . I KNOW WHAT YOU'VE DONE.

With those words, Drew stops struggling – he almost melts into his brother's arms. Silence as they stand together.

Just figured it out. (*Beat.*) I was thinking about it, what you said, and I'm imagining your kids climbing up there and I'm thinking to myself, 'Well, they better be a whole lot braver than Drew 'cause he's a fucking wuss,' and then it just . . . (*Beat.*) You and Todd up in our fort . . . that couldn't've ever happened up there – 'cause Dad tore it down the summer before. It got all mixed together in my head . . . when you told me, but that's the truth. Isn't it? The old man did that the previous August, when he thought I was having too much fun up there so he tore it down, piece by piece, and made a dog house out of it. I 'member that now . . . it's all coming back to me. (*Beat.*) Doesn't matter, Drew . . . I promise. It's . . . it's OK. For a second there, just for a moment I thought 'How? *How* the fuck could you do that to me for a goddam *traffic ticket*? To somebody who you grew up with!' – but I understand why you did it. I GET IT . . . and I forgive you. I do. 'Cause I know what it's like to be frightened all the time . . .

Drew tries to say something, but can't come up with words; just keeps sucking in air. Terry finally releases him.

Terry stands there as Drew moves to him – burying his head in his brother's shoulder, Drew bursts out crying. Long, brutal sobs. Even Terry's eyes start to well up – he hugs Drew with a ferocity that surprises both of them.

Drew Man, don't remember the last time you ever gave *me* a hug – like, one that you started.

Terry It's 'cause that might be the first one. Right there.

Drew nods, still sniffling – he wipes his nose with the back of his suit coat sleeve. Tries to smile.

Drew I knew that you'd . . . you always see through my lies. / Eventually.

Terry . . . Yeah. / It's true.

Drew Even my best ones . . . (*Beat.*) Anyway, I'll call ya. I gotta get back up there, but I'll call . . .

Terry Fine. / Good.

Drew . . . and we can talk about stuff. / I mean, *all* of it. The whole . . .

Terry Yep. One a' these days.

Drew No, I'm *serious* here, Terry – I can say a lot of shit, promise things and all that, but I *mean* this! I'm gonna contact you, OK? I'll call and we can, you know . . . we'll talk. Get all of our stuff out in the open.

Terry Yeah, some time . . .

Drew No matter how hard it is for me, or . . . we'll do that. The two of us.

Terry You bet.

Drew Let's try and make it soon, OK?

Terry Alright then.

Drew We can do that, right? Talk?

Terry Uh-huh.

Drew Yeah. *Soon.* Really soon.

Terry . . . Sure.

> *Drew wipes his eyes and disappears into the woods.*
> *Terry is now alone. Finally, he sits. He reaches into his pants pocket and pulls out Jennifer's key chain.*
> *He holds it up and twists it in the dying light. Watches the glinting splinters dance around him as dusk begins to approach.*
> *Sound of traffic and the woods.*
> *Silence. Darkness.*

IN A FOREST, DARK AND DEEP

In a Forest, Dark and Deep was first performed in London at the Vaudeville Theatre on 3 March 2011. The cast was as follows:

Betty Olivia Williams
Bobby Matthew Fox

Director Neil LaBute
Design Soutra Gilmour
Sound Fergus O'Hare
Lighting Mark Henderson

In a Forest, Dark and Deep was first performed at Profiles Theatre, Chicago, Illinois, on 19 April 2012. The cast was as follows:

Bobby Darrell W. Cox
Betty Natasha Lowe

Director Joe Jahraus
Design Thad Hallstein
Sound Jeffrey Levin
Lighting John Kohn III, Bekki Lambrecht

Characters

Betty
Bobby

Author's Note

The / in certain lines denotes
an attempt at interruption or overlap
by a given character

Silence. Darkness.

We're in a room. It's not the only room in the place, but it seems to be pretty central. Doors and hallways lead off from this rustic space. An obvious front door.

Music was blasting before we started but now it's on the radio. Static but still loud. An eighties station.

Rain beats down on the windows and skylights. Tree limbs tap at the glass. Lightning flashes and thunder rattles.

After a moment, a woman appears above us. She's up in the loft space, moving quickly about as she fills an old box, mostly with books. This is Betty.

She makes her way down a set of stairs and places the box by the door. Wipes her hands on her shirt, turns the radio down and then spins to go back up the way she came. This room and the others are full of stuff, and the characters on stage will pack a lot of it up into boxes, bags, etc.

The lights flicker and go out for a moment, then back on. Betty looks up, then goes and lights a few candles.

Before she's done, a knock at the door. The woman crosses over to the door, peeks out, then tries to open the door but fights the lock. Finally issues in a man – not soaking wet, but he's damp. He carries a six-pack of Bud under an arm. This guy is Bobby.

Betty . . . I need . . . I gotta fix that door. / I owe you one for coming here tonight. (*A quick hug.*) God! Sorry it's so wet out.

Bobby Yeah. / No worries.

Betty No, seriously, I do, though. Owe you.

Bobby Fine. Gimme a towel, then . . .

Betty Honestly . . . (*She throws him one.*) I do.

Bobby OK, so you owe me. I'll jot it down, a piece a paper, stick it in the glove box. See what happens.

Betty You do that.

Bobby I'm gonna. (*Beat.*) Call you up, some night at half past nine when it's pissing down and see what's what.

Betty I would come.

Bobby Maybe.

Betty I would! God, that's not true . . . (*Hands him some cash.*) Anyway, here ya go.

Bobby No, that's . . . I don't need any . . .

Betty Yes . . . just take it . . .

Bobby I thought we said that I'd –

Betty Bobby, no, it's not a big – it's only a hundred bucks. Take it.

Bobby Fine. Whatever. (*Smiles.*) Anyways, you're just paying me now so you don't owe me anything later. I know you.

Betty No, don't say . . . No. That's not nice.

He pockets the cash. Snaps open a beer and takes a drink. Looks at his sister but can't hold her gaze.

Bobby Doesn't have to be nice as long as it's true. 'The truth hurts' – haven't you ever heard that one before?

Betty No.

Bobby What? You're lying . . .

Betty Not at all – is that a saying, or . . . ?

Bobby Jesus, that's the oldest one in the book!

Betty Huh, well, I've never heard it.

Bobby 'Truth hurts, don't it?' You've really never heard that? (*Beat.*) Come on, Dad used to say it. All the time...

Betty No...

Bobby Oh, for Chrissakes! Come on! He did so.

Betty Then I don't remember it... 'Truth hurts.' Hmm. No. (*Beat.*) I thought it 'set you free' or something...

Bobby That's insane. I mean, we sat at the same dinner table for, what, twenty years or so, off and on, and you don't remember the old man saying that? (*Imitating him.*) 'The truth hurts, Bobby. Stings like a bitch. That's why they call it that... the *truth*.' He must've said it, like, a thousand times! At *least* that, if not more...

Betty That's a pretty good imitation...

Bobby Fuck that, it's spot on. *Spot.* He was always saying that kinda shit to me.

Betty Well, then, you must've been a bad boy when you were younger...

Bobby Yeah, right. (*Smiles.*) I did my share... Not a *professional* like you, but still.

This makes them both smile. She reaches over and gives a little tussle to his wet hair. She checks her watch.

You seriously don't know that phrase? 'The truth hurts'? I mean, I'm just...

Betty Bobby! Shit! Of course I know it. Yes... of *course* I do! I mean, please. Everybody knows that one – I was *kidding*! God! I was pulling your leg.

Bobby Really? You were?

Betty Yes, *obviously*. 'The truth hurts', that is so old, it's a . . . Trust me. Yes, I remember him saying that. And not just to you. Others, too. Over the years.

Bobby So you did remember? You were just giving me shit about it, but you do know?

Betty Yeah. 'Fraid so.

Bobby Oh.

Betty Sorry. (*Smiles.*) Truth hurts, don't it?

Bobby . . . Ha. Bitch.

Betty Nope. *Sister*.

He grudgingly smiles then looks round the place. Takes it all in as he drops the towel on a counter-top. Shaking his head. She wanders over to a wine glass, takes a sip.

Bobby Anyways . . . (*Pointing.*) So this is nice. It's very what? *Rustic*, I guess. Cute. With all the little . . . (*Points.*) Whatnots.

Betty Yeah. (*Smiles.*) It's good to see you . . .

Bobby You too. Uh-huh. (*Beat.*) Hey, how'd you fuck up the car there? Your front side-panel and all that?

Betty Oh, God, that's . . . so dumb! I was, this is ridiculous, but I hit one of those carts at the market. Shopping carts?

Bobby Yeah, I know what they are. You did, huh?

Betty Uh-huh. Didn't even see it – you know when people leave them out in the lot after unloading, they won't walk it over to the thingy where you're supposed to –

Bobby The cart corral.

Betty What?

Bobby 'Cart corral'. That's what they ask you to do – return them to the corral. That's the name for it.

Betty Really? I didn't . . . Huh.

Bobby Used to work at Safeway, remember? When I was a kid. (*Beat.*) You used to come in and shoplift . . .

Betty True. (*Beat.*) Anyway, that's what I did.

Bobby Huh. Bet ol' Bruce was pissed . . .

Betty Not really. (*Beat.*) Pretty quiet about it, like usual. Like he is about most things.

Bobby Yeah? I guess so . . . he's kind of a pussy about that sorta stuff. Like . . . 'life'.

Betty Bobby, don't.

Bobby I'm just saying . . . (*Smiles.*) That's all.

Betty What?

Bobby He puts up with a lot of your shit.

Betty What does that mean?

Bobby Nothing. Just that. Dinging car doors and all your, ya know, *conventions* and stuff. Shit I'd never let you get away with . . .

Betty Yeah? You wouldn't?

Bobby Fuck no.

Betty Well then, I'm glad I didn't marry you!

Bobby Ha! (*Laughs.*) I bet you are! You and about a *million* other girls . . .

Betty And I don't go to 'conventions'. I'm not a salesman . . . they're *conferences*. They're a big deal, some of 'em, with people from all over the country speaking. *Authors.* / They're an important part of my job . . .

Bobby Yeah, whatever. / Anyways, I'm sure you got a deductible on it. The car.

Betty We do. It's not bad, really. A scratch . . . Bruce barely did anything when he saw it. I think he said he could 'buff it out'.

Bobby nods at this, seemingly satisfied. He glances about the room, taking it all in. Betty watches him.

Bobby Huh. (*Beat.*) We gotta do all this tonight?

Betty I'd like to, yes. We've got people lined up to come see it and so we'd like to get it all . . . anyway. (*Beat.*) We call it 'semi-furnished' but this is a bit *much* . . .

Bobby No shit! (*Beat.*) You shoulda told Hansel and Gretel to clean up after themselves.

He picks up a book, studies the cover as he finishes his beer. Makes a face and drops the book back down.

Betty I know! It's a lot, right?

Bobby I mean, fuck. *Yeah.* Kinda.

Betty Sorry, but I just . . . anyway, not all of it has to go. Most of the furniture can . . . I'll show you. Sections. In fact a lot of it can stay, but . . .

Bobby OK. Just thinking I coulda brought the 450. Lots more cargo space.

Betty True.

Bobby You shoulda said something, or . . . it's a long way to go back now. In the dark.

Bobby lifts up a couple of magazines. Snooping. Drops them.

IN A FOREST, DARK AND DEEP

Betty I *know*. This just came up. I didn't have anyone to – Bruce had a call he needed to make so he stayed with the boys . . . and so I'm – yeah, I'm sorry. It wasn't planned so I didn't think about . . .

Bobby Doesn't matter now. I'm here.

Betty Right.

Bobby You asked and I came running, so let's . . . just . . . you know? Do it.

Betty True. OK. (*Looking around.*) Let's start in here and move outwards. Do upstairs last.

Bobby 'Kay.

Betty Sound good?

He nods his head and looks around. What to do first?

Bobby Fine. Work's work.

Betty Another thing the old man used to say . . . one of his many 'wisdoms'.

Bobby Yep. (*Beat.*) Thought you might enjoy that – if you could *remember* it. (*Smiles.*) Idiot.

Betty That's me . . .

Bobby Always doing some stupid thing. Right?

Betty Hey . . .

Bobby It's true. When we were kids? That's completely true . . . you were a total dumbshit.

Betty Yeah, well, maybe, but who's making more money now? You or me?

Bobby Fuck that, money's got nothing to do with being stupid.

Betty Oh, really?

Bobby Course not! That's the real 'American dream'. Don't matter if you're a dumb fuck, did shitty on your SATs, you can still drive around in a Cadillac and be a big shot . . .

Betty That's quite a theory there . . .

Bobby Absolutely true. I've made choices, led to where I'm at, what I get paid – same as you and where you are. This big college professor at some *liberal arts* program. So what? Point being, neither one of us ever left *home*. That's kinda pathetic . . .

Betty Hey, it's something – don't say that. I'm proud of what I've . . . Doesn't matter. You think what you want. I'm happy with where I'm . . . Plus, I'm the *Dean* now, which is . . .

He holds his hands up in mock-respect. Makes a face.

Bobby *Awesome*. It's what you do. You make more than me because you're free in the summer and that's all. Same salary, less months. I figured it out on a calculator once.

Betty Ahhh. Thought it didn't matter.

Bobby It doesn't. I was just curious . . .

Betty Sure.

Bobby I was! I don't give a shit how much you make, sis, I promise, or where you live or the house sits up on a *hill*. That's not me, what I'm interested in. (*Beat.*) We're both better off than any dude you meet on the street in Africa, and I mean any country they got down there. *Any*. That true or not? Seriously.

Betty God, the way your mind works, it's –

Bobby It's not racist.

Betty Oh, really?

Bobby It's not! I didn't say who: I mean *any* dude you see, white guy or a black one. Doesn't matter. Poor bastard was born in that shithole, he is just plain fucked and that's all there is. He's gonna get Aids or, or, like, his hands cut off or sold into slavery – I'm saying in the past, but they still do shit like that, taking kids for their armies – It is a fucking *nightmare* down there. The dark continent indeed, right? Fucker's as pitch black as the bottom of their own goddam feet. You know? It'd suck to be African.

Betty Bobby. (*Beat.*) They're white.

Bobby What?

Betty The bottom of . . . Forget it.

Bobby No, what? *What?*

Betty Most African – all black people, I mean, in general – their feet are white. Or pink or whatever . . . on the bottoms.

Bobby *No* . . .

Betty Think about it.

Bobby That's . . . (*Dawns on him.*) Oh yeah. That's true.

Betty See?

Bobby But . . .

Betty I'm just saying. So . . .

Bobby Whatever! You know what I fucking meant. It's an analogy.

Betty Yeah, but not one that works . . .

Bobby I don't give a shit! Dark as their faces, then! Or the inside of their *armpits*. All the rest of 'em's black, correct?

Betty Eyeballs.

Bobby Whatever! Whatever dark spot you wanna pick then, *that's* what Africa is like. BLACK AS FUCK.

Betty Fine. Jesus. (*Beat.*) Can we just . . . ?

Bobby Anyway, that has nothing to do with the first part of what I was saying, anyway. (*Beat.*) *First* bit I said was about being stupid and a pain in everybody's ass . . . which was very much your story. Right?

Betty What are you talking about?

Bobby 'Bout you as a trouble-maker. That's what started the whole conversation . . .

Betty I know, I know, but that's not . . .

Bobby Lemme just finish. I'm just saying that a lot of things happened in our family – all this crying and tension and shit of that nature – due to choices you made. Guys you picked to run around with. You wanna say it's fine, no big deal, you were a *kid*, but lots of lousy times came from what you did. Mom moving out the house for a while even, siding with you – I hated her for all that. Now, it's all crap that you've straightened out, I agree, still at the time it was pretty monumental to them as parents and us as a family . . . but you just had to keep on doing it. You wouldn't listen to anybody in those days, not even Mom, after a while . . . Nobody could tell you shit. So. (*Beat.*) That's me just clarifying what I meant by 'stupid' when I said it earlier. No offence. No harm done, I guess. Off ya go to grad school and life seemed to move on and then, poof! Outta nowhere, back ya come again, teaching at our local college like no one remembers anything you did or all the, like, *heartbreak* you created . . . (*Beat.*) Most normal people can't do that sorta thing: wipe the slate clean and do it all over. I'm just pointing that out.

Betty has stood by and listened to Bobby's little rant.

Betty Ha!

Bobby Seriously. *I* couldn't.

Betty I should've just called the moving guys! Didn't know I'd get a free *Dr Phil* hour.

Bobby Hey, I'm just talking. You're the one who got into the pissing contest about *status* and pay cheques, all that shit.

Betty I stated a fact, that's all.

She turns and moves toward a stack of empty fruit boxes. Bobby watches her go as he cracks open another beer.

Bobby Right.

She stops and turns to him. Tension is starting to build.

Betty I did.

Bobby You pushed a button.

Betty I thought it didn't matter.

Bobby It doesn't, but . . . hey . . . keep pushing.

Betty What? It either does or doesn't . . .

Bobby You know what it does. (*Beat.*) Try it out on your husband there, when you get back home – who makes even less than me, by the way – see what that presses . . .

Betty All I said was –

Bobby You did the same thing you always do, any time we're together . . .

Betty No, that's not at all what I –

Bobby Yes, yes, you do, you get into the money thing a *second* after any argument starts or if we talk about the past, it's all ya got! It's your only ammo so you use it . . . I understand what you're doing, I do, but it gets pretty old pretty fucking quick. You've made a name for yourself in your field, you read *papers* out loud to people every now and then, folks who don't give a fuck what you wrote, they just want to read *their* papers . . . (*Shrugs.*) So what?

Betty Bullshit, Bobby! That is bullshit and I don't do that . . . about my position. (*Beat.*) God, you are *so* like Dad that way, I mean really . . . so goddam judgemental! I think I'm doing fairly OK for me – as a woman, as, as a teacher, whatever! I mean, shit!

She stares him down. Bobby shrugs and leaves it alone.

Bobby Betty, please. Fuck. Come on . . . I didn't mean to start a 'thing'. (*Beat.*) Can we just pack this place up, OK? I do not need to sit up tonight talking about us and where we are in life. I don't. You'd like nothing better than to show me your pay stubs but I have places to be, things that mean more in my life to me now than a *plaque* on my door. I got work tomorrow and I know you're on your whatever-the-fuck-you-call-it so you can sleep in . . .

Betty Sabbatical . . .

Bobby Which sounds all important and religious but really just means you asked for time off to dick around and read *novels*, so . . .

Betty How did we come out of the same womb? I'm being serious, how?

Bobby We didn't. I was raised by wolves.

Betty True.

Bobby And you ran with 'em. Didn't ya?

Betty Who?

Bobby The wolves . . .

Betty Ha! You're funny.

Bobby Whatever. (*Beat.*) I mean, let's be true . . . you had a pretty good go of it when you were younger, like, just the *number* of guys you ended up with . . . for being, you know, a pretty average girl.

Betty . . . And what's that mean? Huh?

Bobby Nothing! No . . . we don't need to get into this stuff and I'm just your brother, so what the hell do I know, but you weren't like some gorgeous person when you were fifteen, sixteen. You were sorta chunky, even. Your legs were OK but you had a kinda dumpy ass. Not so big, but dumpy . . . (*Beat.*) Anyway, that's all.

Betty *Thank you* . . .

Bobby I'm just pointing out some things . . .

Betty OK, I don't need any – Can we get started? Let's just . . . I really need to get through this . . . shit . . . tonight. (*Beat.*) We can get together some other time and fight.

He shrugs his shoulders and stops himself from going on.

Bobby Fine by me. (*Beat.*) When did this happen, by the way? Your little secret?

She stops and looks at him strangely – it takes a moment before she speaks. He gulps down some beer.

Betty . . . What do you mean?

Bobby I'm saying this cabin, when did you guys get into all this?

Betty Oh. Right. Just . . . a while ago . . .

Bobby Yeah? You never told me. (*Beat.*) Strange that you're buying up local . . .

Betty What?

Bobby I dunno . . . *property*. That you guys are out doing that and, you know, in this economy, yet I never knew it. Interesting.

Betty Oh.

Bobby I never heard a word. Per usual.

Betty Sorry. We've been busy, you know, with . . . And it's just *one*, OK? That's all. Just the one unit. (*Beat.*) We always wanted a place near the lake and it's great for us to use it . . . or *rent* it out as we . . . Yeah.

Bobby But they've gotta be converted and shit, right? When you switch them over to being rentals and all that. True?

Betty They're . . . I mean . . . Yes, but . . .

Bobby Huh.

Betty So? What?

Bobby I'm not saying anything.

Betty Yes, you are. *What?*

Bobby No, nothing, just that I'm a *carpenter* and, you know, do that sorta work, so it just seems . . . odd . . . that you'd buy a thing like this and don't even . . .

Betty That's not it at all.

Bobby No?

Betty No, it's not. Bobby. Bruce just wanted to do some of it himself and then we got to the point where it's –

God, you're always so . . . fucking . . . ready to take offence!

Bobby Yeah, well . . . There's a lot of *offenders* out there. And I don't just mean women.

Betty Well, good. How progressive of you.

Bobby I'm not including the cunts I date. (*He smiles.*) That was a joke . . .

He smiles and grabs a box. Starts filling it with books.

Supposed to be, anyway. Probably not for someone as cultured as you . . .

Betty No. Probably not. Or someone, say, *human*.

Bobby That's not true, uh-uh. I knows lots of humans who woulda laughed at that. *Lots*. Only stuck-up pricks don't laugh at funny shit . . .

Betty Nice. Remind me never to accept an invite to one of your bar-b-cues . . .

Bobby Ha! When would I ever have you over to my place?

Betty I was kidding.

Bobby Me, too. I mean, about the 'cunt' thing. But seriously, when? I stopped asking you to hang out with me years ago . . . big sis.

They stop for a moment – they've been circling each other, looking for a place to strike. To move in for the kill. Betty checks her watch again. Bobby finishes his beer.

We should get going, if we're gonna strip this place down. (*Grinning.*) I will not be doing any windows, by the way . . .

Betty Yeah? You're old-fashioned like that?

Bobby Nah, I just hate looking at my fucking reflection. (*Beat.*) I feel like such a failure. Maybe if I made more *money* . . .

Betty Ha! (*She laughs.*) Stupid.

Bobby I know you are, but what am I? (*Beat.*) I told you, *you're* the stupid one, not me.

Betty OK, I got it, I'm stupid, cool – now can we get down to business?

Bobby Yep.

Betty Alright then.

Bobby It's your place, tell me what to do.

Betty Umm, those books are fine, what you were going to do, that's great. I'm gonna grab these . . . along with a few other small bits and then I'll just need to wipe down the fridge and maybe the toilet and tub . . . Oh, and there's a file cabinet that I wanted us to . . . (*Points.*) The loft.

Bobby looks up the narrow stairs to the loft space.

Bobby Ohhh . . . (*Considering this.*) *Why?*

Betty What?

Bobby I'm just asking . . . why're you taking all the books and, and . . . the officey crap?

Betty Because –

Bobby It's none of my business, just tell me and I'll shut up. (*Beat.*) Doesn't matter.

Betty No, it's fine, I'll . . . I'm going to gift a few of them – the good ones, hardbacks – to the library and then, you know, I thought I'd take the rest over to, I don't know, the Salvation Army or somewhere. (*Beat.*) You know how I am about books . . .

Bobby Cool. I was just curious.

Betty And the files are – I mean the cabinet, not anything inside – is mine. From when I was going to make this my office . . . and then I just left them here, but now I figure I'm – Anyway! Blah-blah-blah. Right?

Bobby Hey, you said it. (*Smiles.*) So . . .

Betty Fine. *So* . . . yeah, let's just separate the textbooks and stuff out. You can do all of those. (*Points.*) I already started in the loft but these can go, too.

Bobby Got it. (*Beat.*) Where is this guy? What're we gonna do here, put the rest in storage or you wanna dump it all?

Betty Umm, he's . . . How did you know that? That it's a guy who lived here . . . ?

Bobby Oh, you know . . . stuff. It's guy stuff. The way he keeps it and everything. Sorta in order but messy.

Betty Huh.

Bobby And dusty, too. Guys aren't, like, great at cleaning and shit. We *arrange* good, if we have to, but the actual lifting up of things and sweeping under and around? Not our strong suit. Plus, I don't think a girl is gonna pick out here as her first choice of safe spots . . . way out in the forest. (*Beat.*) So, is it?

Betty What?

Bobby A dude who lived here?

Betty Umm . . . yes, I think so. Bruce does most of the actual . . . But yeah, I believe this was a man. Who stayed here. Yes. A boy.

Bobby Great. (*Looking around.*) Lot of stuff for a guy. Magazines and shit. Was he a fag?

Betty Bobby!

Bobby What? Gay, then. Fuck, you're so . . . was he gay? I mean, look. (*Beat.*) *The New Yorker*.

Betty Why would you ask that? Or care, even?

Bobby I don't. Just curious.

Betty Yeah, but . . . (*Looking around.*) Where does that come from? Whether he's . . . ?

Bobby Just the little shit. Magazines stacked on the coffee table like that. That blanket there, tossed on the edge of the couch.

Betty So?

Bobby *So* – he wants me to notice what he's got. It's all a *look*, which is what gay guys do a lot. He wants me to be aware of it, but not too much. They call it 'studied casual'. I saw a thing about it once. On *Ellen* or one of those fucking shows. (*He looks at Betty.*) What? She oughta know . . .

Betty Wow, that's quite a little . . . theory . . . you got there. About this guy.

Bobby I'm just guessing . . . but I bet I'm right.

Betty I don't know. Sorry.

Bobby Doesn't matter.

Bobby picks up a photo off a shelf and holds it up. Nice-looking young man smiling in the picture.

This the guy?

Betty I dunno. I guess so.

Bobby Picture of himself in a silver frame. From *Tiffany's*. Guy's *definitely* gay . . .

Betty laughs and goes back to picking through stuff. The picture is replaced by Bobby, who continues to browse.

Betty Stop! (*Waits.*) He's a second-year senior, that's all I know. Working on his thesis and, umm . . . needed a quiet place to live.

Bobby Cool.

Crack of thunder and lightning. Lights flicker again.

Betty Yeah, but he . . . I think Bruce said his family – mother, maybe? – has cancer . . . not long to live or something like that.

Bobby Huh.

Betty . . . He took off and left his stuff here. Guess he figured the deposit would cover the . . . you know . . . I'm not sure about the rest, actually. (*Beat.*) We've got people now who wanna take a look, so . . .

Bobby Oh. (*Beat.*) Fine, let's pack it up and we can toss it, or however you wanna do it.

Betty Great. So, you start with books and I'll do the . . . personal effects.

Bobby OK then. (*Beat.*) Can we turn it up? The music, I mean. While we work?

Betty Umm, sure. That's . . . why not?

Betty drifts toward another part of the room – not really cleaning up so much as picking through things. Bobby goes to the radio, searches for a station. Lands on something.
He moves back to the books and begins packing.

One song is just finishing – something from the eighties – and U2's 'I Will Follow' comes on next.
After a moment, both brother and sister are bopping their heads and moving a bit to the music. They notice and then come together, dancing wildly (or as 'wildly' as folks in their forties can dance) until the song is over.
Bobby has to coax his sister to let loose at times, but they both continue.

Bobby Come on! Go for it!

Betty What? I'm *dancing*! These're all the moves I've got!

The music ends. Next song is a slow one and they start to move to it as well but come to a fumbling stop.
They collapse where they are in the room. Betty turns off the radio as they both suck down oxygen.

Bobby Hey! What're you doing? I was just starting to get into it . . .

Betty Can't take it! Oh shit, I'm old! When did that happen?

Bobby You and me both . . . I gotta start to, you know, jog or some shit. I mean, one of these days . . .

They both smile and then laugh. Still both out of breath.

Betty Well, good, we're getting lots done . . . (*Grins.*) Dammit! No more radio . . . come on.

Bobby Aye aye, captain. (*Beat.*) Hey, U2 really used to fucking rock, didn't they? Like, back in the day. / When even that guitar guy had hair . . .

Betty Yep. / Bobby!

Bobby And before the other one started thinking he was Jesus or somebody.

Betty Ha! Who, Bono?

Bobby Whatever. Dude with the sunglasses. Guy decided to feed the world and, like, *two* albums later they sucked ass . . .

Betty Can you just . . . (*She waves him off.*) Go do those shelves.

Bobby Am I wrong? *Bono.* (*Beat.*) And 'The Edge'! Not 'Edge', no, '*The* Edge'. I mean, who in the fuck calls themselves that?

Betty I don't know! I was busy with my own life the last . . . however long. I didn't follow U2 and all their . . . whatever. *Exploits*.

Bobby Well, good, then I can fill you in on all you missed. (*Smiling.*) Don't buy anything after *Joshua Tree*. The rest is crap.

Betty Got it.

Bobby Just a little tip. I mean, seriously . . . *Zooropa*. The *fuck* is that? (*Pointing.*) And now, the books . . .

Betty Thank you! God, you're a piece of work . . .

Bobby Yeah, I know, I've been informed of this at various points in my life. In so many words . . .

Betty Ha! (*Smiles.*) I can only imagine.

Bobby You can more than imagine – you know *both* of my exes.

Betty This is true.

Bobby In fact, I think you sided with both, if memory fucking serves . . .

Betty The first one, absolutely. Second time all I said was 'Save yourself and get the hell out.' Is that siding with her?

Bobby I think technically, yeah.

They both laugh at this – time heals all wounds, I guess.

Betty You didn't speak to me for almost a year after Yvonne left you. Maybe longer. Up until that next Christmas.

Bobby I know.

Betty Which was hardly fair . . .

Bobby You said some shit. Some pretty mean shit at the time which I didn't care for . . .

Betty I know, but . . .

Bobby Seriously, we can laugh about it now but during the break-up –

Betty – during the break-up you were being a really first-class asshole to her . . . *and* I was getting sick of the 911 calls.

Bobby Maybe that was my relationship and you didn't need to have your nose in it . . .

Bobby swoops over and picks up a box. Begins to pile some books into it.

Betty Maybe your wife asked me to help . . .

Bobby *Maybe* you were too fucking close to my wife for your own . . . Fuck it. Whatever. Let's drop it.

Betty Happy to.

Bobby I mean it.

Betty I do, too. Honestly.

Bobby We have hashed all of this out already a lot of times . . .

Betty Too many . . .

Bobby Maybe so, yeah. So let's just . . . Books. I am on it. *Books*.

Betty I'm gonna start in the kitchen now so we can keep this moving . . .

Bobby Fine. Go for it.

Betty moves into another area of the room – just a little kitchen extension – as Bobby continues with the books.

Who the fuck was this kid, Barnes or Noble?

Betty Ha! He was an English major . . . I think.

Bobby Yeah, I figured that one out.

Betty Well . . .

Bobby So he *was* one of yours, then? This guy?

Betty Yes. I mean, no, not really . . . *technically* I suppose he lands in my . . . but I'm not in that department any more. My office is now in the Humanities Building. Across campus from there, actually.

Bobby Oh. But still . . . English falls under your jurisdiction or whatever. Right?

Betty I guess so, yes. It's not really that – 'jurisdiction'. I'm not a cop.

Bobby Whatever! Don't bust my ass over words or you can pack up your own goddam boxes . . . understood?

Betty Sorry. It's a habit.

Bobby Yeah, well . . . it's none of my business, but Jesus! Give these guys a break, why don't ya? (*Pointing.*) This is ridiculous.

Betty What do you mean?

Bobby Kid spent all his lunch money on books! Let 'em watch a *movie* once in a while . . . No wonder he ran away!

Betty Why? What?

Bobby He probably made up that cancer story . . . about his mom. Truth is, he couldn't keep up with the reading assignments! Twenty-two years old and you ruined him for life with all your Tolstoys and Hemingways and those other douchebags.

Betty You really have, like, no respect for anyone, do you?

Bobby Sure, I do . . . not for writing *fiction* I don't, but people who have actually done things, yeah, I've got a ton of respect.

Betty What's that supposed to mean?

Bobby Guy who unclogged my septic tank week ago Thursday? Him I respect. That cop who got shot out on I-94 last month by some Asian dude he pulled over? I respect him a lot. But some rich guy sits down and types up a little novel – *Great Gatsby* or not – who the fuck cares about him? I like people who *work* for a living . . . not some pack of actors or dancers or dickheads like that. *Artists* are a waste of fucking space . . .

Betty That is *so* . . . No . . . this is our usual fight we get into at, whenever . . . Thanksgiving or . . . so, no . . . not gonna do it tonight.

Bobby Fine.

Betty I'm not. NO.

Bobby Whenever you wanna start up again . . .

Betty Another time.

Bobby I'm gonna feel the same way. *Exactly* the same, I promise you.

Betty Fine, rain check then.

Bobby You got it.

Betty I mean . . . *The Great Gatsby*? (*Beat.*) I swear you go out of your way to say things that piss me off. (*Beat.*) How can you even . . . ?

Bobby Only good part's when he gets shot.

Betty Who?

Bobby Gatsby! In the pool. I liked that.

Betty Oh, for God's sake . . .

Bobby Or when he lets that chick drive his car and she smashes into the other – (*Off her look.*) Yeah, I know. Do the books!

Betty Please . . .

He nods and smiles, returning to the task at hand. Betty moves from shelf to shelf in the kitchen.
   Another blast of thunder. The lights flicker and go out.

Awww, shit. Come on!

Bobby You want me to do it?

Betty No, God . . . the box is just in the mud-room there . . . Hold on. (*Hands him a flashlight.*) I got it.

Betty disappears into another room. Flash of lightning.
   Bobby picks up another stack of books and moves to an open box. The book on top slides off and falls

to the ground. A picture slips out of the pages and on to the floor.

Bobby picks it up, goes to shove it back into the volume. He glances at the photo. Stops. Looks at it again.

The lights flicker and come back on. Betty enters again.

Bobby puts the rest of the books in a box, then crosses over to his sister and hands her the picture. Walks away.

She looks at it. Over at him. He has returned to removing books from the shelves.

What?

Bobby Nothing.

Betty No, what? Obviously you're thinking . . .

Bobby No, I'm not.

Betty Bobby, come on . . . BOBBY . . .

Bobby *What?*

Betty Talk to me. (*Beat.*) Please.

Bobby What would I be thinking? Hmm? *What?* (*He shrugs.*) You're the one with the *Master's*. You tell me . . .

Betty Just say something! Ask me some questions or . . . just don't give me the silent treatment. OK? Don't be an idiot.

Bobby You're right – I shouldn't do that, I do not wanna be an idiot, but you know what? It's hard not to be. It is difficult not to be the dumbshit of the fucking month when you're getting played. (*Beat.*) And I am, aren't I? Right now. Oh yeah . . .

Betty What's that supposed to mean? Huh?

Bobby You tell me. Sis. YOU TELL ME WHAT IS UP.

Bobby continues to stack up books as Betty stares at him.

Betty I can explain . . .

Bobby Oh man, I hope it gets better than that.

Betty What?

Bobby That's the worst line ever. *Ever.* 'I can explain.' Of course you can! I bet you've had your *explanation* worked out since the first day you . . . well, whatever the fuck it is you're gonna tell me is going on.

Betty Nothing is 'going on' . . .

Bobby Oh, really?

Betty No, it's not. I mean, not in the present tense. 'Going' on, no, it's not.

Bobby Bullshit. You and your word games . . . don't do the fucking Bill Clinton thing with me here, alright? Do not, because I will . . . fucking . . .

Betty I'm telling you the truth, Bobby. You did ask and so I am telling you.

Bobby Fine. Go ahead.

Betty I am. (*Beat.*) There is nothing going on in the sense that you're thinking. Honest.

Bobby Great. Don't worry about me. I handed you a picture, that's all I did.

Betty I know, but . . .

Bobby The rest is your stuff. It's your shit . . .

Betty That's what I'm saying, though, Bobby, I don't have any 'shit' going on. It's just a photo. (*Holding it up.*) Look.

Bobby Of the guy. From here.

Betty Yes.

Bobby The guy from here *and* you.

Betty I know that.

Bobby Of you two standing there and . . . you know.

Betty Uh-huh. Just 'standing'.

Bobby motions for the rest, jumbling his hands together.

Bobby *Close*. Your faces are close together and he's . . . his arm's around your . . .

Betty I KNOW. OK? Yes, I'm aware of that fact.

Bobby And yet you're . . . all this time . . . you're giving me the whole . . . bullshit!

Betty What?

Bobby Oh, I dunno! He's a 'second-year senior' and 'Bruce is the one who *actually* . . .' (*Beat.*) That's shit, all this is crap you've been saying to me so far! Right?

Betty . . .

Bobby RIGHT? (*Beat.*) I mean, '*cancer*'! Come on!!

Betty Some of it. Yeah. Yes, it is. (*Beat.*) This was taken at a . . . We were at a seminar in, I don't even remember. (*Turns it over.*) . . . There's no date here . . . must've been in, maybe, January or around there. At a conference. On *semiotics*.

Bobby Uh-huh.

Betty And nothing! He was in fact a second-year senior at the time and I . . . yes, I didn't tell the truth earlier. I knew him. *Know* him. Obviously.

Bobby Obviously.

Betty And . . . very bright and, and studying in my field so I was instrumental in moving him forward in the department, I mean, toward his degree. His thesis project. (*Beat.*) We are close here because of the cold – I was worried you'd *overreact* if I told you he was in my . . . So I didn't. I chose not to.

> *Bobby and Betty face each other. Very quiet for a moment. Finally, he turns back to the books and starts packing.*

What're you doing?

Bobby What you asked me here for . . . The fuck else am I gonna do?

Betty I know, but . . .

Bobby Didn't bring me out here to chat, I know that. Not to open your heart up to me . . . I get it, got it, so let's get done.

Betty Bobby.

Bobby I have a truck, I don't ask questions . . .

Betty That's not why I –

Bobby Yes, it is! Please don't make me out to be a retard on top of the rest of it . . . do you mind? Just don't.

Betty I wanted your help. That's why I called you.

Bobby Yeah, to *lift* shit! Because you can't fit all this crap in your goddam *Prius*, that is why – let's not make it into something more than it is, sis.

Betty Yes, but . . . I'm . . . I asked *you* to, to . . .

Bobby To carry crates of this guy's fucking papers and *underwear* outside, not because you actually *need* me.

(*Beat.*) I'm a fucking pack horse to you, that's all . . . a drug mule. I – GET – IT.

Betty Not true. That is not . . .

Bobby Just don't! Please! Your condescending ways are always irritating, but today . . . (*Indicating.*) Right about here. Just in the back of my goddam throat right now.

Betty If you'd just let me . . . just . . .

Bobby I don't need any more explanation from you, I really don't. It's pretty obvious now . . . and the gory details are not what I wanna spend the rest of my night thinking about if you don't mind. OK?

Betty Alright. If that's what you . . . really . . .

Bobby Yeah, it is, thanks very much . . . (*Beat.*) *Now* I see why you're in such a fucking hurry. So you can get home to Bruce . . . and 'the kids', you said to me! That's just . . . fucking . . . creepy and pathetic, just so you know. TO USE THEM LIKE THAT. I mean, Goddam! Your own *children* . . .

Betty I'm not gonna argue about this with you, Bobby . . . You don't know any of the . . .

Bobby And I don't wanna! At all. You and your shiny name on your desk can't make this look any better than it is, no matter if the fucking *French* do it all the time or not. Here in America we pretty much still consider this shit a *commandment* . . .

Betty What does that even mean? You're being . . .

Bobby It sucks, what you've done, that's what it means! SUCKS. (*Beat.*) If I was Bruce I would smash you right in the face . . .

Betty Is that right?

Bobby That is absolutely correct. Right in your goddam uppity little nose . . .

Betty And we wonder why your marriages didn't last . . .

Bobby FUCK. YOU. (*Beat.*) Seriously, sis, I mean that from the heart. Fuck you. You think I hit either of those bitches more than they did me? Huh? I was behind about *two hundred* to one. Yep. Easily. But it's all about the guy in that situation – one shot and you're fucked. One little *tap* and now you're a wife-beater. Scumbag. Meanwhile this girl you married – you used to adore every step she took – she is smacking on you like you're a football dummy . . . every day, just the way she was raised. Screaming at you and wailing away and ya know what? Too much of that shit and I don't care who you are. Anybody – and I mean *any*body on this Earth – at some point, you're gonna take a swing at her in return. I promise you will.

Betty listens to him and doesn't say anything back. Bobby stares her down.

But I never cheated on either one of 'em. No, I did not. We maybe had problems and that's a matter of record –

Betty *Public* record.

Bobby True enough, but I didn't fuck around. On anybody, in fact, that I ever dated, even when I was young and good-looking and had chicks bending over toward me, asking for it – if I was with somebody, that was it. I saw that shit through to the end . . . did not even *think* about another skirt until I was finished with the one in front of me. Seriously. (*Beat.*) Dad taught me that and it stuck with me. To this day . . .

Betty Well, great for you guys. So *noble*.

Bobby Hey, hey, I'm not talking about great or, like, being *Superman* here – this is just a common courtesy that we're supposed to do as people to each other. (*Beat.*) You're in a relationship, OK. You're with Bruce at this point, married with kids, that's it – you're not supposed to be banging anybody else. Get it? And not anybody else's *kid*, either. Thought students were a no-no . . .

Betty We're not . . . (*Beat.*) It was cold out. That is all. I don't know where you get the . . .

Bobby Betty. *Please.*

Betty I'm serious! I don't need you doing any fantasising for me, alright? I can do it for myself if I need to, but I don't. I'm fine with my life and I'll tell you now: yes, I lied about knowing him. *Yes*, I did do that. I was embarrassed. I'm sorry . . . you caught me off guard so I just . . . He's a boy from the English Department who I have given some . . . attention to . . . and . . .

Bobby 'Attention' . . .

Betty Yes, that's right! Believe me, you teach this stuff over and over, middle of what most people would comfortably think of as 'nowhere' and someone shows up. My God . . . he's actually read the material! He *likes* the subject, he can put two sentences to use in a paper . . . it doesn't take much . . . and you make a connection. A connection with another *person*. It's not carnal . . . it doesn't mean you're in heat or about to run away from your loved ones – he's just some boy who understands what I mean when I talk about an author using metaphor and the animal imagery in *Phaedra*. (*Looks at Bobby.*) Doesn't matter. He's my friend. He's just a second-year senior who was trying to live as cheaply as he could and I let him use this place to stay for a while – both of us went to a workshop in Delaware and someone took a picture of us. That's not the end of the world. Or my marriage. *Or* anything else except your imagination on the loose and running wild . . . (*Pointing.*) Look at the photo. Think about what I've just said and *really study* it. Seriously.

She holds out the photo and Bobby looks at it, but doesn't commit to holding it again.

Bobby Yeah, alright. Maybe.

Betty It's not 'maybe', it's the truth.

Bobby Fine.

Betty Listen, I'm . . . this is . . .

Bobby Don't worry about it. You say that's it, then OK. We'll leave it there.

Betty Bobby, please . . . I'm your sister . . .

Bobby Fuck, don't use that as a measure of anything.

Betty Come on.

Bobby I'm serious!

Betty What?

Bobby That's . . . You throw that around when it's *convenient* for you, that little label . . . but otherwise it don't mean shit to you. (*Beat.*) Please.

Betty You are . . . God, you can be cold sometimes!

Bobby Hey, I learned from the pros.

Betty Are you . . . referring to me? Honestly?

Bobby You . . . and Mom . . . others, too. All of you guys growing up were icy bitches to Dad and me, don't act like you weren't.

Betty . . . Bobby . . .

Bobby And you were probably the worst of all. I mean it. (*Beat.*) Just old enough to hate a little brother. You had no time for me . . .

Betty That's not . . .

Bobby Always kicking me outta your room or, or, like, screaming in my face or telling Mom that I'd done shit – usually shit I hadn't touched, by the way – just to get me outta the way. Or if your boyfriends were over. You were a regular fucking *terror* . . .

Betty Oh, come on . . . that's stuff that everybody goes through! I mean, siblings do . . .

Bobby Maybe.

Betty 'Maybe' nothing . . . Why're you even . . . ?

Bobby All I'm saying is you wanna act like you and me are all friendly now or when you needed your kitchen re-done cheap, slip me a hundred bucks that's fine, but let's not lie about it. (*Beat.*) We hardly know each other, sis, and that's the goddam truth. It is and it's pathetic. You and I are complete fucking strangers . . .

Betty Well, I'm sorry you feel that way.

Bobby I'm sorry you did so much shit to make me feel that way . . .

Betty And it's all my fault, right? *I'm* the one who's done everything wrong, is that it?

Bobby No, just enough to piss me off.

Betty You're impossible . . .

Bobby So they keep saying.

Betty I mean, sorry, but I see why you have so much trouble with dating and all that.

Bobby I have trouble when girls turn out to be whores or bitches. That's just me.

Betty Whatever, Bobby, let's not – why don't I do this myself? Alright? (*Beat.*) It's an obvious mistake, me asking you here.

Bobby Why? Because I've found out about you and all the – what'd you call it? – 'attention' you've been given out lately? Huh?

Betty No . . .

Bobby I'm sorry that I find sin offensive.

Betty Fuck you! Stop saying stupid shit like that . . .

Bobby Then tell me the truth – do that once!

Betty About what?

Bobby About this . . . this whole . . . (*Indicating.*) . . . *place* you got here. Your love nest.

Betty You're crazy! Honestly, Bobby, you are just acting so . . . completely . . .

Bobby Bruce doesn't know a goddam thing about what you're doing out here. (*Beat.*) Does he? I bet he's got no sense of what . . .

Betty stops cold and looks at her brother. He looks over at her and shrugs. Her face is slowly draining of colour.

Betty That's . . . you're so full of . . .

Bobby True or not? (*Beat.*) Hey! I'm asking you a question . . .

Betty *What?*

Bobby You heard me. (*Beat.*) Look at your face!

Betty There's nothing wrong with my face.

Bobby You don't look that way very often 'cause you hardly ever feel like you've done anything wrong, it's always the other guy. I know, I've watched you do this a thousand times before, but I can see it there in your eyes . . . I'm telling the truth. What's going on here is as foreign to Bruce as all those fucking *conferences* you sneak off to each year . . . (*Laughing.*) Fuck, he probably bought into this cabin thinking that you guys'd be . . . some *income* and an investment, or . . . like, for weekends and . . . and . . . (*Beat.*) No. That's not . . . no.

Bobby stops and looks around, taking in the cabin in a way he hasn't yet done. Looks over at his sister.

Wait a minute. Wait a goddam minute! Something's not right here. This is . . .

Betty What?

Bobby If it was, you'd be doing this with him here and, and the kids'd be out running around – the whole *line* you fed me before about Bruce needing to be home blah-blah-blah . . . that's made up. Isn't it? BETTY?

Betty No. It's, no . . . he has a . . . he's . . .

Bobby You'd never have me over here, show it to me, if you didn't have to . . . if you weren't completely fucking desperate! I *know* you!

Betty I needed your *truck*, I told you that . . .

Bobby Yeah, but . . . (*Stops.*) Fuck. 'Rental', my ass. I bet that poor bastard doesn't even *know* about this place! Does he? DOES HE?

Betty . . . Of course. Yes. Bruce is . . . he's . . .

Bobby Yeah? Really?

Betty It's . . . it was a joint project. *Yes*, it's been rented out to . . . this guy . . . and it's now . . . but of course Bruce knows about it. I mean, of *course*!

Bobby I do not believe you.

Betty Jesus Christ! You're just acting . . . so . . .

Bobby reaches into a pocket. Pulls out his cellphone.

Bobby Want me to prove it?

Betty What're you doing now?

Bobby Nothing, I'll just call 'em and ask if I should . . . (*Looks around.*) I dunno, if he needs me to fix that door there or if I should just leave it. He probably wants it fixed. With all the new prospects coming by. Right?

Betty You're such a fucker, Bobby.

Bobby It's true. *I* would . . . Lemme just ask.

Betty doesn't say anything. He gives her a chance, then pushes a few buttons. It's ringing. Finally:

Betty ALRIGHT!

Bobby What? (*Pops the phone closed.*) Hmm?

Betty Bobby, stop being a dick, OK? For just one second. Can you?

Bobby If I *really* concentrate . . .

Betty Then do it. *Please.*

Bobby 'Please' always helps.

He smiles and puts his phone away. Turns back to Betty. She moves away and sits.

Betty You don't have any idea about my life . . .

Bobby No, I don't. We're not that close.

Betty Yeah, you said that already.

Bobby And I'm actually sorry about that.

Betty Sure you are.

Bobby I am! I always wanted you to treat me as more of a brother than you ever did – You can't look at me and tell me that's not true. Hmm? Can you?

Betty . . . I'm . . . *Shit* . . .

Bobby Doesn't matter. Now.

Betty Listen, I have made some choices that – you're right about this place. About Bruce. (*Beat.*) I'm doing this . . . alone . . . *investing* for the . . .

Bobby Betty. *Stop.*

Betty I mean, he's . . . *No*, I'm not even gonna try and lie about it to you. I'm tired of it.

Bobby Good.

Betty I helped him find it. A place like this, it was inexpensive and, and out-of-the-way . . . so we just . . . we're . . .

Bobby Which I'm sure you liked . . .

Betty And yes, I paid a few months of rent on it. That's not a crime! (*Beat.*) It's not.

Bobby Matter of opinion, actually . . .

Betty Is it? Really? Do tell, Bobby, I'd *love* to hear this one . . .

Bobby You've got *one* chequebook, right? A savings account or an IRA or some shit, correct? (*Beat.*) Betty! At *home*. Am I right or not?

Betty Yes.

Bobby You throw your pay cheques *together* at the end of each month, don't ya?

IN A FOREST, DARK AND DEEP

Betty We do, but . . . it's not like we're . . .

Bobby Yep. Like most married couples do. (*Beat.*) And then *you* go decide to take some and spend it on yourself. You and your boy's rent and other shit, too, I'm sure, and that doesn't even register to you? Nobody else in your family's the wiser, so you think that means it's OK. You tell me if that's stealing or not. IS IT?

Betty That's a pretty broad . . . Come on, Bobby.

Bobby It's just plain math, Mrs College Dean. And that's not all, either. I bet you're sure it's cool, the time you spend with this guy, running around to bookstores and, and . . . fucking *foreign* films and all the shit you folks enjoy up there on the *quad*.

You don't think those hours add up? Every meal you miss . . . all the times that you spend away from your own kids to be with this guy, to laugh and *wander* and fuck this second-year senior – do not kid yourself, Betty! Your family's crying itself to sleep at night because they know something's wrong in that house of yours. You are a first-class thief, my dear, every day you spend with this dude. (*Beat.*) I'll bet Bruce even knows. Yeah. The back of his mind, he's gotta feel something . . .

Betty . . . I don't think so. No.

Bobby Then you're fooling yourself! Seriously, that's all you're doing . . .

Betty Bruce and I are . . . we're spending a lot of time apart these days. In the same house but you'd never know it. Different beds and, you know . . . all that.

Bobby . . . Oh. (*Beat.*) Well, OK, but still . . .

Betty That's just how life goes sometimes. I am not gonna blame him right now, when he's not here to defend himself but . . . we're . . . it's complicated.

Bobby It usually is.

Betty Yeah.

Bobby And perfectly simple, too.

Betty Ha! Yep. That's true, I guess.

Bobby Yeah. (*Beat.*) So you two are . . . what? Separated, or . . . I dunno. You tell me.

Betty Not yet. We've talked about a lot of . . . I'm not sure what's going to happen. I worry about the children and I need to . . . I'm not gonna just make some stupid quick choice that'll – but we're not gonna make it the way that things are now. (*Smiles.*) Not something I'm proud of, but hey . . .

Bobby No, I get it. It's usually hard to keep a marriage going when your wife's out there fucking somebody else.

Betty GOD! That is so mean! Jesus Christ.

Bobby Well . . .

Betty Can't you even try and understand where I am right now, how all this started? Huh?!

Bobby I am trying . . .

Betty That's bullshit! You're *condemning* me . . . that's all you ever do. You love to see me down and hurting and this is just . . . this is like *nectar* to you. I think you are loving this!

Bobby Hey, I didn't make it happen . . .

Betty Yeah, but you're sure glad it did.

Bobby I'm not *surprised* – let's put it that way.

Betty Everything is ugly through your eyes.

Bobby I'm just a realist, sis. Don't blame me.

Betty It has never been just about . . . *fucking* . . . as you like to put it. With the situation here. I don't care if you believe me.

Bobby What is it, then? Companionship? *Love?*

Betty Would that be *so* impossible . . . ? Hmm? That something like that might happen to me or come my way? Is it *really?* Am I crazy to think that I might find some . . . happiness?

Bobby Kinda. (*Beat.*) Seen you go through a *lotta* relationships . . . not just Bruce, but guys for years and years and it never seemed like 'love' was the number one priority – I'm surprised it's even on the list!

Betty You're disgusting.

Bobby You're just trying to make it look all . . . cutesy and sweet now that it's obviously ended. Guy runs out on you and you're all dreamy about it rather than just calling it what it was. (*Best.*) You had an affair, honey. You screwed a student. I bet it's probably against two or three rules up at the school there, too.

Betty Yes, it is.

Bobby It's sort of morally wrong, as well. Not that I'm gonna throw that in your face right at this minute, but just so you know . . .

Betty That's a big word for you to be using.

Bobby Really? I don't think so – I have plenty of morals. Always have. You used to skip out on Vacation Bible School. Not me.

Betty So you're a religious guy now? That's –

Bobby I didn't say 'religious'. Who said that? (*Beat.*) I'm saying I have a moral *core*, a centre that doesn't waver . . .

and that's a fact about me, whether I swear too much or I've been divorced or, or whatever . . . lose my cool in a bar once in a while, it doesn't change the essential nature of me as a man. What I believe. How far I'll go or not and what I know is just absolutely against the laws of mankind. Not God, not that, but what every person should be willing to stand up and say 'no' to. I've got that in me and I'm not so completely sure that you do, Betty . . . not at all.

Betty Really? You know that about me?

Bobby I know some things. I do. (*Beat.*) I saw a programme on television the other night – I got the History Channel on, like, 24/7 – it was one of those shows where it has a real person on it. A documentary. About a guy who comes home from the war, and I'm saying just recently, from Iraq . . . and he was shot in the spine, he's a cripple now and it follows his journey back. Recovery and his doing rehab, all that shit. Whole time I'm watching I'm looking at his wife next to him. Young, beautiful girl. She's a rock – helping him with his pee-sack and they can't have sex unless he has a shot or, like, one of those pumps in his dick but she's still there, tucking a pillow in behind his . . . and all I'm thinking, the entire show, is how much I'd like to fuck her. Seriously. Find out the place they live and go down there and get her outta that situation. I mean, she's gotta be sick of being on top by now, right?! Now that's a kinda sick thought, I know, but the point being . . . I *won't* do it. I'm not gonna track them down or pretend to run into her in a bar or, or at Chili's and be, like, 'Oh, hey there . . .', because it would be wrong. She loves this fucking guy who can't sit up straight and shits in a bag. He is her man so who am I to go get in the middle of that? Nobody, that's who. It'd be a bad thing and a sin and so she's now off limits. (*Beat.*) See?

Betty What the hell am I supposed to get outta that story? Huh?

Bobby I think it's pretty obvious . . .

Betty Not to me, Bobby. Honestly.

Bobby Yeah, because you've got no sense of fucking morality, sis. *That's* the trouble.

Betty OK, this is getting a little too . . .

Bobby I'm serious!

Betty Just stop now, OK? *Stop*. I get it.

Bobby No, I don't think you do, no, and here is why: 'cause you keep-on-doing-it.

Betty What?

Bobby You keep going out there and having more and more adultery.

Betty Bobby, just . . . and that's not even a word. Not the way you use it . . .

Bobby Bullshit, is too! Yes! 'Adultery'.

Betty It's not! And I'm just . . . Stop it! STOP!!

Bobby We can stop – let's pick up your precious files and I'll be on my fucking way. Get away from your little house of filth . . .

Betty You're not here because of *files*, OK?! That's obvious, so just . . . stop. Please.

Bobby Then why? Huh? *Why* am I here?

Betty Because . . .

Bobby Yeah, go on . . .

Betty Because I wanted somebody around while I did this, went through all of it – You're right, I obviously couldn't have Bruce do it, no. So, who else? All I got is you . . . like it or not, we're family. We're stuck with each other.

Bobby Ha! Too bad you don't have any friends . . .

Betty I know.

Bobby I was kidding.

Betty No, it's kind of true. I'm . . . Women don't like me usually – as friends, co-workers, that sort of thing. Some women are just like that. I do better around men – and I mean just as acquaintances.

Bobby Right.

Betty Women seem threatened by me.

Bobby Maybe because you fuck most of their men. That gets annoying after a while . . .

Betty That's not true!

Bobby Pretty much.

Betty I do not! When I was younger, yes, I was a bit . . . wild, or . . . I don't know. On the prowl. But that stopped years ago . . . I've been whatever, but I did try. Got my head on straight after college and I tried for a while there, to make my marriage work and all that. (*Beat.*) I *really* did . . .

Bobby Except for this new guy. Your second-year senior.

Betty Yes, that's true. He's different . . .

Bobby I doubt it.

Betty And what's that mean?

Bobby Look me in the eye – tell me he's the only one since you've been with Bruce. (*Beat.*) Seriously. Try and tell me that . . .

Betty Bobby, no . . . I'm not gonna . . .

Bobby Say it. You tell me and I'll believe you.

Betty This is not the . . . I'm . . .

Bobby walks over and stands in front of his sister. Waits for her to say something. Faces inches apart. He puts his finger against her chest, pushing her. Again. And again.

Bobby Say it. Go on, say it. SAY IT. SAY IT!

Betty STOP! (*Beat.*) Alright, yes. He's a . . . This was something else. Something wonderful.

Bobby Ha! Bullshit. Bull-fucking-shit – the *lies* you tell yourself to get by! Fuck, you're amazing!

Betty I'm not lying . . .

Bobby Fuck you're not –

Betty I'm not!

Bobby Yes, you are! Yes!

Betty IT'S NOT A LIE! IT ISN'T, BOBBY!! NO!!

Betty explodes and smacks Bobby on the cheek. Hard. This stops him cold.
 A moment of dead silence passes between them.

Bobby . . . Fine.

Betty Fuck. Sorry. (*Beat.*) Look, you don't know him, OK? He's . . . so funny and just, well, really sweet. Very smart and yet not all – he's just a very special person.

Bobby I'll bet.

Betty He is!! Jesus, can't you . . . I mean, try and respect *me* at least, if nothing else?

Bobby Why? (*Beat.*) I mean, why start now?

Bobby waits for her to respond but she doesn't. Silence.

I'm not gonna lie here – I don't at all respect you, what you've done with your life or, or career, and certainly not the way you run around with your pants down. (*Beat.*) You've always been like that and people talk about it behind your back and it makes me sick. Like, *physically* sick. (*Beat.*) Why do I need to pretend I like that or respect you? I am not gonna. No.

Betty Then fine. Just go. I can finish this by myself . . . I'm tired now, so . . .

Bobby Fine. (*Tosses money back at her.*) Doesn't matter to me.

Betty Good. Thanks for nothing.

Bobby Hey, hey, thank your own fucking self, you bitch . . . Shit! Don't blame a single thing on me here. You got that? NOTHING. You're the one who's done this . . . brought all of this down on your own head.

Betty Whatever . . .

Bobby You're goddam right, 'whatever'. (*Beat.*) I can't help it that not even a length of *chain* could keep those fucking thighs of yours closed. The first *whiff* of cock and they part like the goddam Red Sea, so do not point a finger at me! OK?!

Betty You're sick.

Bobby I may be sick – I might also be the only guy in a three-town radius that you haven't fucked, so that's something – 'cept *Bruce*, of course.

Betty JUST GO!

Bobby I am, you bitch! Shut your goddam mouth!

Betty Get out, you fucker! You fucking . . . AAAH!!

Bobby holds his ground, pounding home his message.

Bobby Call me whatever you want – point is, you know I'm not lying. You've brought a *lot* of guys to their knees with that smile of yours . . . over the years . . .

Betty Bobby . . .

Bobby Don't say that you haven't. (*Beat.*) You're just adding to the collection with a new guy. Teacher, student, it's all the same to you. Right?

Betty Let's not . . . I really don't have time for this now. All your . . . foul . . .

Bobby Yeah, why think about the past? You sure as hell don't learn from it, so . . .

Betty Oh, stop! Please! Just . . . just don't. This is the kind of shit Dad would do to me . . . piss me off by bringing up all the things I'd done and rub my nose in it!

Bobby Hey . . . I'm sorry you got involved with a married man once upon a time! I'm very sorry. Wasn't a fairy tale with a happy ending, though, was it? You two didn't ride off into the sunset or anything even close to that. (*Beat.*) Not that *you* cared.

Betty . . . Please stop . . . *please* . . .

Bobby Don't cry now, sis, 'cause you didn't do shit about it at the time and I know that to be a fact. Back when you could've done a thing or two, spared this guy his fucking dignity, at least, you did nothing . . . turned your thumb down like a *Roman senator* and sent the poor son-of-a-bitch to his grave . . . (*Beat.*) You fucked that guy – Mr Freeman or whatever his name was – you were dicking around with him at seventeen and got him booted out of his job at the high school. That's not just hearsay . . . those are cold, hard facts. You wouldn't listen to Dad and that's what it got you.

Betty I *know*.

Bobby You were a fucking *skank* and you let a man throw himself on his fucking sword for you and what'd you do about it? Huh? WHAT?

Betty You know what! Say it if you need to . . . GO AHEAD. (*Beat.*) He was an *adult*, by the way. Alright? Just so you . . .

Bobby He threw his family away, 'by the way'! His kids and every chance he had for a normal sort of life. Kids I used to play with, work that he planned his whole life for . . . *and* you let him!! Let him blab to his friends about it and think you guys would be going to Vegas and that whole deal. The guy wanted to marry you . . . Can you even *imagine* what must've been going through that head of his?! The fucking *delusions* he was living off of . . . and all because of you. Because of the way some teenager was sucking his cock. (*Beat.*) We all knew you hated us – Dad and Mom and me – we figured that part out, but you didn't have to take it out on the whole goddam world. You coulda let that guy go and he maybe woulda limped on back home to his family in the end, maybe even kept his job – but instead you ground him down, let him come off like some fucking jackass in front of everybody and . . . God, it was just ugly and pathetic and, like, sad in the end. I don't know if you've just . . . maybe blocked it out or not, but shit, Betty, I will never forget what that dude was like the last time I saw him. You know? He was a fucking *ghost*. *That* is what you did by living free and easy and not having time to let your parents tell you one goddam thing about life. Nope, you knew everything and just couldn't be bothered in those days . . . so that's what you did. You destroyed a whole person . . . and I'm not sure he's ever bounced back from that. There's every chance he didn't . . . (*Beat.*) I dunno what happened to any of 'em, him or that mousey wife of his or, or any of those three kids. I never saw them again after that summer, but I did happen to be on the street when she drove 'em away . . . I was there on my bike as they passed me. She was looking straight ahead and that girl of theirs . . . I forget her name now . . .

Betty Ellie. His daughter's name was *Ellie*.

Bobby Huh. Look at that – good for you.

Betty Go on . . . tell me . . .

Bobby Ellie was looking out the window and she was staring at me. Not accusing or, or, like angry or anything, but just a look of, like, despair or something. Of having had to grow up, straight up into being an adult, over the course of those few weeks or months or whatever. It was like it was her but also her as an adult, looking out at me. Yeah. (*Beat.*) It was spooky . . .

Bobby and Betty stand still for a moment – a cellphone rings at that moment, breaking the tension. Lightning strikes.
Betty goes to her purse, sighs, then answers.

Betty . . . Hey, honey. Yes. Uh-huh. No, I know . . . I know it's getting late. No, they don't need to stay up and see me, I'll get 'em up in the morning and ready for school . . . It's fine. I know. Yes. What? I'm almost done, I'm just . . . (*Looks at Bobby.*) No, I just want to finish up these few notes on the bibliography and then I'll, yes . . . be home after that. Right. Oh, well, no, I'm not at my desk, that's why . . . no, I'm over at the . . . Can I please just . . . no, I've gone over to the student union building for a cup of coffee. Yeah. Sorry. Don't worry, it's whatever. You don't have to . . . this whole thing is, fine. I thought we were not gonna do this to each other. All the questions and, and . . . then OK. I'm getting a coffee and I'll be back there and I'll finish up. Then home. Alright? (*Beat.*) Do what? When? Bobby called you earlier . . . Oh. I wonder what about? Hmm. OK, yeah, no, I will. (*She turns to Bobby again.*) Well, if he hung up then it was probably a mistake. Yeah. OK. Yes, I'll tell 'that fucking loser' not to call you for any reason when I see him. Alright. G'night. Yeah, I'll be careful . . . yeah, I can *see* that it's wet. *Yes.* Bye.

She clicks off her phone and returns it to her purse.

Bobby Charming . . .

Betty Yep.

Bobby What a fucking asshole . . .

Betty I'm sure you did something to earn it. I mean, in *his* eyes . . .

Bobby *Whatever.* Guy feels that way about *me* and he's got no idea about the woman that he shares his wedding bed with . . . pretty fucking typical. Ha!

Betty Doesn't matter.

Bobby Yeah, to you maybe.

Betty Just let it go. You can never let things go . . .

Bobby Can, too.

Betty Hardly . . .

Bobby Fine. Fuck if I care.

Betty And we're not *sharing* anything much any more. Certainly not the wedding bed.

Bobby Yeah, you say that, but how the fuck do I know what you're doing?

Betty You heard me talking to him, didn't you?

Bobby So what? You sound like a million other married couples . . .

Betty Really?

Bobby Pretty much. Together but, you know . . . just barely. *Every*body sounds like they'd rather be with somebody else these days.

Betty I don't even know what to say to you . . .

Bobby I'm not saying you guys aren't . . . But you just stand there and lie to him. Just as easy as breathing. 'Coffee' and 'over at the student union' like it doesn't matter to you, like the truth is just something that happens once in a while, like one of those *comets* that flies by every hundred years! (*Illustrates.*) Whoosh! I mean, God, don't you even wanna *try* any more? Fuck . . .

Betty You're here with me right now . . . you *know* what I'm dealing with. How do you figure I'm gonna start telling the truth right now? Hmm? *How?*

Bobby You gotta start some time! You have to, I dunno, just fight your way out of the . . . *thicket* of lies you weave and . . . just . . .

Betty Yeah? OK, here. Truth is I've had a few flings over the years . . . Men at work or people from . . . doesn't matter. Guys. I'm quite sure – no, in fact I *know* – Bruce has done the same thing, how long or how many I'm not certain but *before* me. So there.

Bobby *Bruce?* No . . . that pussy? I don't believe it.

Betty Yeah. 'Fraid so. (*Beat.*) *Yes.*

Bobby Jesus . . . I'd've never . . . wow.

Betty First one I found out on my own, I was six months pregnant. I was trying, too, wanted to be his model bride and to put my earlier days behind me – not so easy living in the same town – but I was now a college graduate and a teacher and had even gotten married and had a kid. Just like they tell you to do, in stories and on the TV. And *he* was sleeping with his secretary. Just like they tell men to do, in stories and on the TV. (*Smiles.*) That was how it started up again . . . me paying him back, even while I was carrying his baby. I mean, it's the perfect way not to get pregnant, right? Going to bed with a guy when you're already – and believe me, there's a lot of men out there who are very into that idea. *Very.* So I started up doing that and I guess we just . . . I dunno. We just never . . . stopped. Bruce and I have gone our own ways but we pay the mortgage and keep the lawn mowed and most everybody in town figures we're doing just fine. (*She turns to Bobby.*) I don't care what things you say about this guy . . . he is different and lovely and a really . . . I could just go and be myself with him! Be real and funny and just a, like, a total woman and he was completely into me. Me as a *person* and a writer, and it didn't matter if I was ten pounds too heavy or older or any of that sorta crap. He's kinda perfect. That is the truth of it. Younger than me and from this well-to-do family but just the sweetest, nicest guy you could ever wanna – (*Her eyes are welling up with tears.*) He was not 'nothing' to me. You should know that. Believe what you wanna about me and, and however you feel about the situation, but this was not nothing.

Bobby . . . I see.

Betty I'm just saying. OK? He was special. In my mind . . .

Bobby I hear ya. I mean, if . . . you're . . .

Betty Anyway . . .

Bobby No, that's . . . if that's the case, then you should do something about it. (*Beat.*) Fuck what I say or people think – that's how ya used to be with all of us – so go do that. Just, you know . . . go for it.

Betty I can't . . .

Bobby Sure, you can. (*Beat.*) I'm serious here. If he's *that* fucking great, then go . . .

Betty It's over, Bobby, let's just . . . I wanna do this and get home, so . . .

Bobby No, I think you should go after him, you feel this way about it.

Betty Bobby.

Bobby Betty, fuck, change your life!

Betty Why're you . . . I thought it was a sin?

Bobby Yeah, but, no, this is . . . but there are *circumstances* on occasion. Things that make it more OK than other times.

Betty That's convenient . . .

Bobby I'm saying it's true – you've convinced me here that you love this guy, that you're wanting more than just a *fling* so I think you should, you know . . . go and, and . . .

Betty I can't now . . .

Bobby That's not true! People do this.

Betty I'd like to, but it's not . . .

Bobby Yes, you can, Betty! *Yes!* (*Beat.*) I'd be a lot more proud of you, I'll tell ya that. Doesn't matter if you break up the family because once they know, the kids can make a new life, one that's honest and they'll be able to be more free to love you. Even Bruce would be, he would . . . and you could do what you want without this secret life weighing you down! Every day, you having to pretend and all that, instead you'd be past that and be your own . . . It's true . . . go get a divorce and do it right!

Betty Bobby, I'm telling you I can't, OK?! Why don't you just stay outta my business for once and let me decide if I'm . . .

Bobby Because you do nothing right! You always do the easy thing, the shit where it's no big deal to keep up the facade and forget about anybody else's needs . . . Why not just once think of someone else?! Huh?! Don't always fucking choose yourself . . .

Betty I'm not doing that!

Bobby Yeah, you are . . . you *always* are . . .

Betty No, Bobby, I'm not!

Bobby This would be as much for them as it'd be for you – Your kids need you to – *every*body wins if you'd just . . . go and . . .

Betty Bobby, stop! Stop it!!

Bobby Think about it, it's the only . . .

Betty STOP! STOP IT!! JUST FUCKING SHUT UP!! I NEED TO BE LEFT ALONE, GODDAMMIT!!

Bobby hears this and refrains from any further talking. He holds up his hands as if to surrender.

Bobby Hey, whatever you wanna do . . . Far be it from me to ever make you think twice . . .

Betty No, I actually have thought this through, down to the last detail, and it's not possible for me to . . . This isn't some . . .

Bobby . . . just forget it . . . I mean, listen to me! I'm telling you to dump your husband and your kids . . .

What the fuck is that?! I was trying to be nice to you for once, to say 'go for it' and run off with some dude I don't even know, if it makes you happy . . . and you can't even do that right! I think you wanna be unhappy, 's what I think!!

Betty You don't know anything . . .

Bobby I know it can't be that bad, whatever was the reason this guy left here in such a hurry . . . I know that you could reach out to 'em and probably turn things around if you wanted to . . .

Betty No . . .

Bobby That's not true! You could!! He's a kid and he's probably all mixed up, dealing with you as a woman and, like, a *mentor* at school, that's a lot to take in . . .

Betty I know, but . . . he's . . .

Bobby But you can do it! Call him, Betty, call 'em right now . . . come on!

Betty I SAID 'NO!'

Bobby You *won't*! That's all, you won't, 'cause you're a stubborn fucking bitch, that's why . . .

Betty Bobby, you don't know what the fuck you are talking about . . . so just . . .

Bobby Yes, I do, you're just being cunty about this, like usual!

Betty I'm not! Fuck! *Listen* to me, I'm . . .

Bobby Call him up or shut the hell up about it, OK? That's all I got to say about this . . .

Betty I CAN'T CALL HIM UP, ALRIGHT? I CANNOT! I WANT TO, I WOULD *LOVE* TO, BUT I CAN'T . . . (*Beat.*) He's not . . . He's dead. He died, and so I can't . . .

Bobby . . . *What?* The fuck are you talking about?

Betty I just said it, don't make me say it any more.

Bobby He's dead? This guy . . . your . . . *what?*

Betty Yes. (*Beat.*) He didn't leave me. We didn't have a fight and break up, I never for a minute said that to you . . . No. He died and so . . . so, I'm . . .

Bobby Yeah, but . . . I mean . . .

Betty He was . . . two days ago. That's why I'm here now. Because that happened . . .

Bobby Oh.

Betty So.

Bobby Shit.

Betty Pretty much.

A rumble of thunder and lightning. The lights flicker on and off. Why not? It's perfect timing.

Bobby That's fucking . . . I'm sorry, Betty.

Betty Thank you.

Bobby No, I *seriously* am . . . That's . . .

Betty It's unbelievable, that's what it is. It is right off the charts awful and, like, it's like a curse or something . . .

Bobby No . . . Don't say . . .

Betty Well, feels like it! Like God's punishing me for being *content* for one minute . . . for finally finding someone . . . who I'm . . .

Betty has no more to say. She sits there looking blankly at her brother, who seems troubled by the news.

Bobby I mean . . . Christ. He's . . .? (*Beat.*) Goddam.

Betty *That's* why I asked you here. Not for the books or the . . . the, you know . . . stuff. In the back of my mind I thought I could go ahead and tell you, but we always get – In the end I didn't feel safe enough to do that . . . (*Beat.*) You know how we are. Two *minutes* together and we're . . . tearing at each other's throats . . .

Bobby Yeah. Usually.

Betty Almost always.

Bobby True. But, I mean . . . this is different.

Betty Is it?

Bobby Of course!

Betty Maybe. Somehow I figured it'd just end up the same stuff for us . . . Another thing to misunderstand and fight about . . . and . . .

Bobby . . .

Betty I'm sorry I didn't just say something to you. I am. Please accept that, OK? (*Beat.*) I'm so used to lying to people – you were absolutely right about that – I'm so good at deceiving folks that I just go there most times now. Right off the bat.

Bobby That makes sense . . . I guess . . .

Betty Whether it's my colleagues or the kids or Bruce calling me up – I'm always so ready to filter the truth through some other . . . whatever. Doesn't matter. This is where I'm at in life. (*Beat.*) . . . I need to sit down.

Betty goes to a couch and sits. Bobby follows after her.

Bobby You want some water?

Betty No, that's OK.

Bobby Sure?

Betty Yep. I just need to –

Bobby I got some pot if you want. Do you?

Betty Hmm?

Bobby You know, pot. Weed. Out in the truck if that'd help . . .

Betty Huh. (*Smiles.*) Probably wouldn't hurt any.

Bobby I'll grab it.

He's up and toward the door in two steps. He doubles back and grabs up a box of books. Reaches for his coat – holds it over his head.

Might as well do a run while I'm at it.

Betty Sure.

Bobby Save a little time. Don't worry, I got tarps and shit. (*Beat.*) Right back, sis.

Betty 'Kay.

Bobby shoots out the open door. Betty sits for a moment, taking in the empty room. Her hand goes to her face, up to her eyes. She covers them.
 After a moment, she reaches over and snaps on the radio again. A sappy eighties number fills the room. She looks up and quickly turns it off.
 Bobby returns with a joint – lights it up and takes a good toke. He sits back down, passes it to his sister.

Bobby Huh?

Betty . . . 'S good.

Bobby A kid on my block sells it to me cheap. I buy in bulk . . .

Betty Hmm. So this must not be one of those . . . you know.

Bobby No, what?

Betty On your precious list of commandments. 'Thou shalt not toke.'

Bobby Nope. Not that I've ever seen. I try not to read 'em *too* carefully . . . (*Smiles at her as he hands over the joint.*) So – and if you don't wanna talk about it, then don't, but . . .

Betty No, go ahead. It's probably better . . .

Bobby Maybe, yeah. (*Beat.*) So, what happened?

Betty They don't know.

Bobby Really?

Betty Uh-uh.

Bobby Huh.

Betty Not for sure . . . he was found over on the other side of the lake. There's a bend in the path out where the trees overhang the road and, you know . . . it gets pretty dark, even during the day. He'd been riding – he loved to ride, that's how he got around, to campus and just as, you know, also as exercise . . . so he must've been out doing that. Cycling.

Bobby OK. And?

Betty And . . . we don't know. I spoke to the EMT drivers who brought him in and the police and . . . all from the position of a teacher and adviser, of course, but . . . and that's all they could say. He was found near his bike, down a sort of grassy slope off the road. He'd hit his head on something and his bike was bent, the back tyre, but no obvious cause or time of death.

Bobby So, he fell, right? I mean . . . that's . . .

Betty Probably. There weren't any tyre marks or some pot-hole that he no doubt ran into, but he was alone out there, dead . . . in the forest . . . and it isn't completely clear . . .

Bobby Huh.

Betty Yes.

Bobby An animal darted out? Is that possible?

Betty It is. It's very curvy out there – you've driven that part of the road, you know – it's dangerous.

Bobby Yeah. It can be, sure. Fuck.

Betty Anyway, he's . . . That's what happened. I'm not really able to push for more because it would just . . . it might seem odd.

Bobby Sure.

Betty So.

Bobby And family? You said he's . . .

Betty They're coming soon. Tomorrow morning.

Bobby Really?

Betty Yes. (*Beat.*) He's lying there, all alone in the basement of the hospital and I'm afraid to go see him because it wouldn't make any sense to outsiders and there might be . . . you know, questions about it, so I don't. I've left him there all alone and, and I'm ashamed that I'm doing that but I'm also scared of what happens if I go. (*Beat.*) See? You always think I'm so in-charge and brave . . . but now you can see what a coward I really am.

Bobby Don't say that. No, it's not your . . .

IN A FOREST, DARK AND DEEP

Betty I *know*. I'm just saying. (*Beat.*) Anyway, I got a call at dinner saying they'd be in tomorrow, so I scrambled to get all this done, but . . . And that's when I called you.

Bobby This is . . . fuck, that's shitty. It really is. I'm sorry for you. (*Beat.*) Honestly.

Betty Thanks. Thank you for . . . just being . . .

Betty reaches over and gives Bobby a little shoulder rub. It's only a moment and they both smile after.
A weird silence between them now. Their faces are close together as they sit there. Bobby reaches over to give his sister a hug. She allows it. They slowly separate.
Their lips brush, almost kissing, but they stop. Wait. They go to do it again but this time Betty pushes away. She starts to get up but Bobby pulls her down.

Bobby No, wait . . . I'm not . . . just . . . WAIT!

Betty Don't . . . Bobby . . . DON'T! NO!! STOP!!

They struggle for another moment and then she breaks off from him. They stand there looking at each other.

What the hell? Huh? I mean . . .

Bobby Sorry . . . I wasn't trying to . . .

Betty You hear 'stop', you better do it.

Bobby That's not what I was . . .

Betty I mean Jesus Christ, I'm your *sister* . . .

Bobby . . . I *know*, Jesus . . .

Betty I don't care if we're smoking pot or not.

Bobby That wasn't the . . . No . . .

Betty You don't have to touch me, Bobby. God!

Bobby Fine! Whatever . . .

Betty So fucking . . . *weird* . . . I mean . . . shit!

Bobby has had his fill of this conversation. He kicks the coffee table over, spilling magazines everywhere. Gets in his sister's face.

Bobby Hey, hey! Just watch your big fucking mouth, OK? Can you do that for me? (*Beat.*) You should be so goddam lucky and I mean that. You should have God come down from on high and grant you a fucking wish and it should be *me*. Me or some guy who looks almost exactly like me – same type of dude if you were at all blessed, you hear me? Huh? I mean, you walk around, so pleased with yourself and sure that you're some kind of I-don't-know-what. This *lady* who everybody wants a piece of, but you know what? The only reason anyone feels like that is because they're pretty fucking sure they can . . . have you, I mean. What the fuck, the rest of the *county* has, so why not them? You act like some fucking *graduate* degree erases all your history, you're fooling yourself. (*Beat.*) I've spent most of my life, ever since the first time I walked in on you up in your bedroom there sucking the cock of that kid from our Sunday School – you remember that? Hmm? – I've had to watch you make one shit choice after another, the worst motherfuckers you could find usually, and the nastier they were the better. If Dad didn't like 'em, then that was it far as you were concerned – all the approval you needed. And the little business suits you wear now can't hide the fact that you've got shit for confidence and that you need *every* guy to like you. Was Dad so bad to you, so withholding, that you had to end up like some cheap fucking whore who's out on the sidewalk every night, looking for a twenty-dollar blow-job? Guess so. (*Beat.*) Don't give a shit what society says about the two of us, brother and sister and keep away from each other . . .

you oughta be happy to have me. Least I'd treat you like a man's supposed to . . . not just hoping to fuck you in the ass because you're too drunk to care. Ya know how many times I had to hear that crap in high school? That my sister was fondly remembered not just as the girl who'd put out but the only one that guys could count on to take it in the shitter. 'S nice. Really *nice* . . . (*Beat.*) So don't act like I'm fucking . . . crazy because I might've cared about you all these years, wish I could've taken you away from that kinda thing – I'm sorry that I love my sister and, and that I'd do anything for her. Act like I'm sick or some shit because I have feelings – seems like I'm in a lot better place than your husband or, or, any of these other guys, ya know? Sounds like it to me. Just another group a' people who wanna use you, but not me. I never wanted anything for you but a bunch of good things. Nice, pretty things and you being taken care of. *I'm* the guy who wanted that for you. I am the person who just wanted you to be a little bit nice and show some kindness to me once in a while . . . to act like you needed somebody. This somebody who's your own flesh and blood. (*Beat.*) And you look down your nose at me. That's all you can do, I so much as give you a hug for too long . . . push me off like I'm some pervert over at the 7-11 who's got too close to you up by the register. Well fuck you, that's what I say to that, Betty. Fuck you. You should be grateful to love me and for me to love you. You really should . . . (*Beat.*) 'Cause ya certainly don't deserve it – that much I know. No fucking way.

He stops now and tries to catch his breath. Looks at her.

Flash of thunder and lightning. The lights go out. Betty is the first to stand. A glance at her watch again as she crosses to the fuse box. Flick of a switch and lights up.

Betty . . . God, how did it get so late?

Bobby So let's take whatever else you need and then you can get back. That's fine.

Betty OK, thanks, yes . . . Umm, the books and . . . I've set a few things on the bed that I can grab and then . . . well, also that file cabinet. (*Points.*) Up there.

Bobby Alright.

Betty That should do it.

She exits into another room. Returns with a small stack.

Bobby Great. (*Beat.*) And you don't think . . . ?

Betty What?

Bobby Nothing. I mean, the family is gonna be here, you don't think they might want . . . This isn't against you, I'm just saying it . . . you don't feel like they might be interested in a few of his things?

Betty Of course they would be. I hope so.

Bobby But not any of his books?

Betty No, I think . . . a lot of these are mine he borrowed or, we . . . you know, bought when we were together . . .

Bobby I see.

Betty So they're . . . I'd rather just . . .

Bobby You don't wanna leave any evidence.

Betty Bobby, please.

Bobby I'm not saying anything. I get it . . . but look at what happened with me. Right? I mean . . . what if that happened to his mom or dad as they're standing there? With a picture or whatever. What then?

Betty I'd . . . yes. That would be awkward.

Bobby So that's why. Really. Isn't it? So just say it, then . . .

Betty What?

He points over at the stack of loose items she's holding.

Bobby I know you're doing most of this because of your feelings for the kid, but let's be honest – you're covering your own ass. It is only a matter of . . . whatever until the owner of this place gets nosy and comes down here or, or the police . . . right? Am I right about that or not, Betty?

Betty . . . Fine. Yes. That, too.

Bobby Alright. Just so you know it. (*Beat.*) You oughta try and be a bit more honest with yourself sometimes – 's good for the soul.

Betty Because it's important for me to do that now, right? Even after all I've told you?

Bobby Just keeping it real, sis . . .

Betty O–K. Are you done?

Bobby Yep. Mostly.

Bobby looks over and points to a stack of valuables as he speaks:

Lemme ask you this, though: why are you taking that?

Betty . . . What?

Bobby His laptop. (*Pointing.*) I mean, isn't that kinda risky? I get all the rest of it but something like that – how do you know his parents won't miss that? Wonder where it is and then you'll have to lie about it.

Betty No, because . . . that's not . . .

Bobby What? You will . . . You'll make up some damn story and then you'll be caught in a –

Betty I bought it for him. Last year. It was his birthday and I bought it for him. So.

Bobby I see.

Betty I bought it for him and so I wanna, you know . . . keep it as something to remember him by. Is that so hard to understand?

Bobby No, it's pretty . . . that's quite clear. (*Beat.*) Except you're lying and I don't know why . . .

With a sigh Betty carefully puts down her stack and turns to her brother. Throws her hands up, exasperated.

Betty God, Bobby . . . what do you mean now?! We need to get out of here. Can we maybe talk about this after we've –?

Bobby Just answer that and I'll hoist all of this other shit up on my shoulders and be gone. 'Kay? No pointing fingers, nothing.

Betty Fine. (*Beat.*) What?

Bobby That thing's, like, five years old. Maybe more. I have the same one and I know what the new ones look like . . .

Betty Well, good for you. (*Beat.*) I really don't know what you're driving at. *What?*

Bobby That's a G4 right there. The new ones are something different. MacBook Pros or some shit. They all have a different design . . . Up close you can tell, but you gotta know what to be looking for. I fucking hate computers and even I know that.

Betty SO WHAT?

Bobby Why lie to me about it? That's all I'm saying – just like that . . . right here at the end? I don't get it. Can't explain it . . .

Betty I'm not lying. (*Beat.*) Bobby, look at me – I am telling you the truth. I LENT HIM THE MONEY TO BUY IT. OK?

Bobby I don't care – *nobody* bought that computer last year, Betty.

Betty How do you know that?! Hmm?! (*Beat.*) You are so damn . . . I mean, you're gonna say that to me now, after I open up to you?! *Un*-believable!

Betty goes to pick up the stack again but stops when:

Bobby What, you got your boyfriend some used computer? Is that the story?

Betty It is possible, isn't it? They do still sell them . . . I mean, people out there, on Craigslist or, or eBay or whatever . . . IT COULD BE TRUE, RIGHT?

Bobby Maybe. I'd be surprised, though . . . somebody who rents this guy a place and buys him all this stuff –

Betty I didn't say that I *personally* got on . . . Fuck, Columbo! WHAT IS YOUR POINT?!

Bobby I'm just saying! You paint a certain deal when you're talking about him, all these glowing memories and then . . . I dunno. This one just doesn't fit. And I question it.

Betty stands and looks at her brother. Who is this guy?

Betty What're you saying to me? I think that . . . you want to say something so just do. GO AHEAD.

Bobby OK. I will. Because I'm nothing if not a fucking honest guy. Mostly. Try to be.

Betty Just . . . OK, what? Seriously, WHAT?

Bobby I think you're still holding shit back from me. Obviously from everybody else but even from this conversation we had here. Tonight.

Betty Yeah?

Bobby I do. I feel it and I believe it's true.

Betty Well, you think what you want. I need to get home.

Bobby I think there's something on that laptop you don't want people to know about.

Betty . . .

Bobby Am I right?

Betty This is . . . Why do you have to do this to me? Right now? Huh?!

Bobby I'm not doing anything that you didn't do already. This is your mess, sis. This one right here . . . it's all yours. Like usual. You fuck shit up and then you want it to be all better, to just go away . . . Well, it doesn't, Betty. OK? Bad shit lives on and you can't outrun it. You can't.

Betty I just . . . I bought him this computer! Gave him the money to purchase it, and he –

Bobby No, you didn't. That just isn't true . . .

Betty You don't know *every*thing!!

Bobby I know enough. I know that machine is not new and . . . Well, doesn't matter. (*Beat.*) So why?

Betty . . . Because.

Bobby Yeah, I know there's a reason. I'd like to hear it, now that I know I'm looting the house of a dead man.

Betty Please don't talk like that.

IN A FOREST, DARK AND DEEP

Bobby Then tell me. NOW.

Betty AHHHH! You're right . . . OK?! Feel better? You are *right* about this . . .

Bobby About what?

Betty It's old. I wanted to buy him a new one, was going to but he had all his . . . shit . . . on this one, you know how people can be about their own – he was always so particular about his computer and all his whatever, I dunno, his, his *iPhone* and . . .

Bobby Yeah. And?

Betty *And* he didn't want it . . . I got him a gift certificate instead. I did that but I was going to buy him the one you mentioned . . . the Mac-something. Pro.

Bobby OK. Fine. So why are you . . . ?

Betty *Because*, Bobby! Shit. Isn't it obvious?

Bobby It's getting to be . . . yeah. GO ON.

Betty There ended up being *things* . . . some stuff on it that wasn't . . . doesn't matter! Just things. Things *all* over this place that I want to get rid of. (*Beat.*) And that's not all . . . I mean, God knows what's up in that file cabinet that he kept locked for some reason . . . so . . . just . . .

Bobby I think it does.

Betty What?

Bobby I bet it does matter. *All* this stuff.

Betty Oh, for God's sake! STOP! Just . . .

Bobby No, I'm not going to . . .

Betty Bobby!

Bobby We're gonna do this right now and I don't give a shit what you think. You put me in the middle of this so here we go. You're gonna tell me EVERYTHING YOU KNOW. *NOW*.

Betty shakes her head – drifting a bit before she speaks.

Betty There are files on there I wouldn't want his parents – or anybody else, really – seeing. Emails from me and just other things. OK? (*Beat.*) A couple *pictures* . . . I also found out that – by peeking at a time that I shouldn't've, when he wasn't aware of it – I saw . . . things of his that were . . . other girls on there . . . He was *friendly* with *many* more people than I was led to believe. So that was another thing . . . my golden boy wasn't as lovely and shiny as I'd imagined him to be. (*Beat.*) And then there was one more find, too . . .

Bobby What's that?

Betty It was so simple . . . Just a few little bits of his diary . . . notes that he kept with all his thoughts and wishes and dreams . . .

Bobby Yeah? And?

Betty *And* I wasn't one of them. I was – how did he put it? – 'old' and 'expendable'. 'OK in bed,' he wrote. 'Sex with her is kind of like fucking grey Jell-O.' (*Beat.*) Ha! For *so* long I've been chased and wanted and – a *prize* . . . and now some boy, this second-year senior reduces me to nothing in just a few words . . . less than nothing. *Jell-O.* Well, you can imagine how something like that might take your breath away . . .

Bobby . . . I'm sure.

Betty I suddenly saw what it was like to become invisible. You know? To be seen through. (*Beat.*) I mean, I felt it coming. 'Campus' is not for the weak of heart, trust me. New, beautiful girls every semester, year in and out, and yet . . . I could still turn a head or two. You know, when I tried. Some make-up on and my heels or whatever, yeah. I still had a little something. But hey, college guys are easy, I suppose – looking to get laid and they don't really care by who, so that wasn't any great accomplishment. Still, didn't hurt at eight a.m. as you're walking across the lawn there. A bunch of guys whistle at you . . . It's stupid, but it at least makes you feel alive or whatnot. *Wanted*. Even just for a second. (*Beat.*) So with him . . . this beautiful young guy who I find in my office one day, needs help on a scholarship application and he makes me smile and laugh and, and he's . . . he likes my 'hair' . . . It doesn't take long. To get sucked in. To believe in something, even if you know it's probably not the truth. You want it so bad, *need* to believe in that illusion so, so much because it's all you ever were – this pretty face and a girl who would say 'yes' – it's not so easy to give that up. For it to pass you by. And so later, you'll do almost anything to keep it, to hear it again just once. And from whomever. Kid down at the pharmacy. Some old man getting his *coffee* in Dunkin' Donuts. That's how pathetic ya get. Shit. (*Beat.*) But it does pass. Yes, it does and one day you are transparent. People walk by and don't see you, they say, 'Excuse me, Ma'm,' and you just want to scream, you wanna grab them and shake them and yell, 'I am a fucking beautiful, desirable woman,' but you don't. You don't do anything like it because you've started to know, inside somewhere, you've begun to recognise the truth. You are not that any more. You're just normal now and, and middle-aged and tired most of the day and everyone, from your husband on down, has begun to see right past you. Through you. As if you're no longer even there. (*Beat.*) I'm not making any excuses here, Bobby, but I'm just saying. I'm saying that's how it is for me these days, that's all . . .

Betty looks at him but past him, too. Lost in thought. Silence for a moment.

And that's everything, Bobby. I promise.

Bobby Yeah?

Betty Yes. That is the truth. As ugly and as, you know . . . terrible as it seems. That is what has happened. And why I'm doing all this.

Bobby I see.

Betty So now you know. (*Beat.*) I don't care what you say . . . I gave myself to this boy. I believed in him. In *us*. (*Beat.*) I hadn't done that in a long time. Trusted someone like that . . . and he . . . he said he was staying another year for me . . . so that we would . . . taking time to finish his thesis for me. So he could be with *me*, he said.

Bobby I'm sure.

Bobby doesn't know what else to say but knows enough to keep his big mouth shut at the right moments.

Betty He did! That we might – It seemed like he was offering me this whole new universe – but instead he shit on that . . . (*Beat.*) I know I did a lot of bad things to get here and so why should it work out for me, but I just . . . (*Beat.*) I did love him, Bobby. That is not a lie . . . I loved him and he was using me. I wasn't ever going to be anything but a *footnote* to him. In the end. (*Beat.*) And then, just to make the *entire* thing pointless and painful and sad – this past weekend, on a beautiful afternoon . . . he was out biking and he died.

Bobby turns to Betty and looks at her. Long and hard. He nods, thinking carefully before speaking:

Bobby He was out biking . . .

Betty Yes . . . around the lake . . .

Bobby And he died.

Betty He did. Yes.

Bobby Oh.

Betty shakes her head dimly. Lost in all of her thoughts.

Betty They're continuing to investigate . . . said they'll be in touch, but . . . for now . . .

Bobby I see.

Betty So you never know. I can't ask about it without people being suspicious . . .

Bobby Yeah, you said that.

Betty And his parents are coming – I told you all that, didn't I? Did I?

Bobby Yes . . . 'tomorrow', you said.

Betty That's right. I spoke to the father.

Bobby Uh-huh.

Betty And I wanted to give away a lot of this stuff – books and things – but we already talked about that.

Bobby Yes.

Betty So you know what I'm doing? Right?

Bobby You want to get your things outta here before they show up. Before anyone can come over here and start – I get it. It's understandable.

Betty Is it?

Bobby Sure. What good does it do for everybody if your relationship came out now? Right? It's just sadness, that's all this'd be, especially for his family. And yours.

Betty Exactly! That's what I thought, so I . . . That's why I tried to get all the . . .

Bobby You did this.

Betty Yes. Came here after calling you up. I am trying to do a good thing . . .

Bobby I get it now. I do . . . (*Beat.*) So just one more question.

Betty OK. I'm getting tired, though . . .

Bobby Just hold on. Just this. Tell me now – tell me *one* true thing and I will help you in any way I can. I promise . . . (*Beat.*) He died in the afternoon, you just said.

Betty Yes.

Bobby But before . . . *before* you said they didn't know how. Or when. That it was . . .

Betty No. I don't think they do. Nope.

He looks long and hard at Betty. The truth is just ahead.

Bobby I see . . . (*Beat.*) Then how did you know it was in the afternoon? Betty? I mean, how could you possibly know that? Hmm?

She stares up at him silently. Only her eyes blinking rapidly.

Betty . . . I dunno.

Bobby And I'm not saying anything here, I'm not some cop, but . . . if he did hit a bump or, like, some shitty patch of pavement out there *or* an animal, some fucking *squirrel*, a deer, whatever, jumped out in front of him – and maybe it did, it's possible –

Betty They think that's what happened . . .

Bobby Yeah, I heard that before, I did, but . . . *if* that was the case? How come it's his *back* tyre that's messed up now and not the front one? Why would that be? (*Beat.*) I want you to think about that . . .

Betty doesn't say anything – just keeps looking at Bobby.

You didn't scratch your car at the store, did you?

Betty . . .

Bobby Did you?

Betty What?

Bobby Betty?

Betty I don't know . . . I don't remember now.

Bobby Yes, you do. YOU DO KNOW.

Betty I do?

Bobby Say it to me and I'll help you. Just come clean for one time – and I mean, with *all* of your stuff, the whole pile of fucking shit you carry around – do that and I can help you . . .

Betty I'm . . . I'm not sure that . . . I . . .

Bobby Say it.

Betty . . . But . . .

Bobby Come on!

Betty I can't . . . Bobby . . . I can't do that . . .

He grabs her by the shoulders and shakes her. Violently.

Bobby Yes, you can! Say it, Betty. SAY IT TO ME NOW, GODDAMMIT! JUST SAY IT!!

Betty Owww! You're hurting me!! STOP!!

Bobby Then say the fucking words!

Betty No . . .

Bobby SAY IT! *SAY* THE TRUTH OR I SWEAR TO GOD THAT I'LL . . . !

Betty Stop it! Stop yelling at me!!

Bobby Then do it! Come on, just do it!!

Betty I can't!

Bobby Yes, you can, people can do anything they want, they do it all the time and so can you! YES!!

Betty No, Bobby, stop it . . . stop!

Bobby No! I'm not stopping this time, I'm not!

Betty Leave me alone!

Bobby Tell me the truth! Say what you've done!

Betty No! Stop it, no!! I don't know what I'm –

Bobby lets go of Betty and goes to the door and swings it open. The rain pouring down.

Bobby I WILL WALK OUT RIGHT NOW, WALK THE FUCK OUT AND LEAVE YOU HERE!! YOU WANT THAT?! HUH?! DO – YOU – WANT – THAT?!

Betty . . . I'm . . .

Bobby DO YOU?! IS *THAT* WHAT YOU WANT, BETTY?!

Betty . . . I don't know any more!

Bobby Then fine. That's . . . you know what? You're on your own. Just how you like it.

Nothing from Betty. Bobby slowly turns and starts to go out. At the last moment, Betty calls out to him:

Betty Please don't! Bobby! PLEASE!!

Bobby (*turning*) . . . What?

Betty *Please.* I'm not . . . (*Starts to cry.*) I need you. OK? I'm asking now because . . . I just really do *need* you. PLEASE. DON'T LEAVE ME HERE. I CAN'T . . . I'M . . . PLEASE DON'T . . .

Bobby closes the door and turns back to his sister. After a long silence:

Bobby So tell me then. Say it now. The *truth*.

A long silence. Betty finally speaks up and breaks it:

Betty I was never at the store. Or by . . . what'd you call it? The thingy there.

Bobby Cart corral?

Betty Yes. That. (*Tries to smile.*) . . . Bobby, I can't . . . it's so hard to be . . . I didn't go to the store that day. That's *all* I can say . . . is I didn't . . .

Bobby lets this soak in. He looks around the room, taking it all in. This time in the harsh light of reality. For a second it looks like the truth is too much to take. Bobby braces himself and lets the emotion pass. After a moment:

Bobby So listen to me – I'm gonna pack up the rest of this shit and I'm gonna take it back to my place. Leave it in the garage.

Betty OK.

Bobby Did you hear me?

Betty Yes. I think so.

Bobby Betty, fucking listen right now! OK?

Betty . . . I am. You're taking it all with you. (*Beat.*) Thank you.

Bobby Yeah, and I'm . . . tomorrow morning I want to see your car. OK? I want you to bring it over to my place and I'm gonna take care of those marks on it . . .

Betty We can . . . But Bruce said we can always . . .

Bobby Fuck Bruce. He's not here now – you didn't go to *Bruce* with this. You listen to *me* and do what I say, alright? Take it to my house tomorrow and I'll fix it for you . . .

Betty You will?

Bobby I can sand that down and repaint it and I think it'll be fine. You hear me? OK?

Betty Alright.

Bobby *Yes?* First thing.

Betty . . . I will.

Bobby You should go home now. Right now. I can do the rest and I'll take the keys . . .

Betty Really?

Bobby Yeah. I got it. Just go.

Betty I will, in a second. I just need to rest for a minute.

Bobby OK. But hurry. You need to go.

Betty But . . . if you do . . . ?

Bobby What? I can lock a fucking door. Promise.

Betty No . . . the other. If you do that – help me – is it a sin, Bobby? Is it?

Bobby stops and looks at her. A funny look on his face as he finally shrugs his shoulders.

Bobby You know what? I dunno any more.

Betty You don't?

Bobby Nope. I do not know that answer.

Betty Well, that's a first . . .

Bobby Yeah, it's true. I know a lot of shit, but not that one.

Betty It's not a commandment or anything, is it?

Bobby Betty . . . I'm not even gonna check. I don't know and I'm not gonna look into it right now . . . So . . .

Betty OK.

Bobby It is what it is. It's me helping out my sister, that's all I can see.

Betty Thank you. Because I do need you . . . I *do*.

Bobby I know you do.

Betty Thank you . . . Bobby. Thank you.

Bobby . . . You're welcome, sis.

Bobby walks over to where Betty is sitting. Stands above her. He reaches down and touches her hair. He brushes it slightly.

Betty smiles. Looks up at her brother for a moment, then leans her head against his hand. One real moment finally passes between them.

Bobby goes to the stairs and climbs quickly up into the loft. Grabs the file cabinet and hoists it up into the air and tosses it over the railing to the floor. Smash!

The sound is deafening and Betty jumps. Looks up.

Bobby comes downstairs, grabs it up and starts out the door. Scoops up the laptop on his way out.

Betty . . . Bobby? Do you . . . you wanna at least know his name or anything like that?

Bobby No. I don't. I don't wanna know anything about 'em. Alright? Just . . .

She nods. A crack of thunder. The lights flicker and go out. The rest happens by candlelight.

It's OK, don't worry. I can still see what I'm doing . . .

Betty 'Kay. (*Beat.*) Hey, Bobby . . . ?

Bobby What?

Betty The truth . . .

Bobby Uh-huh? What about it?

Betty It hurts . . . don't it?

Bobby Yeah, it does. It stings like a bitch. (*Smiles.*) That's why they call it that . . .

They look at each other for a moment. She nods. He exits.

Betty sits on the couch. Turns to the radio and turns it on. Modern English is singing 'I Melt with You'. She smiles lightly and closes her eyes. Puts her head back on to the cushion.

Betty resting. Lights slowly fading. Music blaring. Silence. Darkness.